PASSED! The Ultimate California Civil Engineering Surveying Test Preparation

Jakob Stanford, P.E.

First Edition

ISBN Paperback: 9798445152002

Publisher: On-Demand Publishing LLC, Scotts Valley, CA, USA

Preface

We civil engineers play a monumental role in society. We plan and help to construct, maintain and operate our national infrastructure. In our daily work we hold the lives of millions of Americans in our hands. Oftentimes it is said we save lives. In contrast to medical professionals, we engineers save lives by ensuring the safety and resiliency of our country's infrastructure in the face of natural and man-made disasters. We take pride in safeguarding the public's life, health, property, and welfare.

In the densely populated state of California, earthquakes, landslides, floods and wildfires are just a few of natural disasters that persistently threaten the safety of Californians and over 200 million annual visitors of our state. Under the circumstances, it is of utmost importance to restrict our practice to those only, who are able to demonstrate a minimum of relevant knowledge, practice, and education. Understandably, BPELSG (Board for Professional Engineers, Land Surveyors, and Geologists) has set the bar high for admitting applicants into California family of civil engineering professionals. The sometimes as low as 39%[1] pass rate of California PE exams is a clear testament to that.

In my personal pursuit of becoming a licensed civil engineer in California, I was faced with a shortage of up-to-date adequate training material for the state specific exams. Some of the material I obtained did not correspond with the official exam format, some included several incorrectly solved questions. Thanks to years of experience in our field, I passed the state specific exams at the first attempt. Subsequently, I felt compelled to author the book you are currently reading. My goal was to make a contribution however small, and give back to our community. Particularly, aiding the dedicated zealous young engineers, who are at the beginning of their careers.

The purpose of this book is to develop the reader's math, logical reasoning and problem-solving skills. The reader will be working through two full-length practice exams that cover the most common and challenging topics included in the official test. Every single question is carefully crafted to be uniquely challenging and to adequately prepare the applicant for the official test. Step-by-step solutions and additional graphics will offer adequate explanation and teach the most efficient problem-solving approach necessary for success in the PE surveying test. The first three chapters supply the reader with helpful insight and technical advice, which would prepare them to get the most out of practice examples.

For some, the California Civil Engineering Surveying Exam is the major roadblock to their path to licensure. Each failed attempt results in about a half-year postponement in the application process, additional costs, and increased anxiety. Many who fall under this category are bright young civil engineers that feel stuck not because of low talent and marginal skills, but as a result of unfamiliarity with the current structure and assessment criteria of this specific exam. If *PASSED! The Ultimate California Civil Engineering Surveying Test Preparation* succeeds in helping this group to overcome the last roadblock before them and to achieve the long-desired prestigious honor of receiving the title of California PE, this book has fulfilled its promise.

Jakob Stanford, P.E.
April, 2022

[1]For example, Q3/2018. https://www.bpelsg.ca.gov/applicants/exam_statistics.pdf

Contents

Chapter 1

Introduction

1.1 How to Use this Book

The main purpose of this book is to provide civil engineers with practice material for the California Civil Engineering Surveying Exam (CCESE). Feel free to skip the following and head directly to the exams section if you already know the basics, and the only reason you purchased this book was to go over some more tests before the official exam. If hearing about useful tips and valuable insight captures your interest, then what follows next is certainly worth a read.

1.2 About the Exam

The California Civil Engineering Surveying Exam (CCESE) is one of the five required exams every engineer has to pass before qualifying to become a licensed Professional Engineer in the State of California. It is a two-and-a-half-hour computer-based exam with 55 questions of equal weight[1]. Passing scores are not published and results are reported as either pass or fail only. What sets this exam apart from all other required tests for obtaining a California PE license, is its relatively limited mastery requirement. In fact, a three page cheat sheet would probably get you through 75% of the exam and for 50% of the questions you don't even need to look up a single equation. What causes CCESE to have the lowest pass rate among all California PE prerequisite exams, is its short duration. As you will have a very limited amount of time for each question, I can only suggest that you divert your efforts to enhancing your competency by practicing as much as possible. The following pages show you how.

1.3 Useful Resources

The Board for Professional Engineers, Land Surveyors, and Geologists hosts a comprehensive set of information. My suggestion is to go straight to *Examination Candidate Information* page [2]. This page has further links to all relevant information such as:

- **Examination Schedule**: Deadlines for application and test-taking. Despite computer-based nature of this exam there are certain deadlines for application submission.
- **Test Plan**: Offers an outlook on topics that are covered in the exam.
- **Candidate Information Bulletin (CIB)**: This key document is written by the testing services provider, Prometric. It provides the applicants with the A to Z of scheduling and taking tests at their centers.
- **Recommended References:** A list of literature that might be helpful for exam preparation. Also see the list below.

Apart from the references suggested by the board, the following free resources can also come in handy:

- **FE Reference Handbook**, published by NCESS, contains useful area and volume formulae, and trigonometry (law of cosine, etc.)
- **FS Reference Handbook**, published by NCESS, includes a good number of surveying and geometry equations relevant to the surveying exam.
- **PS Reference Handbook**, published by NCEES, is a way more advanced resource than FS Reference Handbook. Nevertheless, several topics in this handbook are relevant to the CCESE (such as spiral curves).
- **Open Access Surveying Library** (`jerrymahun.com`) provides textbooks covering surveying to the depth adequate for CCESE.

[1] According to the Candidate Information Bulletin (CIB)

[2] URL at the time of writing this book: `https://www.bpelsg.ca.gov/applicants/candidate_info.shtml#california_civil`

- **Caltrans Surveys Manual**, is also a reference worth mentioning, especially chapter 12.4 on Construction Stakes.
- **Caltrans Highway Design Manual**, chapter 200: Geometric Design and Structure Standards, contains helpful equations for vertical curves that are not commonly found in other reference books.

If by the time you are reading this book the URL to any of these resources has changed, simply find the current link through a quick internet search.

1.4 About the Practice Exams

The two practice exams in this book will give you ample examples to test your knowledge and practice your exam strategies. Due to exam confidentiality, the questions in this book neither represent examples from the actual surveying exam; nor can it be claimed that they match the difficulty level of an official exam. However, even engineers who pass the official surveying exam find it impossible to go through all the exam questions within 2.5 hours. Therefore, do not set such an impossibly high expectation for yourself. Rather, use the exams provided in this book, as previously mentioned, as an opportunity to study as best as you can.

Refer to the next chapter on how to constructively prepare for the test and utilize the practice exams in this book. As a side note, do not let the length of the reference solutions intimidate you. They are intentionally expanded for extra clarity. Oftentimes finding the right answer can also be achieved through shorter but less clear ways.

1.5 The Last Word

Before moving on to the next chapter, I would like to thank you for including *PASSED! The Ultimate California Civil Engineering Surveying Test Preparation* in your self-curated study plan. I hope this book proves to be effective in fulfilling your expectations, and I wish you a smooth path to licensure in the state of California.

If you found value in this book, please spread the word and consider adding a review on Amazon. If for any reason this book did not turn out to be what you had hoped, I would like to hear from you too. Please share your feedback on Amazon, and I will keenly take your feedback into account in my next work.

There is no reason to hold off any longer. Do your best, do your part, never give up, and victory will be yours!

Chapter 2

Strategies for Success

2.1 Recommended Exam Preparation Strategies

Everyone has their own personal method to prepare for exams. The following tips are generally very helpful:

1) Inform yourself about all the exam details. Read through the information provided by BPLESG and Prometric and keep the references handy.
2) Skim through a textbook on basic surveying. The purpose of this exercise is to improve your general understanding of the field of surveying and to have secured a secondary learning source for topics that common exam preparation text books might not adequately touch on.
3) Get your exam calculator and only use this calculator from that point on. Note that CCESE calculator policies are less stringent than NCEES [1]. You might be able to use your current calculator for the exam after all. If you end up needing a new calculator, make sure it has the following features:
   a. Handling of angles in degrees minutes seconds (DMS) format.
   b. Storage of values in variables.
   c. Sophisticated calculation history, with the option to recall previous calculations in order to modify and refresh them.
   d. Numerically solving nonlinear equations.
4) Thoroughly work through the classic California surveying exam preparation text books. Go through every single example. Add any new equation you come across along your personal notes to your collection of formulae as you go. Feel free to skip the chapters that are not on the current test plan anymore.
5) Move on to practice exams. Get your hands on as many practice exams as possible. Don't be shy to ask! Many fellow professionals will be more than happy to help you out. When taking practice exams, always simulate the real exam conditions: Have a timer running, only use approved pencils and your collection of formulae. After each practice exam, analyze your performance meticulously. See 2.3 Performance Review for details.
6) Between practice exams, familiarize yourself with all relevant features on your calculator. Competency in using your calculator will make you significantly faster. See chapter 3 Technical Tips for details.

[1] Refer to the CIB for specifics.

What you need for the exam and exam prep:

- Your calculator*
- Pen per CIB
- Your own collection of formulae*
- An exam prep textbook
- A surveying textbook
- As many practice exams as you can get

The ones marked with * are the only two items you really need to bring to the official exam.

2.2 Recommended Test Taking Strategies

An effective strategy is essential for success in both the official and the practice exams. Since the most suitable strategy for every exam varies from another, consider the following tips for the practice exams in this book.

1) Try to simulate the exam environment as closely as possible. Always have a timer running. Only

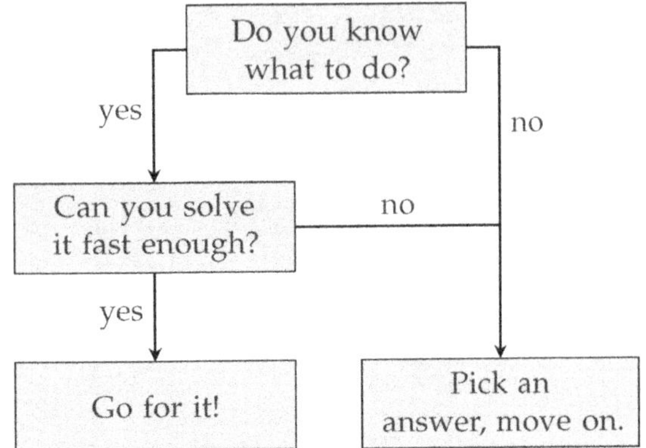

Figure 2.1: Exam Problem Decision Tree

use the permitted writing utensils and reference material. For efficiency, print or cut out the answer sheet so you don't need to flip pages during the exam. (In the official exam you won't need to flip any pages to mark answers on the computer either.)

2) Keep in mind that the CCESE is a computer based exam, so resist the temptation of annotating the sketches in this book. Highlighting a text is fine.

3) The practice exams in this book are very time-sensitive to simulate the official exam. This means you need to be prepared to solve about 50% of the problems without looking up equations. About 25% of the questions would require looking up a specific formula that you know where to find it in your compilation. Be prepared to skip the remaining 25% of the examples you cannot solve right away.

4) Learn to walk away from any example you cannot solve right away. If you would need to look up some information in textbooks, then this is a clear sign that you need to skip that example for the meantime. Follow the steps shown in the flowchart above before each example. As a reminder, there are no penalties for wrong answers[2]. Sometime you just have to pick any answer and move on.

5) Every so often keep an eye on the time and adjust your speed accordingly. Remember, you have 30 minutes for 11 questions.

6) Figure out and create a personal convention regarding this exam. For example, decide on approximately how much and which steps of your calculation better be written down on paper and which data should always be directly inserted into your calculator. You can also create your own abbreviations to save yourself some time. For example, use α for azimuth angles, β for bearing angles and ΔH for elevation differences. Use ′ for [ft] and ″ for [inch].

7) Before starting to solve a problem, take a peek at the answer options. Check what units you need to convert your answer into and how many digits you need to carry through your calculations. When the problem statement is asking for grid coordinates, see if some answer options have same northing or easting values. Based on that, it should be clear if easting, northing or both need to be computed in order to pick the right answer option.

2.3 Performance Review

It is extremely important to review your performance after each practice exam. Merely checking how many answers you got right would not suffice. Read the solution description to each problem you got wrong, and figure out what mistakes you made. Here is a suggestion on how you to classify wrong answers and what lessons you can learn from them:

- **Misread the question**: Remember, the time spent on understanding the task is a time well spent.
- **Mistyped a number, misread a number:** Double check every input before moving on to the next.
- **Identified a knowledge gap:** Note down the topics you don't know enough about yet. Go after studying them in depth through different resources, then come back to this book and take a mini exam of the questions you had got wrong.
- **Hadn't come across this equation before:** Add the equation to your collection.
- **Ran out of time:** Speed up your typing. The expectation determines the outcome. Try to solve a few examples as fast as you can, and soon you will realize many questions can be answered in much less time than what you thought.

While these suggestions might sound obvious, following them rigorously works every single time. Record a thorough assessment of each exam to help you determine your strategy moving forward: "I am going to practice increasing my speed.", or "I will remember to double check every input." (This is an iterative process that takes a few practice exams to get it right.)

[2] According to CIB.

Chapter 3

Technical Tips

This chapter is mainly helpful for individuals who struggle with some of the elementary concepts, and have already had unsuccessful attempts at CCESE.

3.1 Choose a Rational Approach Over an Intuitive One

Compute Departure and Latitude Using Azimuth Only

This tip applies to computing angles from departures and latitudes, or vice versa. Consistency is very important, when you intend to compute departures and latitudes from angles. Stick with using an azimuth angle, which is always counterclockwise and positive. Because then you can always compute departures as $\Delta E = L \sin\alpha$ and latitudes as $\Delta N = L\cos\alpha$. Resist the temptation to use a bearing angle. The reason is that during the exam it would be very difficult to correctly determine the direction of a trigonometric function based on the pictured direction of the bearing angle alone. Add the conversion between azimuth and bearing angle to your collection of formulae.

Compute Azimuth Using *atan2* Only

When computing direction angles from departures and latitudes, it is tempting to use the tangent function ($\alpha = \tan \frac{\Delta N}{\Delta E}$). The caveat is that in order to determine the actual direction, the signs of ΔN and ΔE have to be carefully considered. As an alternative, many calculators (and virtually all programming languages) offer a function called **atan2(ΔN, ΔE)**, which directly gives the right azimuth angle. Oftentimes this function is accessible in the polar to rectangular coordinate converter section. On TI calculators this function is called **R▶PΘ** and is used as **R▶PΘ(ΔN, ΔE)**.

Use the DMS Feature on Your Calculator

In land surveying it is customary to use the degrees minutes seconds form for angles, and this practice

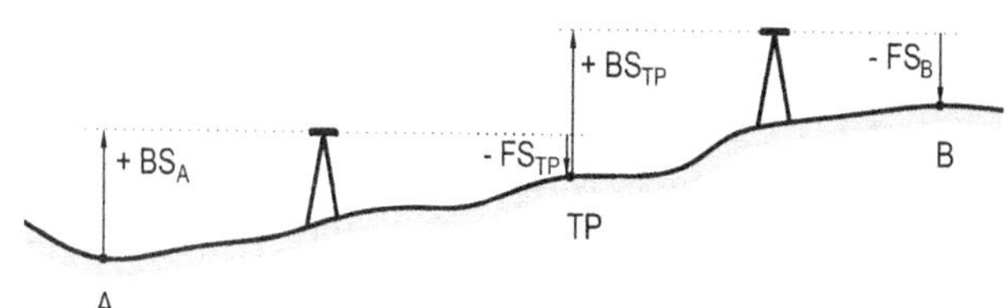

Figure 3.1: Visualizing Vertical Distances

exam book is no exception. Most calculators have a **▶DMS** function, which receives the decimal angles and displays them in DMS format. When dealing with angles given in DMS format, it is highly recommended to use the method already included on the calculator. Check your calculator's manual on how to input angles in DMS format.

Use the Numeric Solver on Your Calculator

Sometimes it is necessary to rearrange equations such that the unknown variable is isolated on one side of the equation. Oftentimes it may be faster and less error-prone to utilize the numeric solver functions that are included on many board-approved calculators. Check the manual of your calculator for instructions.

3.2 Visualize What is Behind the Numbers

Leveling and Vertical Distances

When dealing with leveling field notes, instead of following the foresight minus backsight rule, visualize the distance measurements along a horizontal line instead. This way it will immediately become clear which measurements should be subtracted or added.

Angles

Sometimes, it is required to derive angles from a sequence of angular measurements. The nice thing about an angle is that it represents a direction, which is easy to visualize mentally.

If you need to determine the azimuth of the right segment below (the gray angle), imagine how you would have rotated a transit level: First, set up the transit level at point A and turn it towards north, which is the direction the azimuth is measured from. Mentally set the measured angle to zero, then turn it towards point B. Now it should read the azimuth angle from A to B (add 50°). Next, move the transit level to point B. In order to consider the interior angle, rotate the transit level back towards point A. Note that you need to do a 180° rotation for this (add or subtract 180°). Now, turn the transit 131° clockwise. Which means you have to subtract 131°, as counterclockwise rotations are negative. The transit level is now looking at point C, and should read the sought azimuth angle. The resulting equation is:

$$50^\circ + 180^\circ - 131^\circ = 99^\circ$$

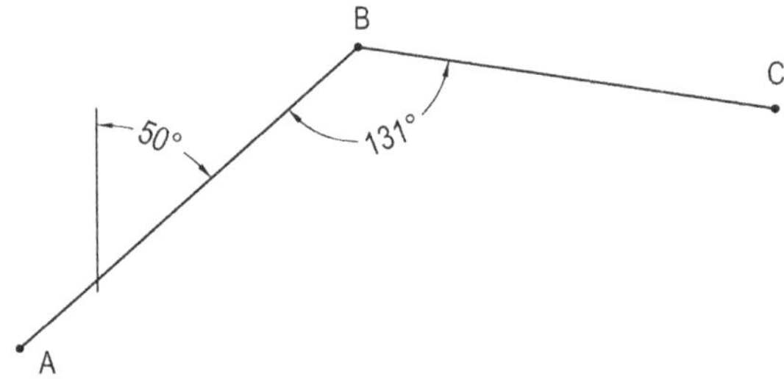

Figure 3.2: Visualizing Angles

Chapter 4

Practice Exam I

Answer Sheet to Practice Exam I

Question	Flag?	Option				Correct?
1.	⚐	A	B	C	D	○
2.	⚐	A	B	C	D	○
3.	⚐	A	B	C	D	○
4.	⚐	A	B	C	D	○
5.	⚐	A	B	C	D	○
6.	⚐	A	B	C	D	○
7.	⚐	A	B	C	D	○
8.	⚐	A	B	C	D	○
9.	⚐	A	B	C	D	○
10.	⚐	A	B	C	D	○
11.	⚐	A	B	C	D	○
12.	⚐	A	B	C	D	○
13.	⚐	A	B	C	D	○
14.	⚐	A	B	C	D	○
15.	⚐	A	B	C	D	○
16.	⚐	A	B	C	D	○
17.	⚐	A	B	C	D	○
18.	⚐	A	B	C	D	○
19.	⚐	A	B	C	D	○
20.	⚐	A	B	C	D	○
21.	⚐	A	B	C	D	○
22.	⚐	A	B	C	D	○
23.	⚐	A	B	C	D	○
24.	⚐	A	B	C	D	○
25.	⚐	A	B	C	D	○
26.	⚐	A	B	C	D	○
27.	⚐	A	B	C	D	○
28.	⚐	A	B	C	D	○
29.	⚐	A	B	C	D	○
30.	⚐	A	B	C	D	○
31.	⚐	A	B	C	D	○
32.	⚐	A	B	C	D	○
33.	⚐	A	B	C	D	○
34.	⚐	A	B	C	D	○
35.	⚐	A	B	C	D	○
36.	⚐	A	B	C	D	○
37.	⚐	A	B	C	D	○
38.	⚐	A	B	C	D	○
39.	⚐	A	B	C	D	○
40.	⚐	A	B	C	D	○
41.	⚐	A	B	C	D	○
42.	⚐	A	B	C	D	○
43.	⚐	A	B	C	D	○
44.	⚐	A	B	C	D	○
45.	⚐	A	B	C	D	○
46.	⚐	A	B	C	D	○
47.	⚐	A	B	C	D	○
48.	⚐	A	B	C	D	○
49.	⚐	A	B	C	D	○
50.	⚐	A	B	C	D	○
51.	⚐	A	B	C	D	○
52.	⚐	A	B	C	D	○
53.	⚐	A	B	C	D	○
54.	⚐	A	B	C	D	○
55.	⚐	A	B	C	D	○

Tip: You can also download and print this answer sheet from: `https://tiny.cc/ccese-answersheet`

Problem I.01

The shaded area of an intersection is proposed to be repaved. Determine the area to be repaved. Assume a road width of 30′ and an 8′ curb radius.

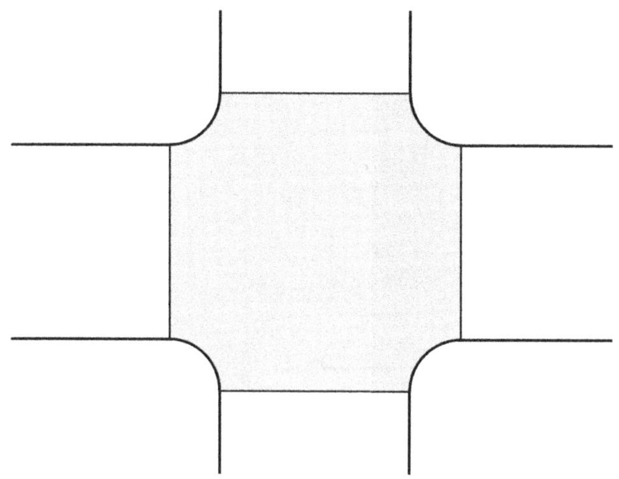

(A) 699[ft^2]

(B) 1243[ft^2]

(C) 1915[ft^2]

(D) 2066[ft^2]

Problem I.02

To verify the intactness of the control points shown below the distance between the control points is being taped in the field. What is the expected distance between points *B* and *D*?

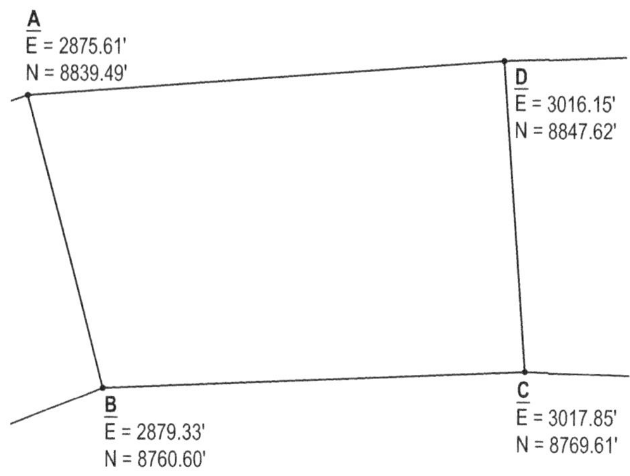

(A) 87.02[ft]

(B) 123.06[ft]

(C) 136.82[ft]

(D) 162.15[ft]

Problem I.03

Referring to the curve shown below, the azimuth from PC to station (202+00.00) is?

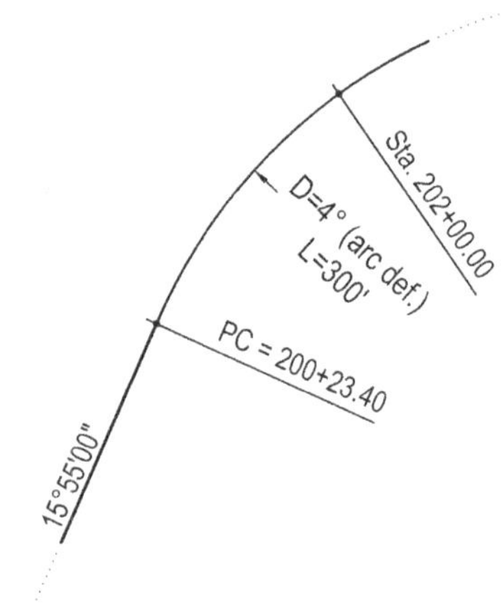

(A) $8°8'47''$

(B) $12°1'53''$

(C) $19°48'7''$

(D) $23°41'13''$

Problem I.04

For a water reservoir, the water surface area for certain elevations was determined using GIS software. Determine the volume of water that can be stored between elevation $1500'$ and $1375'$. Use the contour area method.

Elevation [ft]	Surface Area [ac]
1500	1702.5
1450	957.6
1425	665.0
1400	425.6
1375	239.4
1350	106.4
1325	26.6

(A) 33915[ac ft]

(B) 75479[ac ft]

(C) 96760[ac ft]

(D) 99752[ac ft]

Problem I.05

A cross section for a proposed road is shown below. In the figure, the row *Dist.* denotes the horizontal distance between dimensioned points, and *Cut* indicates the elevation difference between a proposed and the existing grade. Compute the total area of cut required in this section.

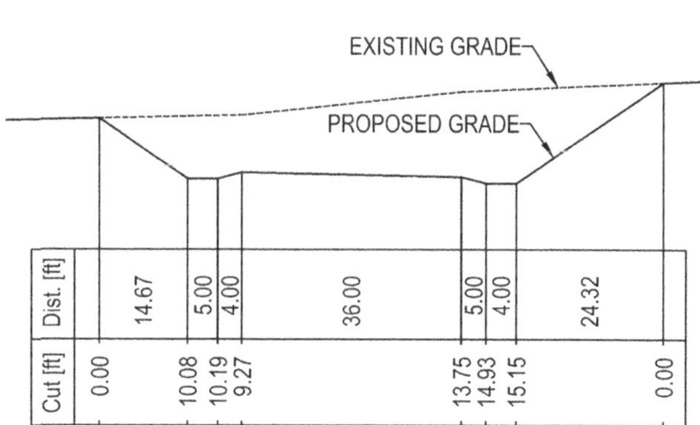

(A) 429.3[ft²]

(B) 503.3[ft²]

(C) 687.5[ft²]

(D) 894.7[ft²]

Problem I.06

In order to determine the height of a building, a total station (height of instrument: 5′8″ above ground) was set up in front of the building and measurements to the top and base of the building were taken. See the table below. Determine the height of the building.

#	Zenith Angle	Sloped Distance
1	38°59′13″	111.26[ft]
2	94°37′42″	70.23[ft]

(A) 70.00[ft]

(B) 80.81[ft]

(C) 92.15[ft]

(D) 140.0[ft]

Problem I.07

The concrete pad for a bus stop is shown in the figure below. What is the required concrete volume if the pad thickness is 8″?

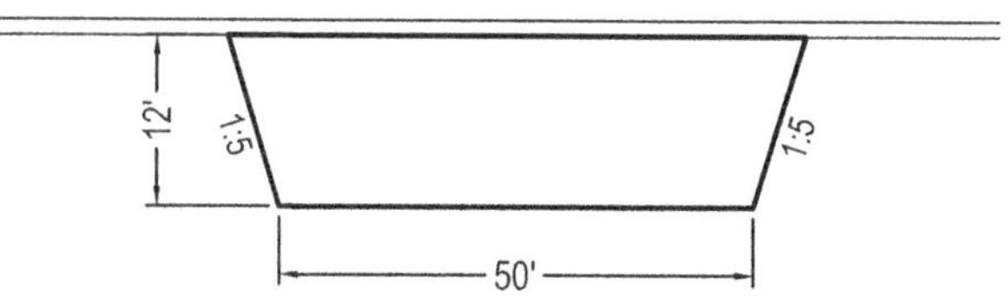

(A) 14.8[yd³]

(B) 15.5[yd³]

(C) 22.2[yd³]

(D) 32.6[yd³]

Problem I.08

Referring to the figure below, points A and B have been established in a previous survey. Later, a third point, C, was added to the survey. But, because only a tape measure was available, no direction angles are available. Determine the area enclosed by A, B, C.

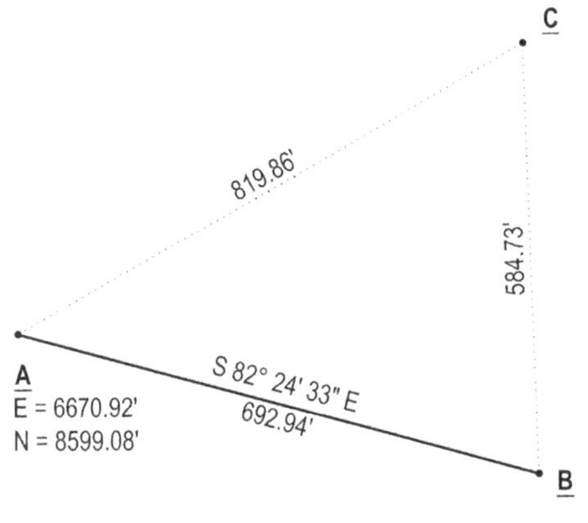

(A) 4.57[ac]

(B) 13.1[ac]

(C) 24.5[ac]

(D) 54.2[ac]

Problem I.09

The two construction stakes shown below were set for rough grading of a highway segment according to Caltrans' Surveys Manual. Determine the cross slope between the hinge points (assuming there is no additional grade point in between).

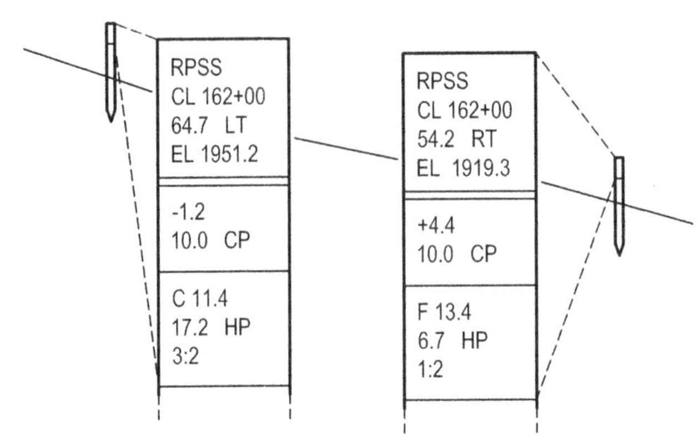

(A) 0.5%

(B) 2.0%

(C) 3.5%

(D) 5.0%

Problem I.10

A construction pit, shown below, is about to be excavated to an elevation of 234.40′. The construction pit is shored using pile sheet walls. The spot elevations shown in the figure represent existing soil elevations. Determine the excavation volume using the borrow pit method.

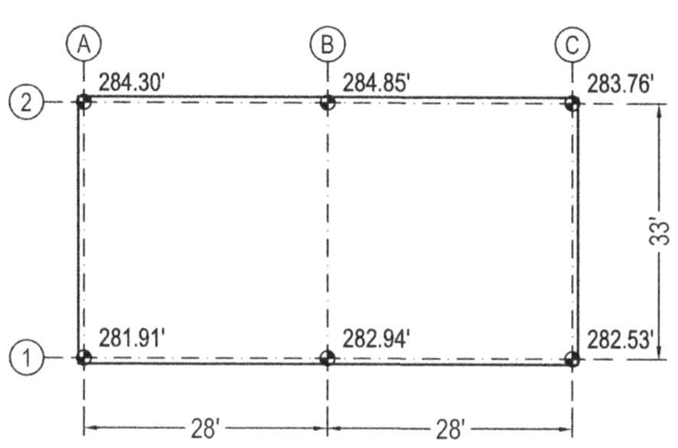

(A) 2514[yd^3]

(B) 2852[yd^3]

(C) 3361[yd^3]

(D) 3962[yd^3]

Problem I.11

A two-lane urban street is to be extended to have a third lane. Based on the data in the figure below, what is the length L of the transition zone?

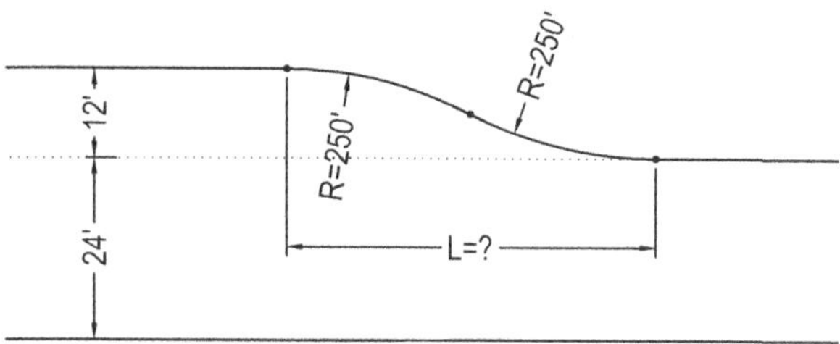

(A) 108.88[ft]

(B) 153.05[ft]

(C) 217.77[ft]

(D) 306.10[ft]

Problem I.12

A planned road has a stormwater drain running parallel, as depicted below: The flow line is 3′ below center line of the road; except where the road has a sag vertical-curve, in which case the flow line follows the straight line extension of the vertical alignment. At the point of vertical intersection, the storm drain passes through a 2′6″ diameter culvert.

Determine the required length L of the vertical curve such that the culvert has a 4′ clearance between top of the culvert and center line of the road.

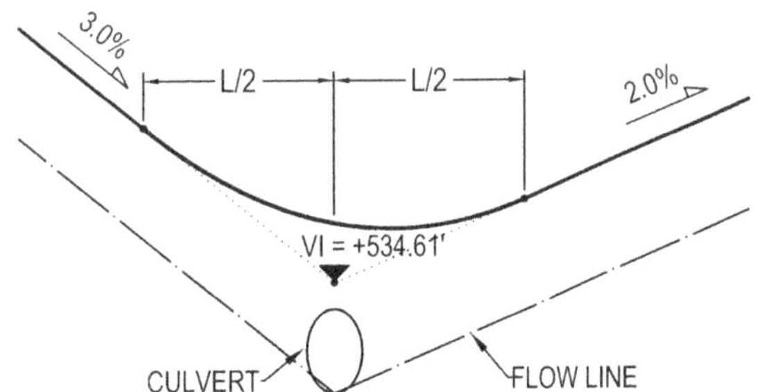

(A) 2.6[sta]

(B) 4.8[sta]

(C) 5.6[sta]

(D) 7.2[sta]

Problem I.13

A crest vertical curve, with 4.0[ft/sta] slope on both sides has its point of vertical intersection at elevation 2463.50′. Determine the required length of this vertical curve as such that the top turning point of the curve is at elevation 2450.00′.

(A) 1.7[sta]

(B) 3.4[sta]

(C) 6.8[sta]

(D) 13.5[sta]

Problem I.14

A drain is running parallel to a road but keeps running straight as the road takes a turn, as shown below. Determine the required length of the culvert.

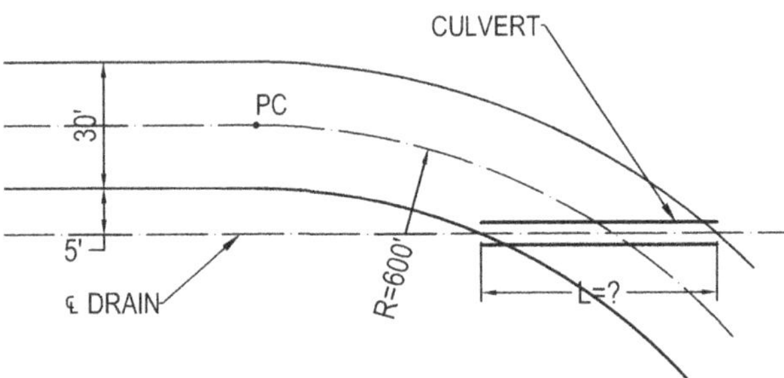

(A) 71[ft]

(B) 91[ft]

(C) 99[ft]

(D) 128[ft]

Problem I.15

A proposed power line is to run through an undivided, typical township section. The power line requires a 120[ft] wide right of way. Determine the required area for the power line's right of way within the township section.

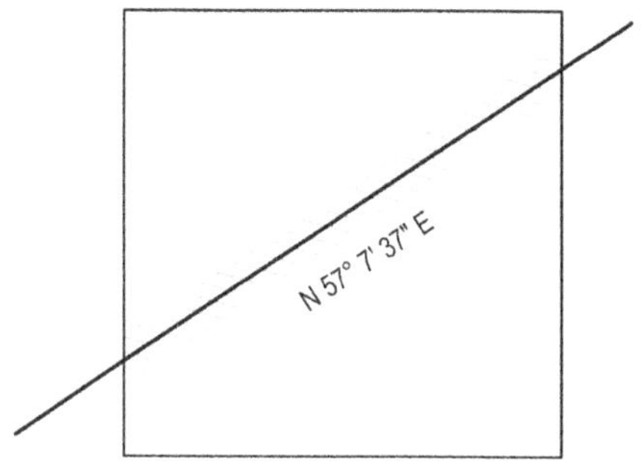

(A) 12.2[ac]

(B) 14.5[ac]

(C) 17.3[ac]

(D) 26.8[ac]

Problem I.16

A proposed, 32[ft] wide road is laid out to follow existing property lines. At a property line kink, the road takes a 500[ft] long curve, measured along the road center line. The area enclosed by the curve and property line, as shown in the exhibit, is to be greened. This area is most nearly?

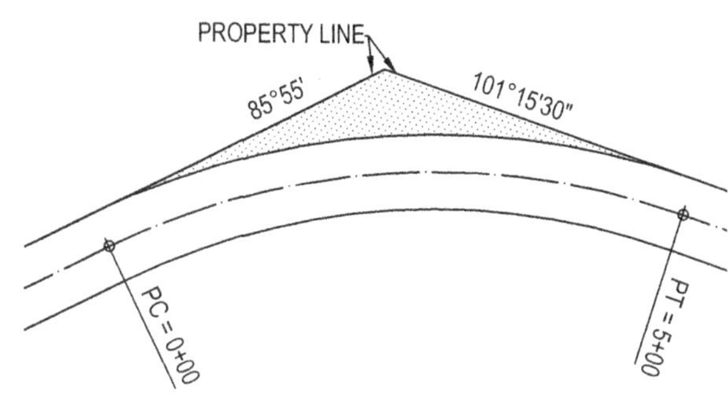

(A) $2,713[ft^2]$

(B) $2,761[ft^2]$

(C) $2,809[ft^2]$

(D) $2,858[ft^2]$

Problem I.17

A 32[ft] wide road follows a property line, as shown below. At a property line kink, the road takes a 500[ft] curve (measured along the road centerline). Determine the minimum distance from the property line kink to the edge of the road.

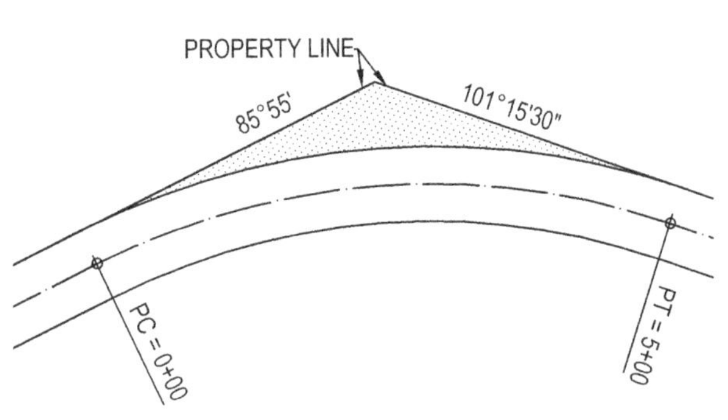

(A) 13.01[ft]

(B) 16.72[ft]

(C) 16.86[ft]

(D) 17.01[ft]

Problem I.18

A new pipeline is to be constructed, as shown below. Regulations require barriers for when the pipe line is closer than 200[ft] to the shoulder of the road. At what pipeline station may the special barriers end?

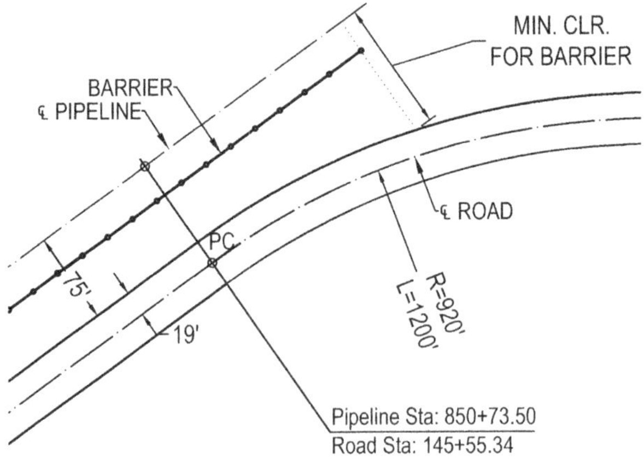

(A) Sta. (855+36.51)

(B) Sta. (855+41.61)

(C) Sta. (856+46.21)

(D) Sta. (856+52.81)

Problem I.19

For a construction project a temporary benchmark with elevation 591.63[ft] (project elevation: $-2.64'$) has been established.

If the excavation for a foundation needs to reach project elevation $-16'3''$, and the backsight rod reading is $4.61'$, what is the required foresight rod reading to verify the excavation elevation with a laser level?

(A) $13.61'$

(B) $18.22'$

(C) $18.89'$

(D) $20.68'$

Problem I.20

The underpass shown below requires an elevation difference of $\Delta H = 26[\text{ft}]$ using two vertical parabolic curves. If the maximum allowed slope is $G_{\text{max}} = 7.5\%$, what is the minimum length L of the transition?

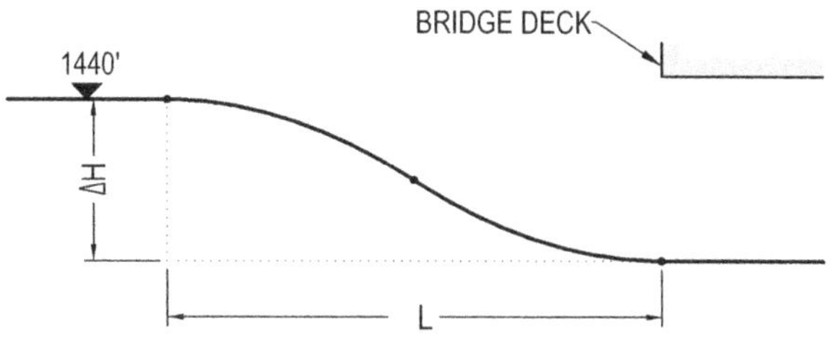

(A) 1.73[sta]

(B) 3.47[sta]

(C) 6.93[sta]

(D) 13.86[sta]

Problem I.21

The same physical distance between two points is measured twice using the same metal tape. The first measurement was taken at a temperature of $72.6[^\circ\text{F}]$. The second measurement was taken at a temperature of $93.2[^\circ\text{F}]$. If the physical distance between the points did not change between the readings, which of the following statements can be made regarding the recorded lengths of the measurements?

(A) The first measurement reads a lower distance.

(B) The second measurement reads a lower distance.

(C) Both measurements read the same value.

(D) None of the above statments can be made.

Problem I.22

A $D = 12^\circ$ (arc definition) curve is being staked out in the field. If stakes are to be set every 100[ft] along the curve, what must be the corresponding chord length between the stakes?

(A) $99.635[\text{ft}]$

(B) $99.817[\text{ft}]$

(C) $99.909[\text{ft}]$

(D) $99.954[\text{ft}]$

Problem I.23

The trapezoidal cross section of a riverbed shown below is being surveyed with 3-wire leveling. See the table below for field notes. The slope of the right riverbank is most nearly?

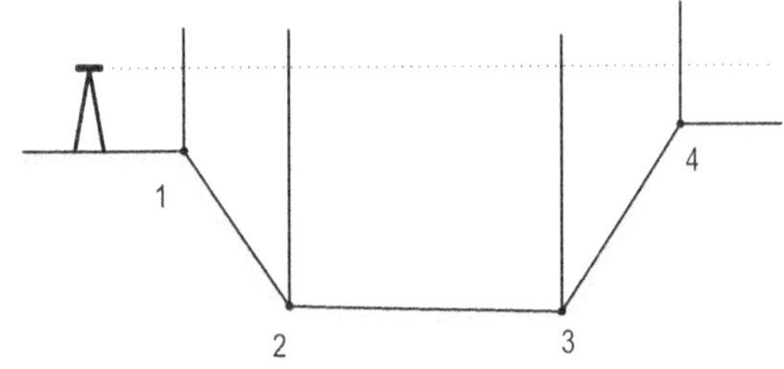

	FS	
1	5.67 5.64 5.61	
2	12.90 12.82 12.74	
3	13.72 13.57 13.42	
4	2.93 2.72 2.51	

(A) 89.6%

(B) 90.4%

(C) 99.3%

(D) 101.3%

Problem I.24

To verify the reflector constant of a newly bought EDM device, measurements of three points along a straight line were taken. See the table below for the measurement results, with A and C being the outer points. The reflector constant is most nearly?

Line	Distance [ft]
A–C	78.446
A–B	6.324
B–C	70.768

(A) 0.190[ft]

(B) 0.338[ft]

(C) 0.676[ft]

(D) 1.354[ft]

Problem I.25

In order to track the movement of an earthquake fault, the field measurements depicted below were taken. The azimuths noted are corrected for magnetic declination. Determine the magnitude of fault displacement based on the provided recordings.

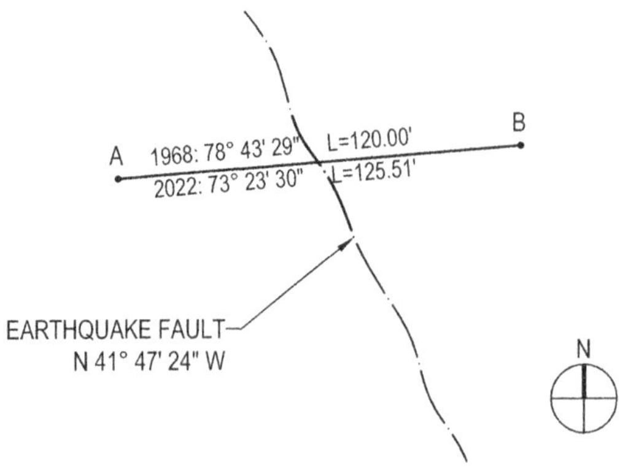

(A) 2.7[ft]

(B) 5.5[ft]

(C) 11.2[ft]

(D) 11.7[ft]

Problem I.26

A cross section of a proposed highway is shown below. Determine the net amount of cut or fill for this cross section.

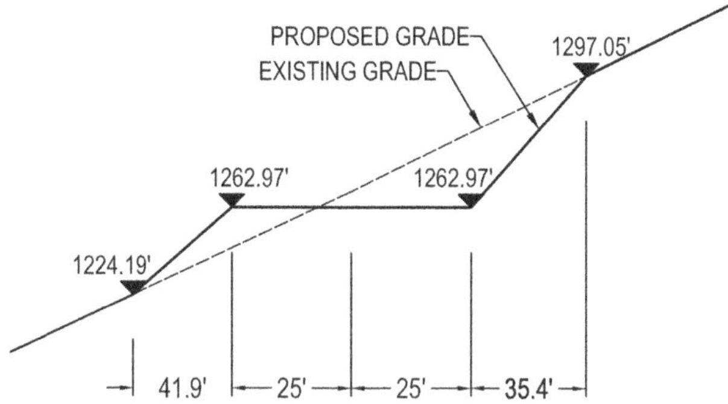

(A) 27.6[ft^2] cut

(B) 27.6[ft^2] fill

(C) 89.9[ft^2] cut

(D) 89.9[ft^2] fill

Problem I.27

The results of a differential leveling exercise are depicted below. The linear misclosure was distributed equally to each measured elevation. Later on it was discovered that the actual elevation of BM 6281-05 is at 923.28′. Based on this, what is the actual, corrected elevation of point C?

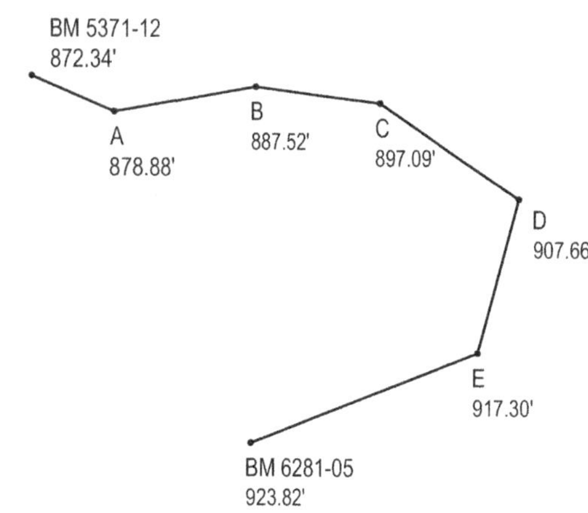

(A) 896.69′

(B) 896.82′

(C) 896.91′

(D) 897.00′

Problem I.28

Referring to the topographic map below, the average slope between which two points is the steepest? Assume the map is drawn to scale.

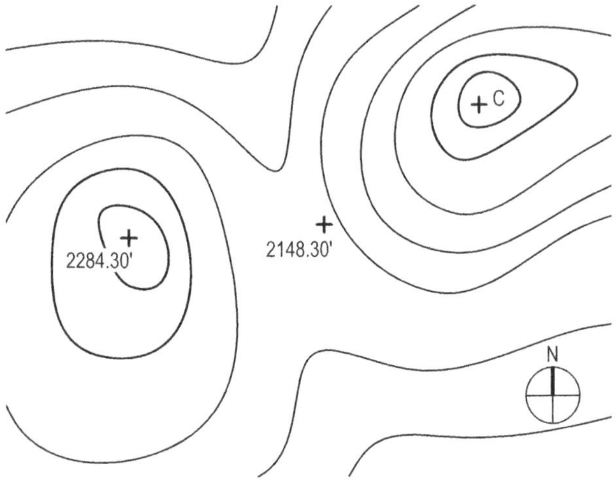

(A) Between point at elevation 2284.30′ and point at elevation 2148.30′

(B) Between point at elevation 2284.30′ and point C

(C) Between point at elevation 2148.30′ and point C

(D) None of the above can be concluded without additional information.

Problem I.29

To demolish an existing concrete building, a temporary 22[ft] tall and 15[ft] wide ramp needs to be built. If the maximum allowed slope is 12%, what is the minimum required ramp length?

(A) 100[ft]

(B) 125[ft]

(C) 147[ft]

(D) 183[ft]

Problem I.30

A 260′ long and 3′ wide ditch with 2.5[ft/sta] slope along the flow line is being excavated. A dumpy level is used to verify the excavation depths. If the rod reading at beginning of the ditch is 6.54[ft], what should be the rod reading at the end of the ditch?

(A) 0.04[ft]

(B) 6.50[ft]

(C) 12.74[ft]

(D) 13.04[ft]

Problem I.31

The construction drawings for the existing horizontal curve shown below were destroyed in a wild fire. Based on the conducted field survey, which is shown below, determine the centerline radius of the curve.

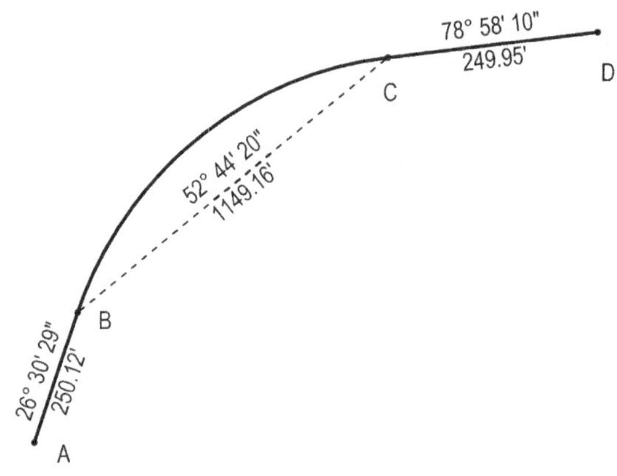

(A) 1130[ft]

(B) 1200[ft]

(C) 1300[ft]

(D) 1450[ft]

Problem I.32

For a horizontal curve with $R = 600[\text{ft}]$, the azimuths of the forward and backward tangent are $89°40'0''$ and $32°30'15''$, respectively. With the coordinates of PI being $(N = 15884.23[\text{ft}],\ E = 416.55[\text{ft}])$, determine coordinates of the point of PC.

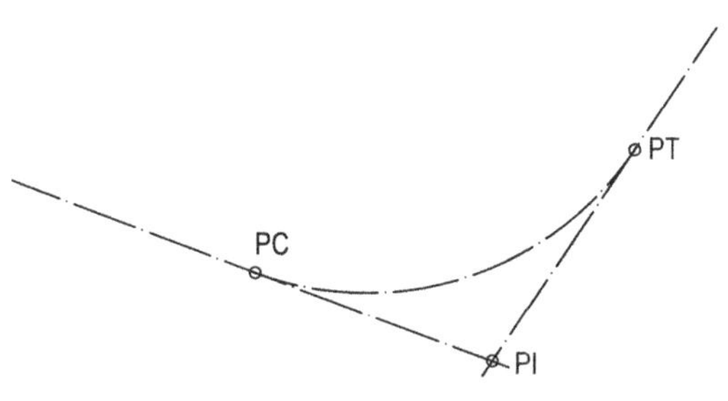

(A) (15100.181[ft], -83.024[ft])

(B) (15100.181[ft], 240.900[ft])

(C) (15608.558[ft], 240.900[ft])

(D) (16159.902[ft], 592.200[ft])

Problem I.33

An existing railway fork, as shown in the figure below, is to be extended with an additional turn. Determine the distance between point PC_1 and PT_2.

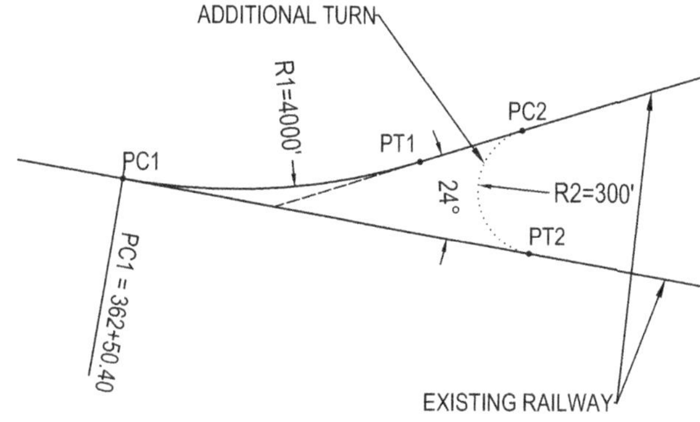

(A) 1045.05[ft]

(B) 1647.35[ft]

(C) 2261.62[ft]

(D) 2454.73[ft]

Problem I.34

A proposed road network was staked out in the field. The construction drawings specify the curves through coordinates of their end-points and the degree of curvature using chord basis. However, the surveyor mistakenly staked out using the arc basis definition for degree of curvature.

How do the proposed curve radii (R_{plan}) compare to the staked out(R_{field})?

(A) $R_{\text{plan}} < R_{\text{field}}$

(B) $R_{\text{plan}} = R_{\text{field}}$

(C) $R_{\text{plan}} > R_{\text{field}}$

(D) Cannot be determined without further information.

Problem I.35

Consider the curve of a 32[ft] wide road with deflection angle $I = 23°52'14''$. Project specific regulations require that PT_i remains visible from PC_i. This is enforced by defining a setback distance of $S = 15$[ft] in which no obstructions may be built. What is the minimum possible centerline radius of this curve?

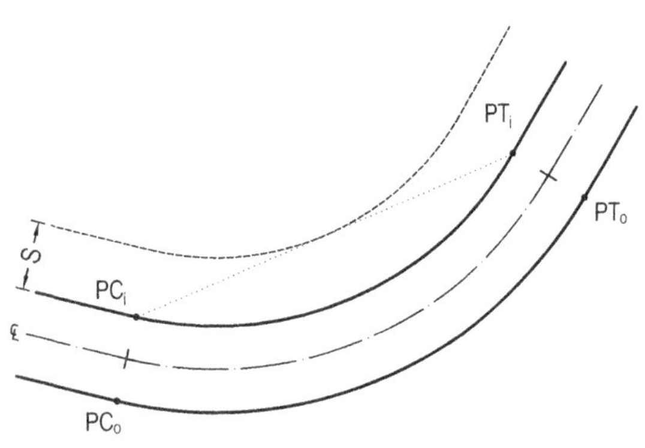

(A) 191.36[ft]

(B) 709.86[ft]

(C) 756.12[ft]

(D) 1496.24[ft]

Problem I.36

A storm drain—currently starting at point E—is to be extended to start at point A. It is planned to use a 48″ (inside diameter) reinforced concrete pipe with 5″ wall thickness. At point E, the invert elevation is 950.04′. The storm drain requires a minimum cover of 4′6″ above the pipe top. The maximum slope is 6.0% and can change at every full station.

Determine the highest possible pipe invert elevation at point A.

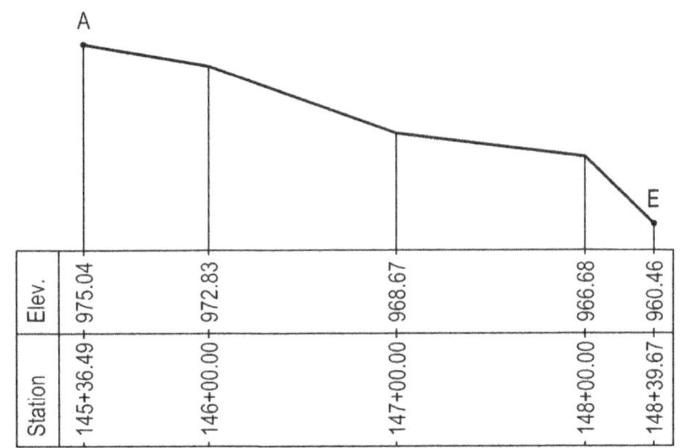

(A) 963.81′

(B) 964.64′

(C) 966.12′

(D) 968.23′

Problem I.37

In order to track the movement of an earthquake fault, the field measurements depicted below were taken. The azimuths noted are *not* corrected for magnetic declination. Determine the magnitude of fault-parallel displacement based on the provided recordings. Assume the line $B-C$ is initially perpendicular to the fault and points A, B were not displaced relative to each other.

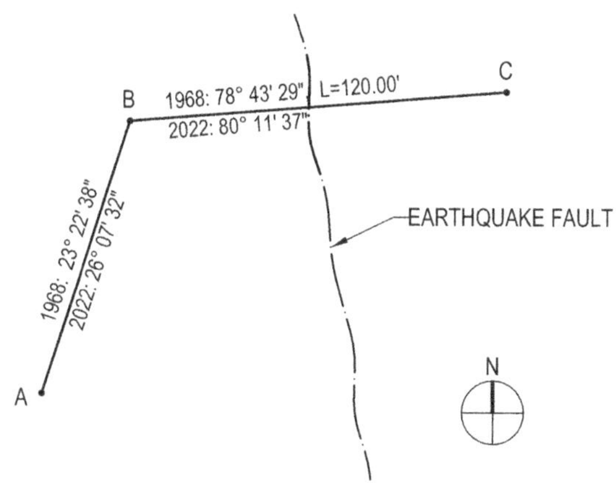

(A) East side moving 2.68[ft] northwards.

(B) East side moving 3.08[ft] northwards.

(C) East side moving 8.85[ft] northwards.

(D) East side moving 14.66[ft] northwards.

Problem I.38

The excavation plan for a construction pit is shown below. Determine the excavation volume using the average end formula. For determination of excavation depth, assume an existing elevation of 342.50′ and a final grade of 321.40′ for the excavation.

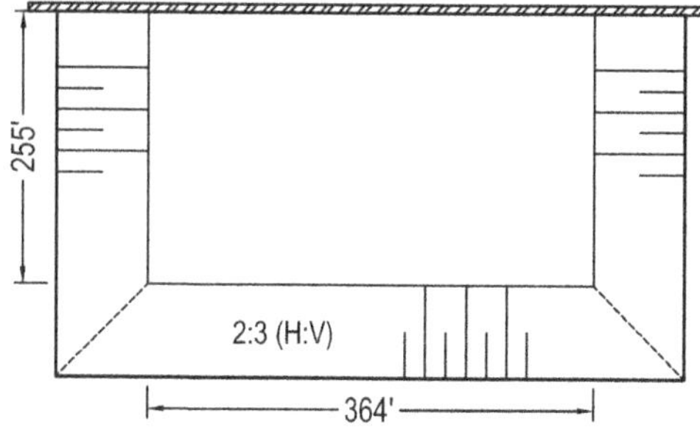

(A) 76000[yd^3]

(B) 77500[yd^3]

(C) 79700[yd^3]

(D) 84100[yd^3]

Problem I.39

A curve with radius $R = 1800$[ft] and deflection angle $\delta = 28°$ is to be laid out in the field using stakes at 100[ft] chord distance. The number of stakes between PC and PT is:

(A) 4

(B) 5

(C) 8

(D) 9

Problem I.40

Determine the slope of the ramp shown below.

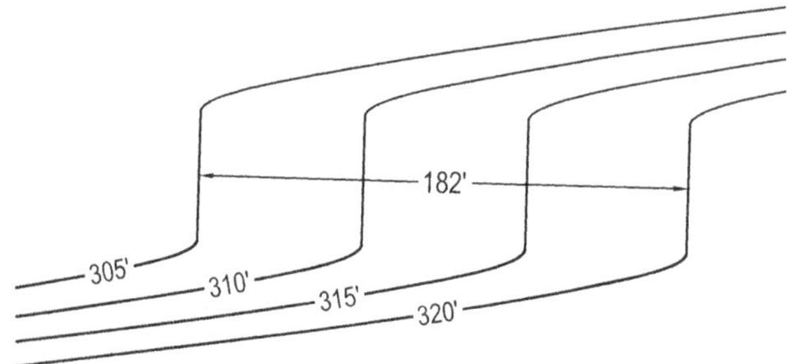

(A) 8 : 1 (H : V)

(B) 12 : 1 (H : V)

(C) 15 : 1 (H : V)

(D) 18 : 1 (H : V)

Problem I.41

The underpass shown below realizes an elevation difference of $\Delta H = 28$[ft] using two vertical parabolic curves. If the horizontal length of the two horizontal curves is 12.5[sta], what is the maximum grade in the transition?

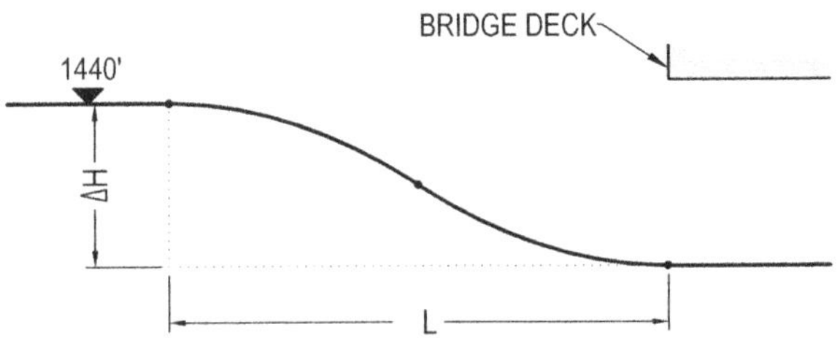

(A) 4.5[ft/sta]

(B) 9.0[ft/sta]

(C) 13.0[ft/sta]

(D) 18.0[ft/sta]

Problem I.42

Measurements were taken from point C to points A and B, as shown below. What is the distance between points A and B?

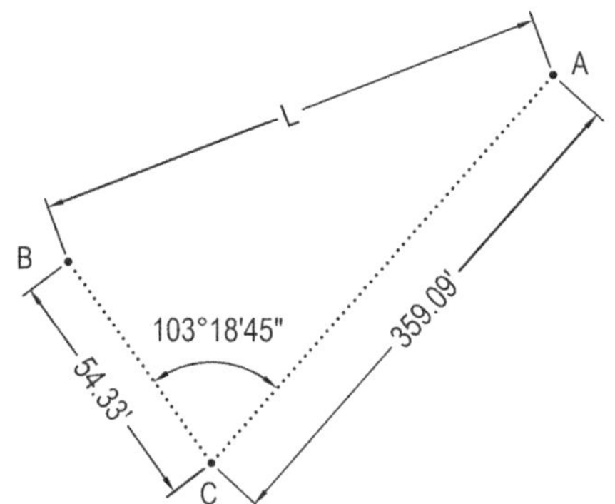

(A) 306.47[ft]

(B) 350.58[ft]

(C) 375.34[ft]

(D) 359.09[ft]

Problem I.43

Flight planning for a photogrammetry flight mission: The plan is to shoot with a 6[in]-focal length lens on 9 × 9[in] photos. The altitude above ground will be 3000[ft] and the plane will fly with a speed of 105[mph]. What is the required timing between photos to achieve a forward overlap of 50%?

(A) 1.2[sec]

(B) 3.6[sec]

(C) 7.3[sec]

(D) 14.6[sec]

Problem I.44

The open traverse shown below represents centerline points of a natural creek. The creek is to be streamlined from A to D in a straight line. Determine the bearing from A to D.

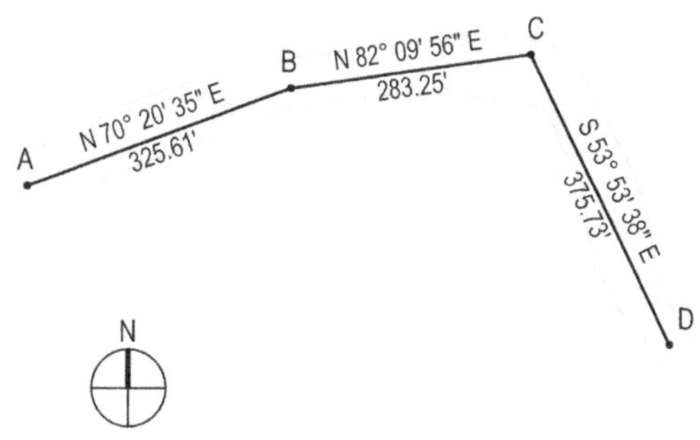

(A) N 4°42′7″ E

(B) N 86°42′7″ W

(C) S 4°42′7″ E

(D) S 86°42′7″ E

Problem I.45

Using the differential leveling field notes below, determine the elevation of the lowest surveyed point (out of A,B,C,D,E).

	BS	HI	FS	Elev
BM 574-5	5.34			875.36
TP 1	3.92		7.38	
A			7.54	
B			7.61	
C			7.83	
TP 2	10.55		8.54	
D			5.84	
E			6.04	
TP 3	5.64		3.5	
BM 574-5			6.13	

(A) 868.31[ft]

(B) 869.41[ft]

(C) 873.21[ft]

(D) 868.7[ft]

Problem I.46

For the traverse shown below, determine the bearing angle of the segment $D - E$.

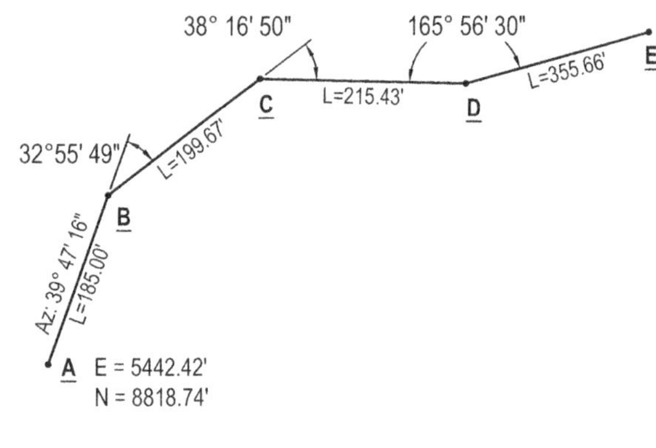

(A) S 7°3′35″ E

(B) S 21°0′5″ E

(C) S 54°56′35″ E

(D) S 83°3′35″ E

Problem I.47

Using the leveling field notes and the sketch below, determine the misclosure for point 2′.

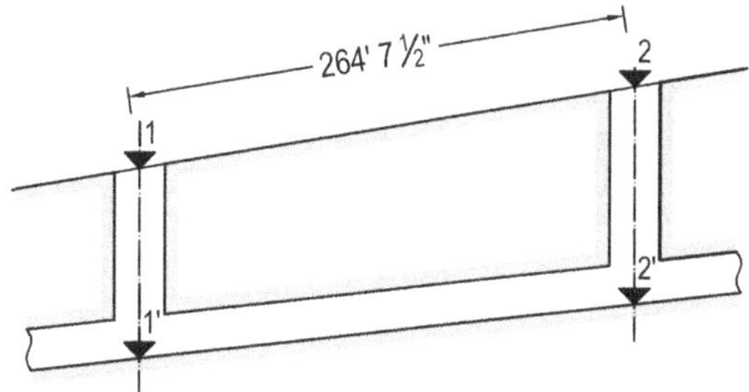

	BS	HI	FS	Elev
BM 12-06431	5.54			263.383
1			10.54	
1′			16.41	
2			5.37	
2′			12.46	256.472

(A) -0.015[ft]

(B) -0.009[ft]

(C) ± 0.000[ft]

(D) 0.015[ft]

Problem I.48

The intersections in a residential neighborhood are to be changed to have raised cross walks. For the typical intersection shown below, determine the area of asphalt to be replaced (shaded area). For determining the north ramp length, assume a 6″ height difference between the road and cross walk.

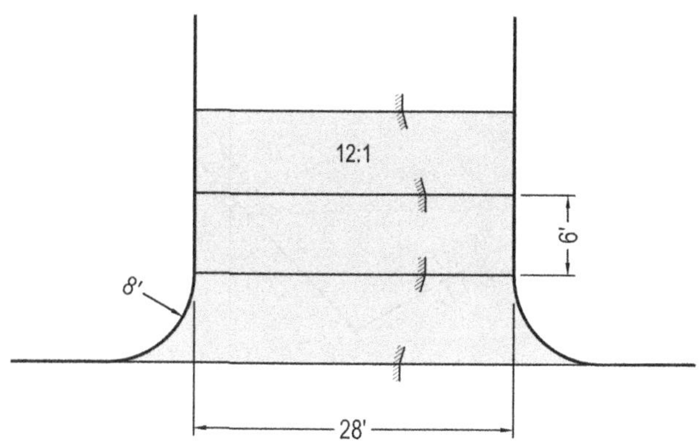

(A) 573.7[ft^2]

(B) 587.4[ft^2]

(C) 610.3[ft^2]

(D) 660.5[ft^2]

Problem I.49

The figure below shows field notes of a closed traverse. Determine the enclosed area.

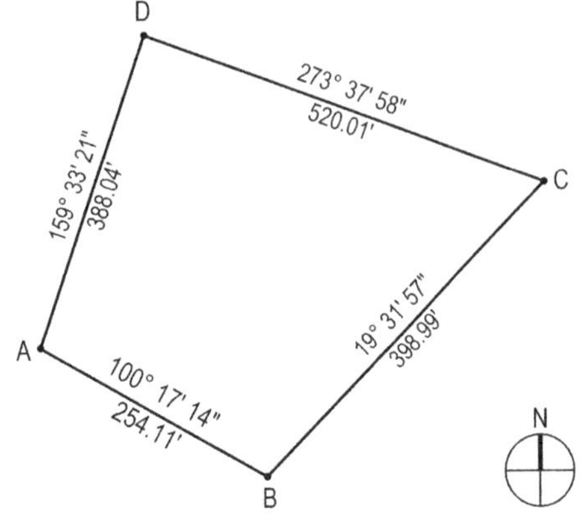

(A) 0.76[ac]

(B) 1.93[ac]

(C) 2.09[ac]

(D) 3.26[ac]

Problem I.50

Determine the shaded area of the turnaround shown below. The incoming road is 50[ft] wide and the radius of the turnaround is 45[ft].

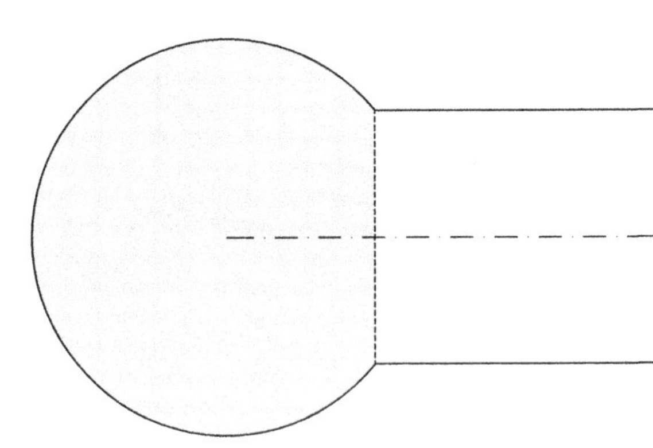

(A) 6104[ft^2]

(B) 6328[ft^2]

(C) 6357[ft^2]

(D) 6396[ft^2]

Problem I.51

For the storm drain shown below, determine the amount of water in the cross section if freeboard f is 3[ft].

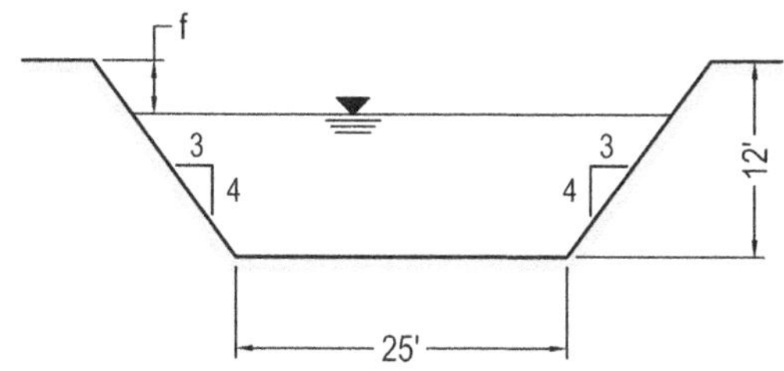

(A) 255[ft^2]

(B) 279[ft^2]

(C) 286[ft^2]

(D) 333[ft^2]

Problem I.52

For the traverse shown below, determine the bearing angle of the segment $A - D$.

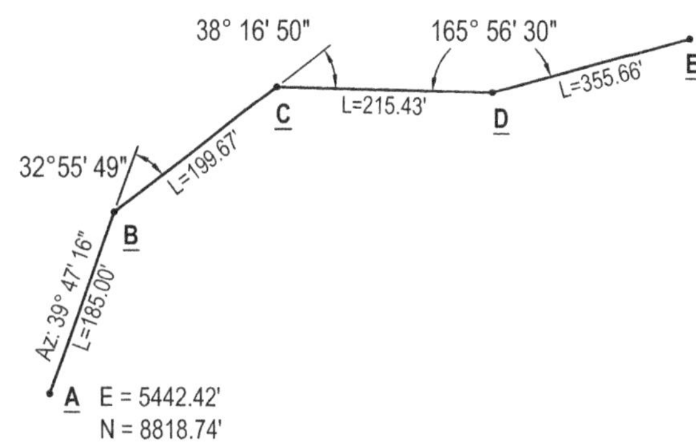

(A) $(E, N)_D = (5566.7, 9328.91)$[ft]

(B) $(E, N)_D = (5629.64, 8842.54)$[ft]

(C) $(E, N)_D = (5873.29, 9197.89)$[ft]

(D) $(E, N)_D = (5952.59, 8943.02)$[ft]

Problem I.53

A cross section of a proposed highway is shown below. Determine the net amount of cut or fill for this cross section.

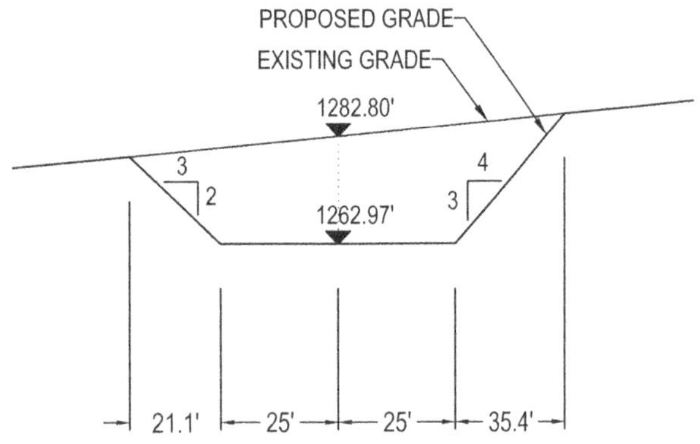

(A) 1564[ft^2] cut

(B) 1783[ft^2] cut

(C) 1821[ft^2] cut

(D) 2042[ft^2] cut

Problem I.54

A hillside sewer pipe is daylighting after a landslide. To asses its continued functionality, the measurements given below were taken. Determine the current slope of the sewer pipe using the information provided.

Point	BS	HI	FS	Notes
A			5.67	to manhole cover
B			27.18	to top of pipe

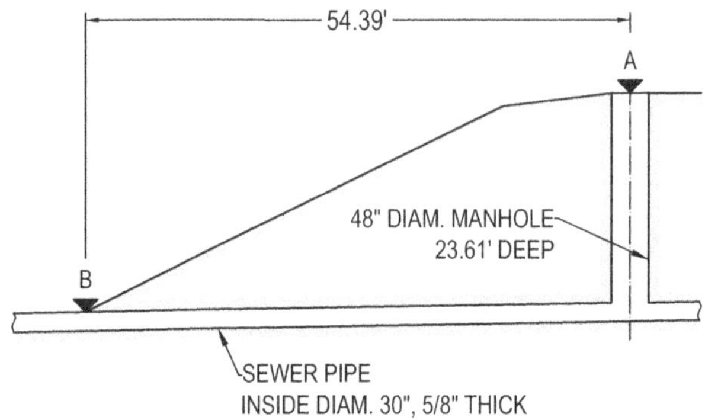

(A) 0.64%

(B) 0.83%

(C) 3.86%

(D) 3.96%

Problem I.55

A certain typical section in the Public Land Surveying System is occupied by a 128[ac]-lake. What percentage of this section is occupied by the lake?

(A) 10%

(B) 20%

(C) 25%

(D) 33%

Chapter 5

Practice Exam II

Answer Sheet to Practice Exam II

Question	Flag?	Option	Correct?	Question	Flag?	Option	Correct?
1.	⚐	A B C D	○	29.	⚐	A B C D	○
2.	⚐	A B C D	○	30.	⚐	A B C D	○
3.	⚐	A B C D	○	31.	⚐	A B C D	○
4.	⚐	A B C D	○	32.	⚐	A B C D	○
5.	⚐	A B C D	○	33.	⚐	A B C D	○
6.	⚐	A B C D	○	34.	⚐	A B C D	○
7.	⚐	A B C D	○	35.	⚐	A B C D	○
8.	⚐	A B C D	○	36.	⚐	A B C D	○
9.	⚐	A B C D	○	37.	⚐	A B C D	○
10.	⚐	A B C D	○	38.	⚐	A B C D	○
11.	⚐	A B C D	○	39.	⚐	A B C D	○
12.	⚐	A B C D	○	40.	⚐	A B C D	○
13.	⚐	A B C D	○	41.	⚐	A B C D	○
14.	⚐	A B C D	○	42.	⚐	A B C D	○
15.	⚐	A B C D	○	43.	⚐	A B C D	○
16.	⚐	A B C D	○	44.	⚐	A B C D	○
17.	⚐	A B C D	○	45.	⚐	A B C D	○
18.	⚐	A B C D	○	46.	⚐	A B C D	○
19.	⚐	A B C D	○	47.	⚐	A B C D	○
20.	⚐	A B C D	○	48.	⚐	A B C D	○
21.	⚐	A B C D	○	49.	⚐	A B C D	○
22.	⚐	A B C D	○	50.	⚐	A B C D	○
23.	⚐	A B C D	○	51.	⚐	A B C D	○
24.	⚐	A B C D	○	52.	⚐	A B C D	○
25.	⚐	A B C D	○	53.	⚐	A B C D	○
26.	⚐	A B C D	○	54.	⚐	A B C D	○
27.	⚐	A B C D	○	55.	⚐	A B C D	○
28.	⚐	A B C D	○				

Tip: You can also download and print this answer sheet from: `https://tiny.cc/ccese-answersheet`

Problem II.01

A 1800[ft] long, 5[ft] deep utility trench as shown below is to be built. Determine the volume of sand bedding required.

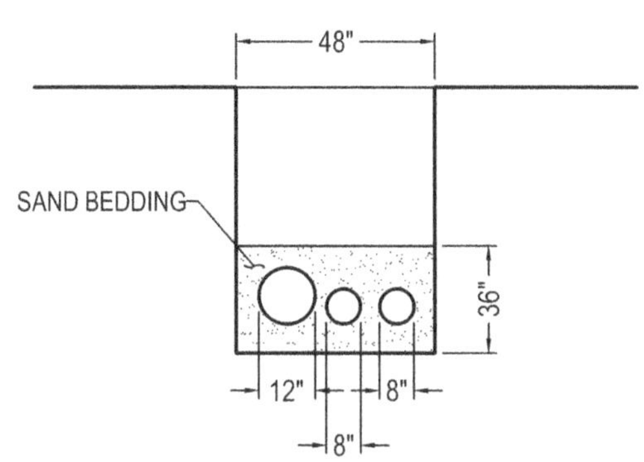

(A) 643[yd^3]

(B) 672[yd^3]

(C) 701[yd^3]

(D) 730[yd^3]

Problem II.02

What is most likely the elevation of point *C* shown in the topographic map below?

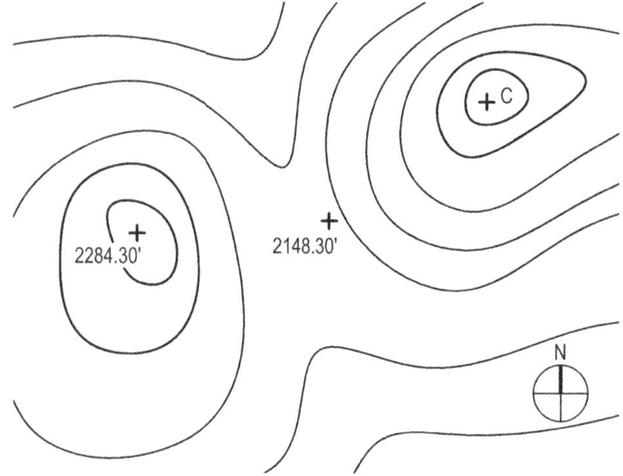

(A) 2282′

(B) 2382′

(C) 2557′

(D) 2588′

Problem II.03

A new tunnel, as shown below, requires a 7[ft] clearance to the vertical curve crossing it. Determine the required length L of the vertical curve to keep the required clearance.

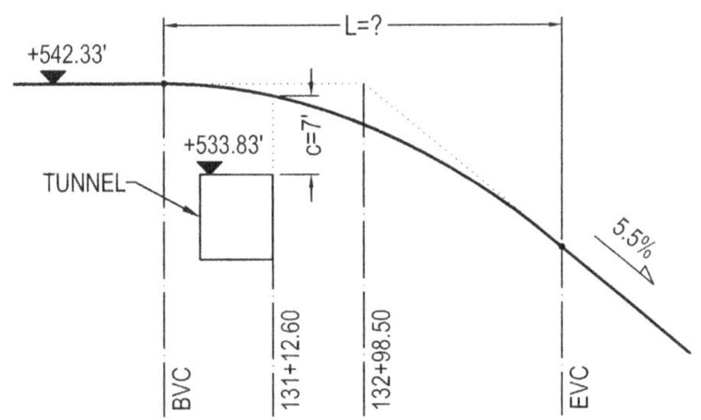

(A) 1.7589[sta]

(B) 3.9294[sta]

(C) 7.8588[sta]

(D) 8.9853[sta]

Problem II.04

The top of a retaining wall is continuously monitored for creeping deflections. The table below shows raw tape measurements taken between a stable point and the top of the retaining wall. After applying temperature corrections, what is the top-of-wall movement between 01/01 and 07/01?

Date	T[°F]	L[ft]
01/01	9	88.53
03/01	36	88.96
05/02	64	90.12
07/01	83	90.57
09/01	71	90.62
11/01	23	91.57

(A) 2.01[ft]

(B) 2.08[ft]

(C) 2.33[ft]

(D) 2.64[ft]

Problem II.05

A road alignment is passing through a bridge, as shown in the figure below. Determine the minimum clearance between the road and the underside of the bridge deck at the left side of the bridge deck.

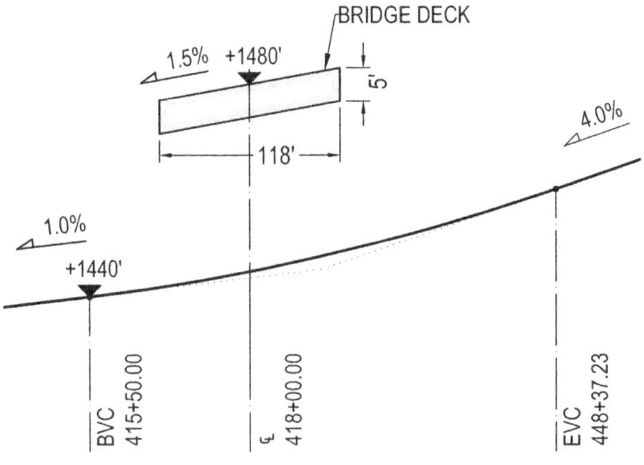

(A) 29.30[ft]

(B) 31.42[ft]

(C) 32.04[ft]

(D) 34.30[ft]

Problem II.06

A theodolite, set up above a point A, was used to determine the height of a point B. The height of instrument was $5'9''$ above point A and the foresight reading to point B was $5.34'$ under an elevation angle of $\alpha = 48°13'54''$ and a sloped distance of $L = 52.75'$. Determine the elevation of point B if the elevation of point A is $1252.48'$ above datum.

(A) $1224.23'$

(B) $1252.89'$

(C) $1292.23'$

(D) $1297.16'$

Problem II.07

For the given river channel cross section shown below, determine the required slope of the storm sewer pipe, such that the pipe daylights 1 feet above the mean river elevation.

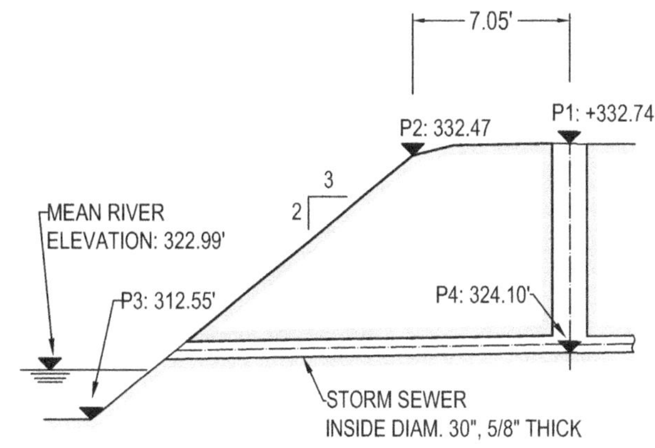

(A) 0.6%

(B) 1.5%

(C) 5.2%

(D) 7.9%

Problem II.08

Referring to the curve shown below, the bearing of the curve tangent at station (202+00.00) is?

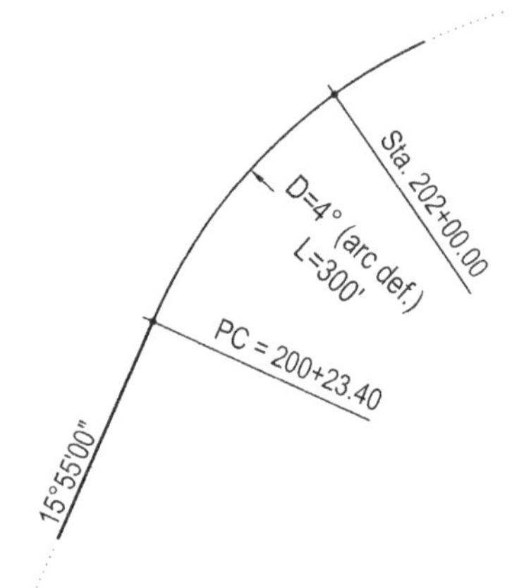

(A) 22°51′10″

(B) 22°58′50″

(C) 27°3′50″

(D) 28°51′10″

Problem II.09

The traverse shown below contains uncorrected field notes. Determine the linear misclosure of the traverse.

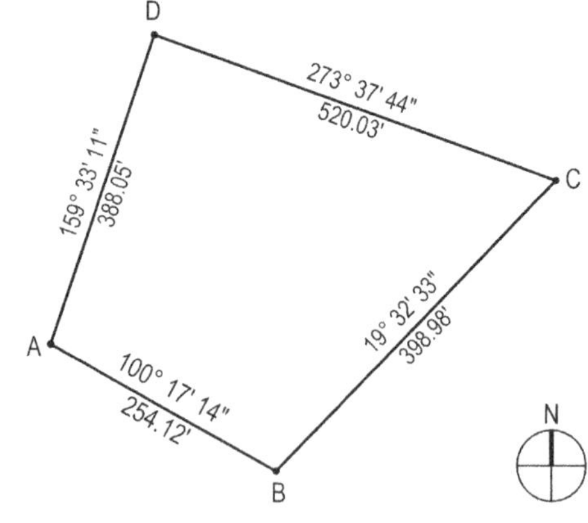

(A) −0.19′

(B) −0.09′

(C) 0.09′

(D) 0.19′

Problem II.10

For a tapered precast concrete manhole, determine the amount of concrete required, while neglecting the geometry around the joints.

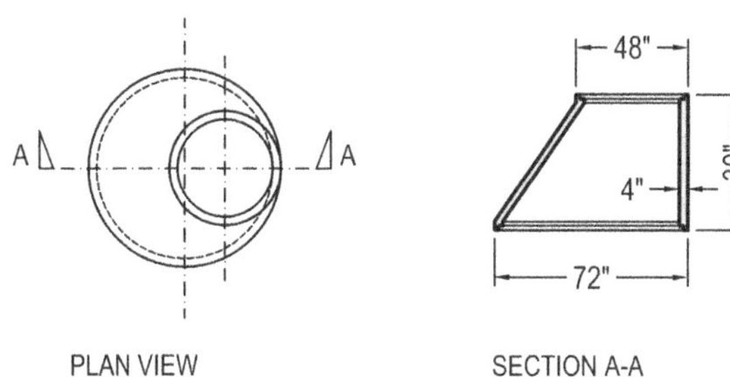

(A) 12.2[ft^3]

(B) 13.1[ft^3]

(C) 14.0[ft^3]

(D) 14.9[ft^3]

Problem II.11

The ramp of the excavation pit shown below is to be removed. The slope angle of the ramp side was constructed at 35°. Assuming the construction pit is 18[ft] deep, determine the excavation volume to remove the ramp.

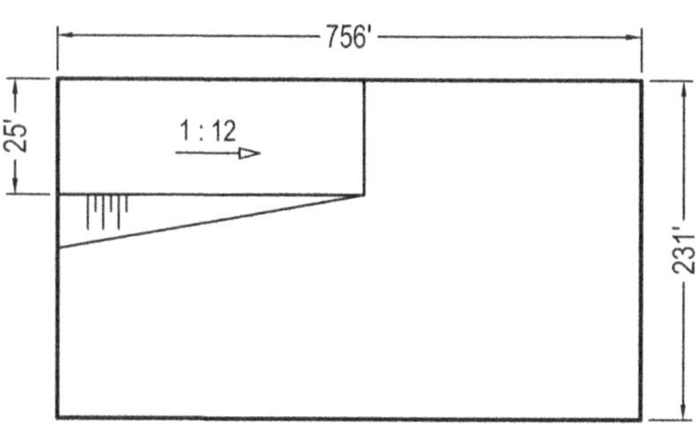

(A) 2033[yd^3]

(B) 2417[yd^3]

(C) 2725[yd^3]

(D) 3651[yd^3]

Problem II.12

The leveling field notes below were taken to survey the corner points of the parcel shown beneath. Based on the leveling notes, determine the direction in which water flows toward.

	BS	HI	FS	Elev.
BM 627-95	8.54			746.37
TP1	14.59		2.66	
A			10.26	
B			10.77	
TP2	6.15		9.54	
C			9.42	
D			9.86	

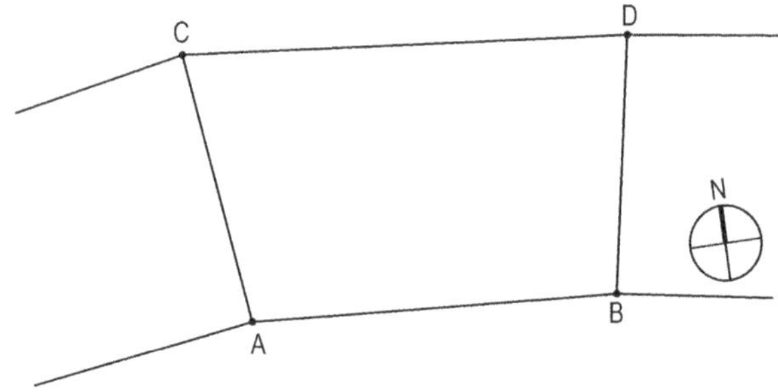

(A) North

(B) East

(C) South

(D) West

Problem II.13

For the traverse shown below, determine the length of a straight line connecting A and C.

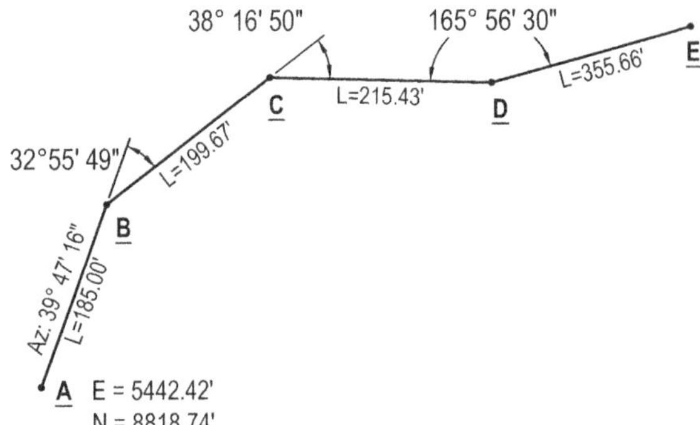

(A) 368.92[ft]

(B) 383.08[ft]

(C) 383.98[ft]

(D) 384.67[ft]

Problem II.14

In the survey shown below, point C was surveyed from both points A and point B. Determine the linear misclosure in grid coordinates when grid coordinates are computed based on point A and point B respectively.

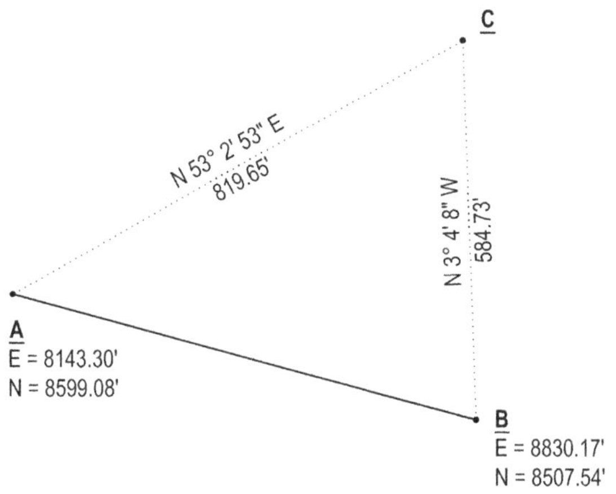

(A) 0.037[ft]

(B) 0.377[ft]

(C) 0.550[ft]

(D) 0.667[ft]

Problem II.15

Which of the following Public Land Surveying System sections might measure 5076[ft] along the south edge and 5215[ft] along the east edge?

(A) Section 1

(B) Section 6

(C) Section 31

(D) Section 36

Problem II.16

An excavation for a pad foundation needs to be dug 3[ft] deep from existing soil. To regularly check the progress of the excavation, a level is used. If the rod reading to existing soil is 5.56′ and to current excavation depth 7.18′, how much deeper the excavation needs to go to reach the required depth?

(A) 1.38′

(B) 1.62′

(C) 2.22′

(D) 2.56′

Problem II.17

Using the surveying records below, determine the distance from B to the closest point on the line $\overline{AC}$.

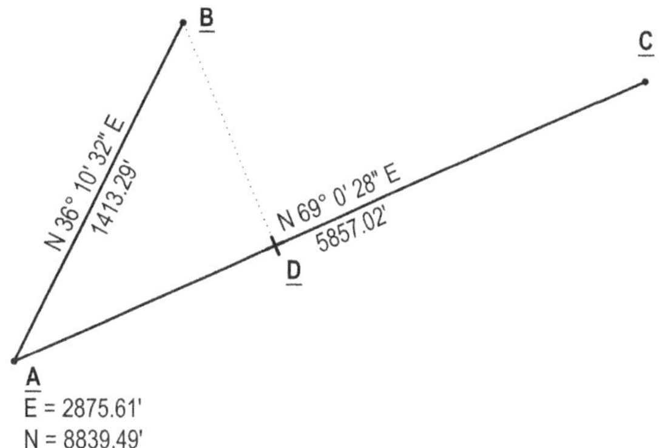

(A) 370.15[ft]

(B) 766.26[ft]

(C) 1187.53[ft]

(D) 1363.96[ft]

Problem II.18

Based on the field notes shown below, determine the vertical clearance between the road and the bottom of the bridge.

	BS	FS	Elev
BM 12-06431	5.54		263.383
TP 1	4.38	13.69	
CL Road @ edge of bridge		6.87	
Bottom of bridge [1]		10.62	

[1] *Rod was held upside down.*

(A) 3.75[ft]

(B) 6.87[ft]

(C) 10.62[ft]

(D) 17.49[ft]

Problem II.19

The pile cap shown below couples six cast-in-place piles. Determine the total concrete volume for pouring the six piles and the pile cap. Assume the length of each pile starts at the bottom of pile cap. Neglect the volume of reinforcement.

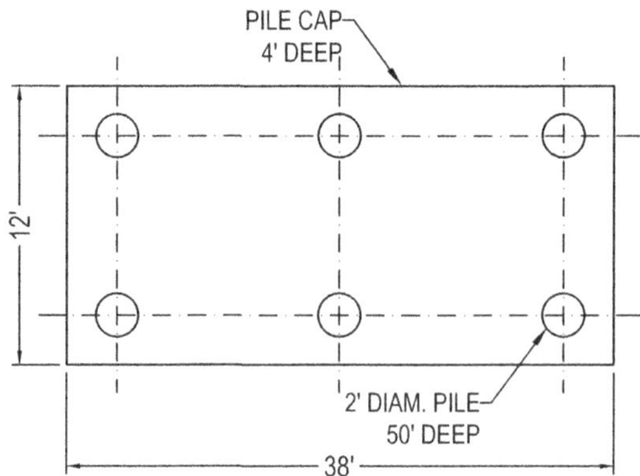

(A) 65.9[yd^3]

(B) 71.5[yd^3]

(C) 99.7[yd^3]

(D) 102.5[yd^3]

Problem II.20

For the rectangular parcel shown below, determine the coordinates of point C.

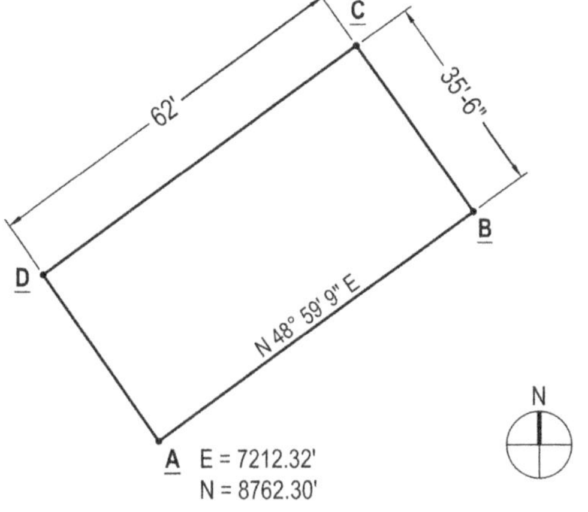

(A) $(E,N)_C = (7226.22, 8832.38)[\text{ft}]$

(B) $(E,N)_C = (7235.81, 8829.77)[\text{ft}]$

(C) $(E,N)_C = (7253.01, 8809.08)[\text{ft}]$

(D) $(E,N)_C = (7282.40, 8776.20)[\text{ft}]$

Problem II.21

An existing railway fork, as shown in the figure below, is to be extended with an additional turn. Determine the distance between point PT_1 and PC_2.

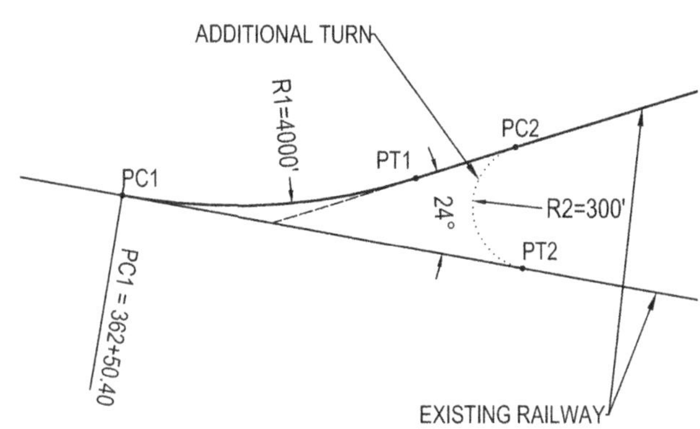

(A) $561.16[\text{ft}]$

(B) $786.46[\text{ft}]$

(C) $913.99[\text{ft}]$

(D) $2261.62[\text{ft}]$

Problem II.22

A solar power plant is to be built on the semi-circular lot shown below. Determine the area of the lot.

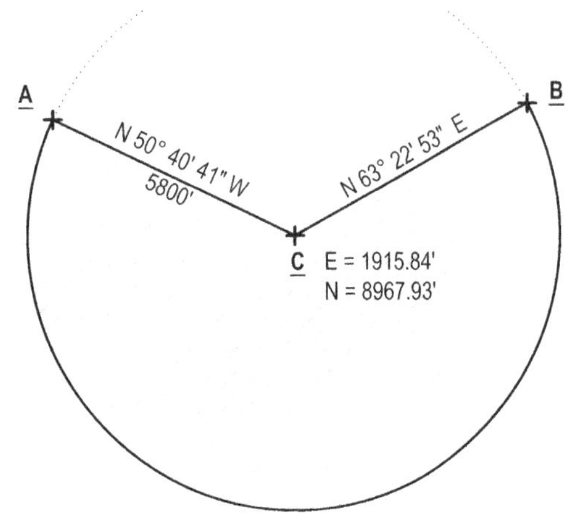

(A) 161[ac]

(B) 769[ac]

(C) 1375[ac]

(D) 1657[ac]

Problem II.23

The parcel shown below is to be refurbished. Currently, the lot (excluding the building) is paved with concrete. Determine the area of concrete that needs to be removed (assuming all concrete will be removed).

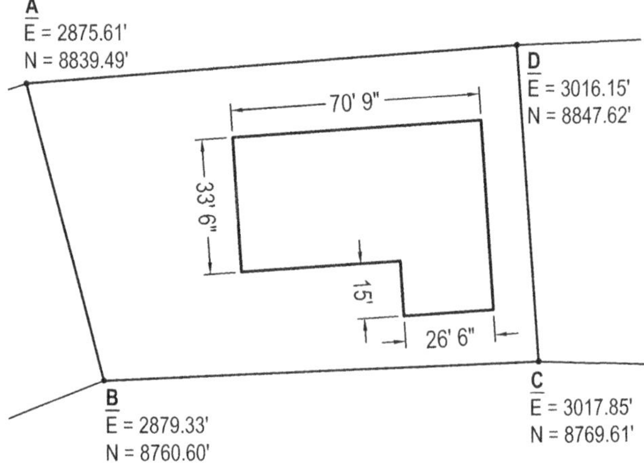

(A) 8202[ft^2]

(B) 8996[ft^2]

(C) 19171[ft^2]

(D) 19966[ft^2]

Problem II.24

Using the differential leveling field notes below, compute the misclosure for BM 574-5.

	BS	HI	FS	Elev
BM 574-5	5.34			875.364
TP 1	3.92		7.38	
A			7.54	
B			7.61	
C			7.83	
TP 2	10.55		8.54	
D			5.84	
E			6.04	
TP 3	5.64		3.5	
BM 574-5			6.13	

(A) −0.10[ft]

(B) −0.01[ft]

(C) +0.01[ft]

(D) +0.10[ft]

Problem II.25

A drainage ditch is to be dug along the stations shown in the table; starting at point 0, ending at point 5. The ditch requires a minimum depth of 4[ft] at each point. Assume the ditch starts with a 4[ft] depth and the ditch slope doesn't change. What is the minimum ditch slope required to maintain the minimum depth along its length?

Point	Station [sta]	Elevation (existing) [ft]
0	(145+36.49)	975.04
1	(146+00.00)	972.83
2	(147+00.00)	968.67
3	(148+00.00)	966.68
4	(149+00.00)	932.05
5	(149+39.67)	929.46

(A) 10.72%

(B) 11.31%

(C) 11.83%

(D) 12.93%

Problem II.26

For the flared sidewalk ramp shown below, determine its area (the shaded portion). Assume a height difference of 6″ between sidewalk and road.

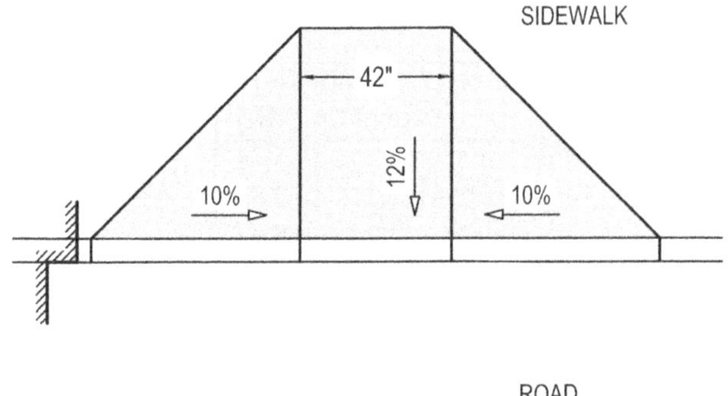

(A) 31.9[ft^2]

(B) 35.4[ft^2]

(C) 39.6[ft^2]

(D) 56.3[ft^2]

Problem II.27

The vertical grade of a highway changes from $G_1 = 3.5\%$ to $G_2 = -0.5\%$ with a rate of change of grade of -0.1627 percent per station. Determine the station at the end of the vertical curve, assuming the beginning of vertical curve is at station (1034+71.16).

(A) (1053+15.04)

(B) (1059+29.67)

(C) (1071+58.93)

(D) (1083+88.19)

Problem II.28

The two construction stakes shown below were set for rough grading of a highway segment according to Caltrans' Surveys Manual. Determine the rough grading elevation of the centerline. Assume a constant slope of the proposed grade between the catch points.

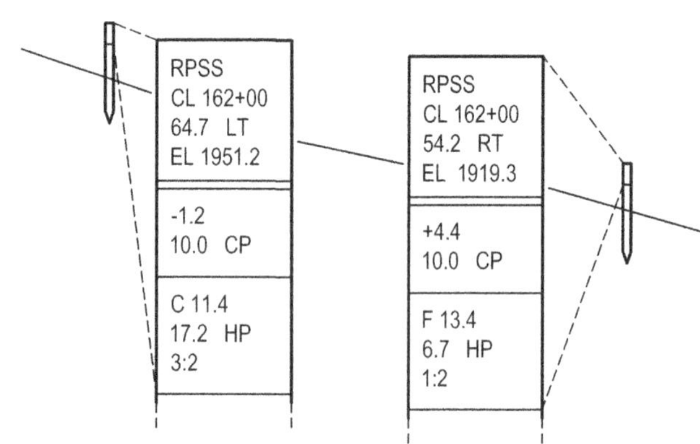

(A) 1920.0[ft]

(B) 1921.2[ft]

(C) 1924.4[ft]

(D) 1937.8[ft]

Problem II.29

Field tape measurements, broken into three segments, are recorded in the table below. Readings were taken at a temperature of 92.5[F] using a nominally 100′ steel tape with calibrated length of $\ell = 100.34$[ft]. What is the corrected total length of the field measurements?

#	Measured Distance
1	54.782[ft]
2	98.462[ft]
3	14.325[ft]

(A) 167.569[ft]

(B) 167.595[ft]

(C) 168.112[ft]

(D) 168.165[ft]

Problem II.30

The table below shows existing grades at certain stations of a proposed road extension. The proposed road extension starts with a 2.5% upward slope at point 0 at existing grade and ends at point 5 meeting the existing grade again. Determine the project station with zero fill. Assume the existing grade varies linearly between stations measured.

Point	Station	Elevation
0	(145+36.49)	949.54
1	(146+00.00)	926.25
2	(147+00.00)	930.41
3	(148+00.00)	932.40
4	(149+00.00)	967.03
5	(149+39.67)	959.62

(A) (148+26.15)

(B) (148+41.54)

(C) (148+62.64)

(D) (148+73.85)

Problem II.31

A shipping container is to be buried in sand. Two 12′ long ramps are to be dumped adjacent to long sides of the container. Determine how deep the container needs to be buried, such that the ramps can be built from the excavation material and no excess material remains.

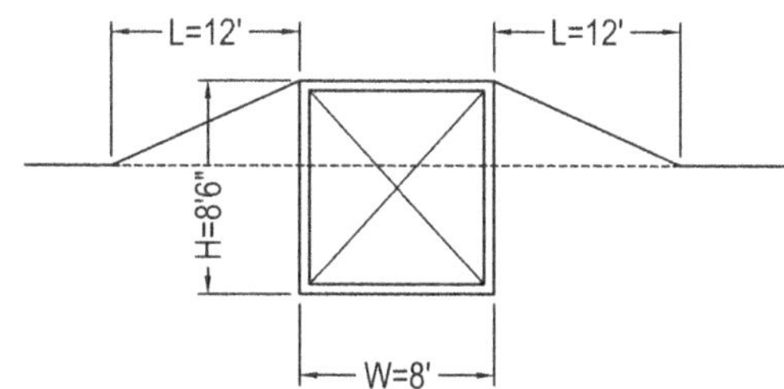

(A) 3.3[ft]

(B) 3.6[ft]

(C) 4.7[ft]

(D) 5.1[ft]

Problem II.32

From the field notes of a leveling exercise shown below, determine the linear misclosure of the vertical clearance of the bridge underpass.

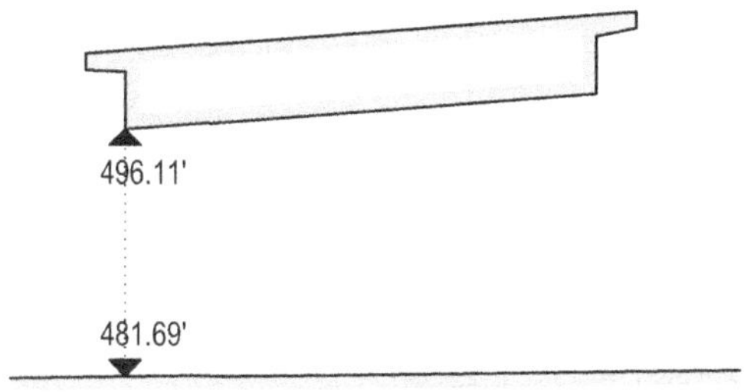

Point	BS	HI	FS	Elev	Notes
CL of Road	8.53			481.69	
Bot. Edge of Bridge			5.92	496.11	Rod held upside down.

(A) −0.01′

(B) −0.03′

(C) 0.01′

(D) 0.03′

Problem II.33

A $R = 900$[ft] curve is being staked out in the field. The table below contains layout data from the previous stake. Determine the required chord distance between points 3 and PT for backchecking the stakes.

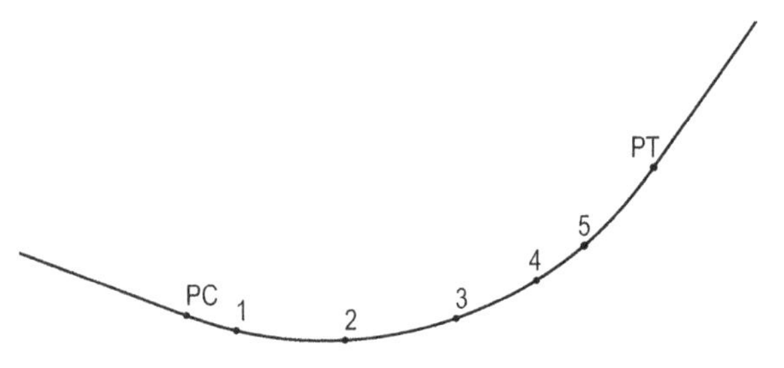

Point	Curve Length x[ft]	Deflection Angle $\delta[^\circ]$	Chord Length c[ft]
PC	—	—	—
1	31.000	0.9868	30.998
2	100.000	3.1831	99.949
3	100.000	3.1831	99.949
4	70.000	2.2282	69.982
5	30.000	0.9549	29.999
PT	22.560	0.7181	22.559

(A) 122.181[ft]

(B) 122.465[ft]

(C) 220.298[ft]

(D) 221.993[ft]

Problem II.34

The temporary benchmark at point B got lost. Determine distance and azimuth to re-establish the benchmark from point A.

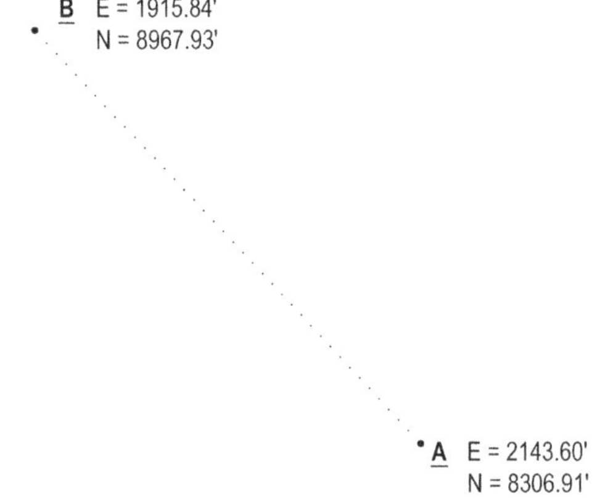

(A) $L_{AB} = 699.16$[ft], $Az_{AB} = 19°0'43''$

(B) $L_{AB} = 699.16$[ft], $Az_{AB} = 71°0'43''$

(C) $L_{AB} = 699.16$[ft], $Az_{AB} = 161°0'43''$

(D) $L_{AB} = 699.16$[ft], $Az_{AB} = 341°0'43''$

Problem II.35

The table below shows existing grades at all project stations of a proposed road. The proposed road starts with a 2.5[ft/sta] upward slope at point 0 at its existing elevation and ends at point 5 meeting the existing grade. Determine the project station with greatest cut. Assume the existing grade varies linearly between measured stations.

Point	Station	Elevation
0	(145+36.49)	949.54
1	(146+00.00)	926.25
2	(147+00.00)	930.41
3	(148+00.00)	932.40
4	(149+00.00)	967.03
5	(149+39.67)	959.62

(A) (146+00.00) (Point 1)

(B) (147+00.00) (Point 2)

(C) (148+00.00) (Point 3)

(D) (149+00.00) (Point 4)

Problem II.36

The two construction stakes shown below were set for rough grading of a highway segment according to Caltrans' Surveys Manual. Determine the distance between left and right catch points.

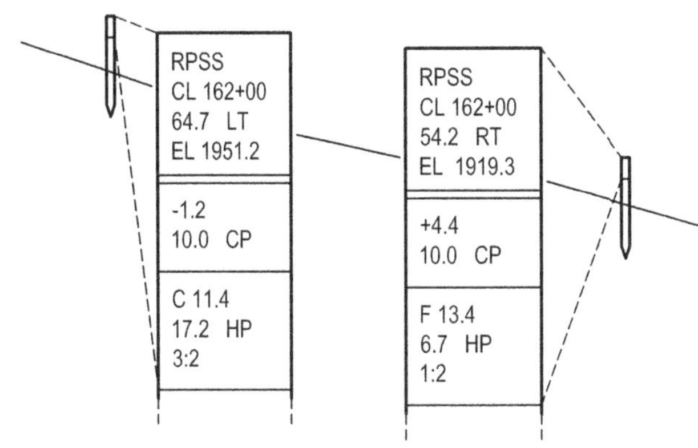

(A) 88.9′

(B) 98.9′

(C) 108.9′

(D) 118.9′

Problem II.37

For a construction project, two benchmarks—A and B—have been established. A third temporary benchmark C has been set out in the field; see the sketch below. Determine the easting and northing coordinates of this new temporary benchmark.

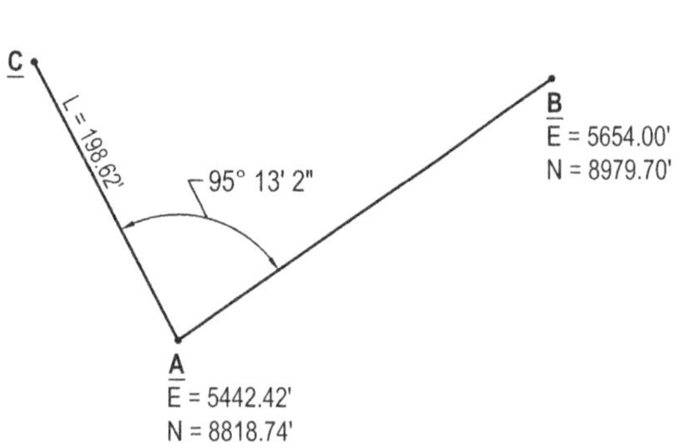

(A) $(E, N) = (5308.29[\text{ft}], 8965.23[\text{ft}])$

(B) $(E, N) = (5337.04[\text{ft}], 8650.38[\text{ft}])$

(C) $(E, N) = (5547.80[\text{ft}], 8650.38[\text{ft}])$

(D) $(E, N) = (5576.55[\text{ft}], 8965.23[\text{ft}])$

Problem II.38

The figure below shows a typical cross section of a proposed, 75[ft] wide highway. Using the tabulated dimensions and the prismoidal method, compute the excavation volume between the three cross sections.

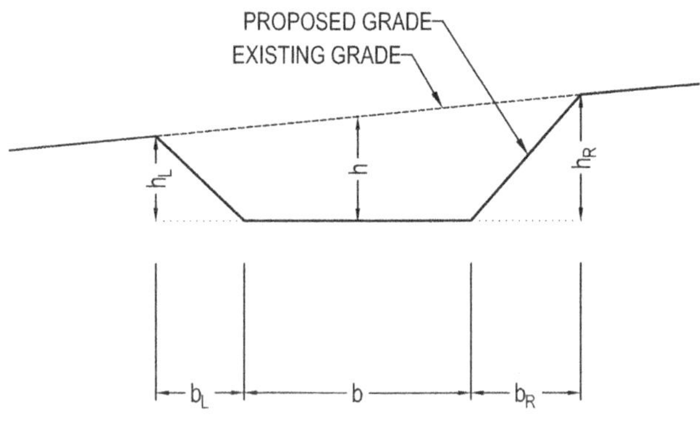

Station [sta]	b_L [ft]	b_R [ft]	h [ft]	h_L [ft]	h_R [ft]
161+00	19.62	39.35	18.85	13.08	26.23
162+00	25.15	50.54	23.81	16.77	33.69
163+00	40.62	52.96	29.00	27.08	35.31

(A) $13696[\text{yd}^3]$

(B) $13838[\text{yd}^3]$

(C) $17458[\text{yd}^3]$

(D) $20462[\text{yd}^3]$

Problem II.39

For the all-rectangular building shown below, only the two corner points at the front have coordinates. Determine the coordinates for corner F.

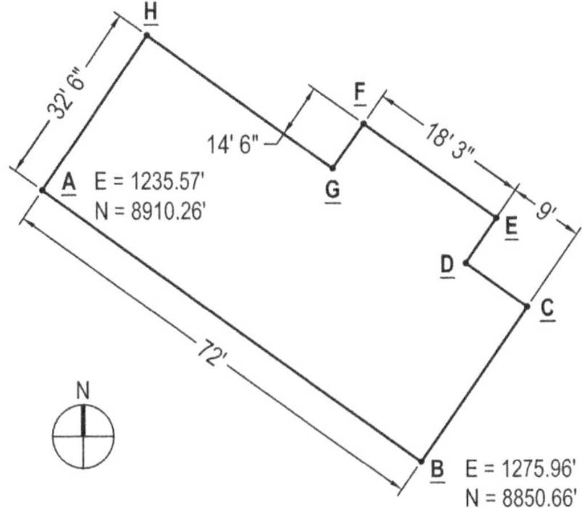
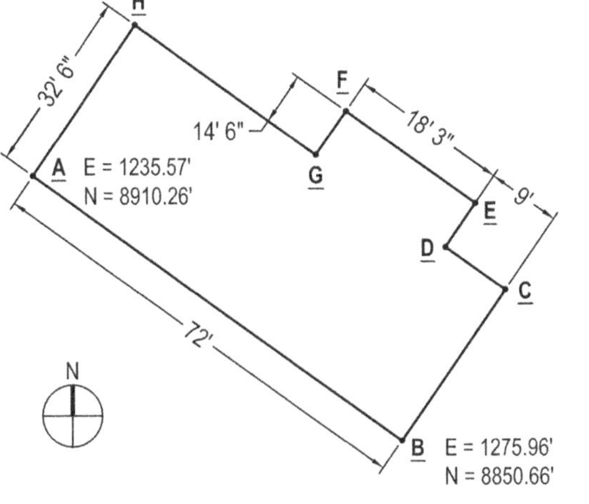

(A) $(E, N)_F = (1228.90, 9003.89)[\text{ft}]$

(B) $(E, N)_F = (1299.58, 8899.58)[\text{ft}]$

(C) $(E, N)_F = (1309.68, 8884.68)[\text{ft}]$

(D) $(E, N)_F = (1320.06, 9003.89)[\text{ft}]$

Problem II.40

A $3^1/2''$ deep speed table, as shown below, will be added to a residential road. Compute the volume of this speed table using the average end area method.

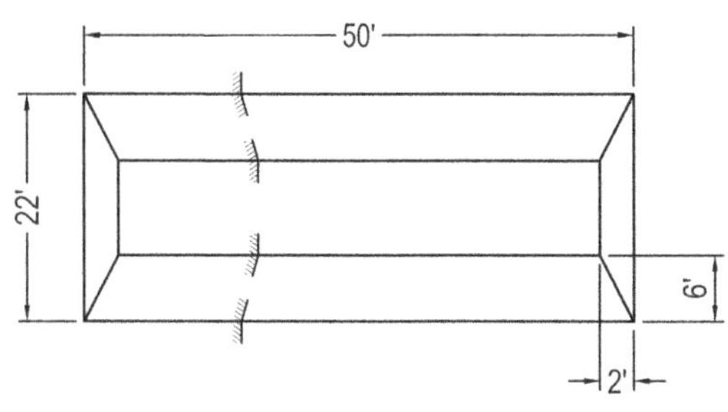

(A) $228[\text{ft}^3]$

(B) $233[\text{ft}^3]$

(C) $308[\text{ft}^3]$

(D) $321[\text{ft}^3]$

Problem II.41

The creek on the topographic map shown below is most likely to flow in which direction?

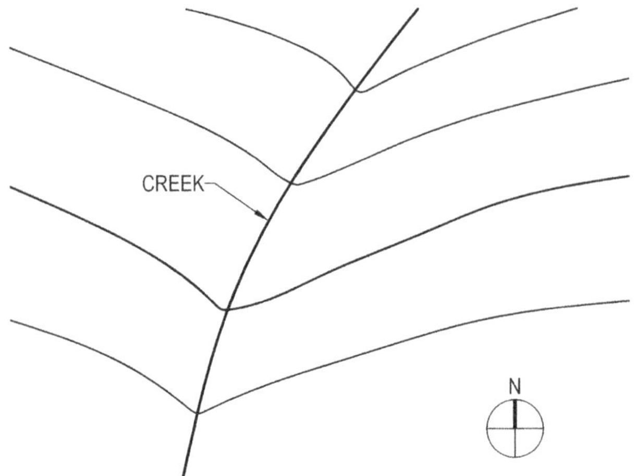

(A) North

(B) East

(C) South

(D) West

Problem II.42

For the turnaround shown below, determine its length L.

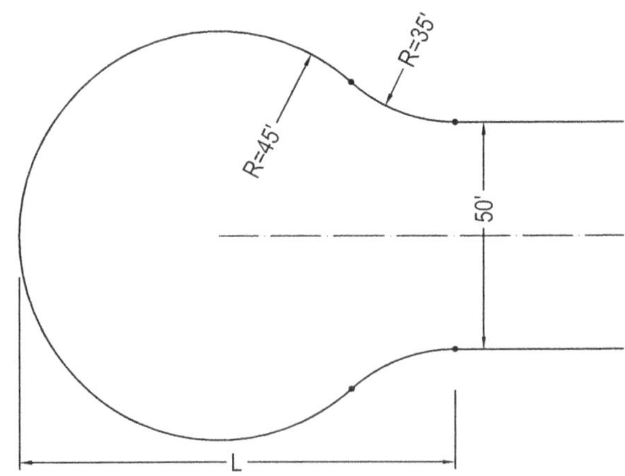

(A) 52.92[ft]

(B) 97.92[ft]

(C) 106.80[ft]

(D) 145.00[ft]

Problem II.43

A brand-new metal tape was used to measure a distance at a temperature of 85.6[°F]. The distance after temperature correction is 68.72[ft]. After taking the measurement, the tape was sent in for calibration. The calibration gave a length of 99.94[ft] for this 100[ft]-tape. What would be the actual distance when incorporating the tape length correction?

(A) 68.679[ft]

(B) 68.687[ft]

(C) 68.720[ft]

(D) 68.761[ft]

Problem II.44

A 9×9[in] aerial photo was taken at 2400[ft] above ground level using a 152[mm] focal length lens. A feature was measured to be 4.35[in^2] on photo. Determine the actual area of the feature.

(A) 145.38[ft^2]

(B) 2312[ft^2]

(C) 16.06[ac]

(D) 824[ac]

Problem II.45

For the highway section shown below, if the minimum curve radius for each lane (measured at the lane centerline) is 2100[ft], what is the minimum possible curve radius at the median line M?

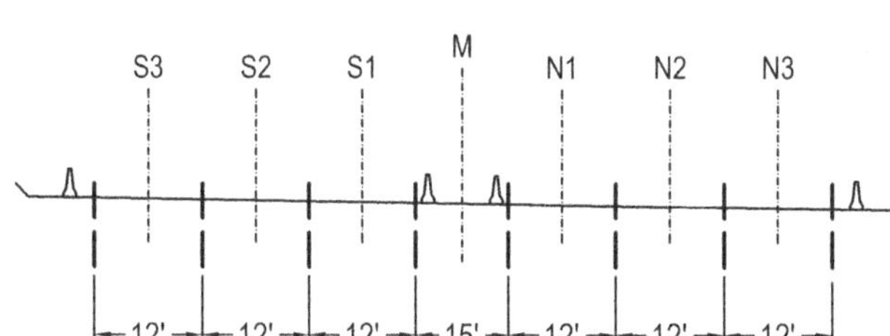

(A) 2064[ft]

(B) 2136[ft]

(C) 2138[ft]

(D) 2151[ft]

Problem II.46

The air strips of an airport are to be paved with asphalt. Each runway is 8000[ft] long and 300[ft] wide. Determine the total area to be asphalted.

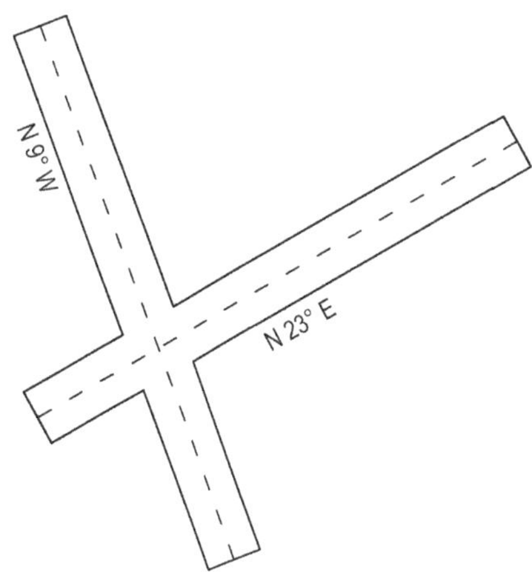

(A) 106.29[ac]

(B) 107.76[ac]

(C) 108.13[ac]

(D) 114.09[ac]

Problem II.47

For the road segment depicted in the figure below, determine the station of the high point.

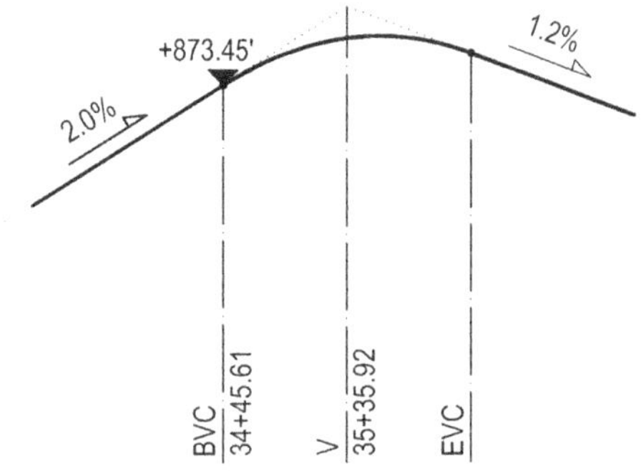

(A) (35+58.50)

(B) (35+13.34)

(C) (36+02.05)

(D) (36+26.23)

Problem II.48

The open traverse shown below represents centerline points of a natural creek. The creek is to be streamlined from A to D in a straight line. If the average slope of the original path is 5.5%, what would be the slope of the streamlined path?

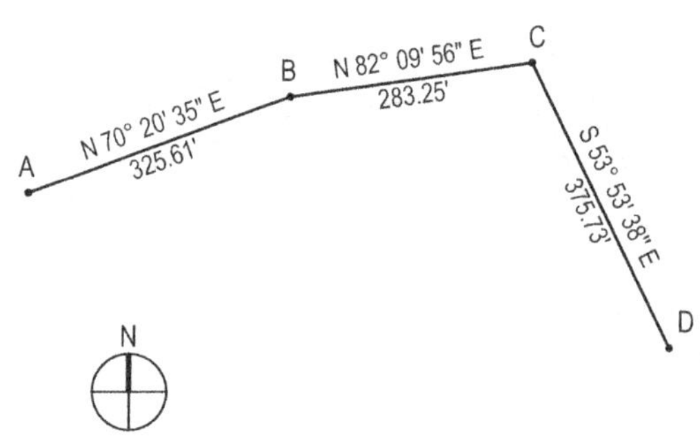

(A) 6.1%

(B) 8.5%

(C) 11.6%

(D) 18.5%

Problem II.49

The two construction stakes shown below were set for rough grading of a highway segment according to Caltrans' Surveys Manual. Determine net cut or fill area of this cross section. Assume the horizontal distance between hinge points is 75[ft] and that there is no additional grade point in between hinge points. Also, the existing slope is constant between the catch points.

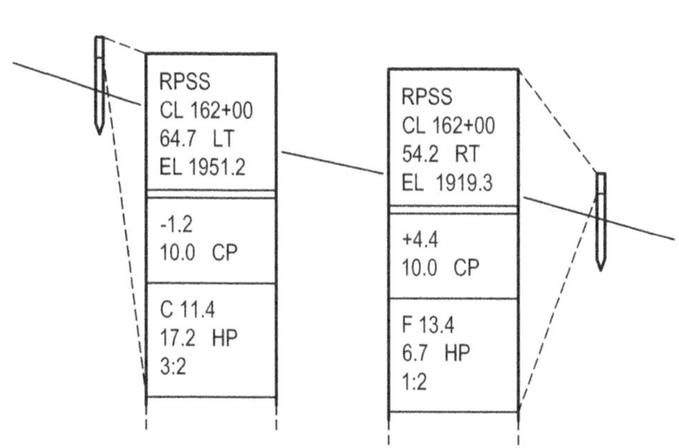

(A) 135[ft^2] (net cut)

(B) 135[ft^2] (net fill)

(C) 160[ft^2] (net cut)

(D) 160[ft^2] (net fill)

Problem II.50

A shipping container is to be buried in sand 6′ deep and covered 1′6″ on top with sand and ramps along the long edges. Determine the ramp length, such that the excavation material can be used to build the ramp and the top cover and no excess material remains.

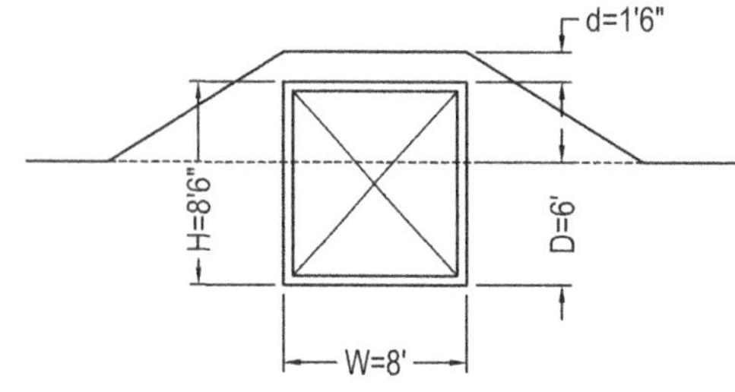

(A) 4.5[ft]

(B) 6.0[ft]

(C) 9.0[ft]

(D) 14.4[ft]

Problem II.51

Determine the area of the rectangular parcel shown below.

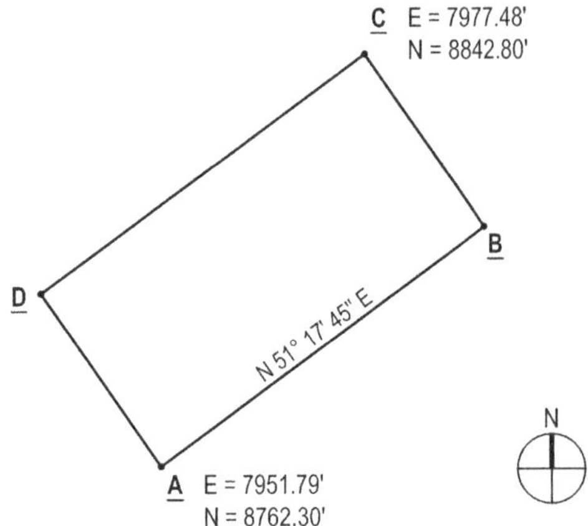

(A) 2389[ft^2]

(B) 3291[ft^2]

(C) 4954[ft^2]

(D) 7140[ft^2]

Problem II.52

Using the leveling field notes and the sketch below, determine the slope of the flow line.

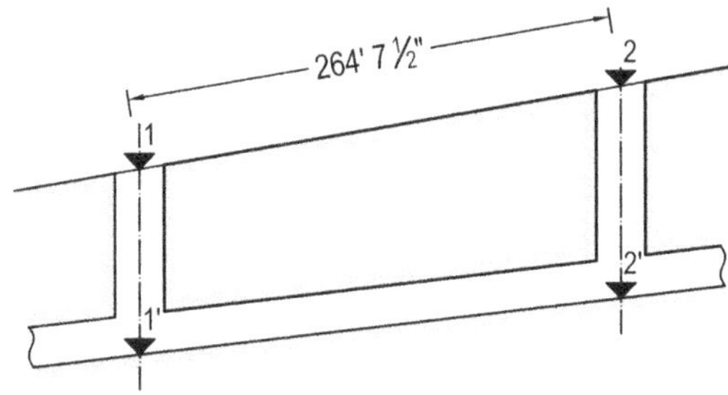

	BS	HI	FS	Elev
BM 12-06431	5.54			263.383
1			10.54	
1′			16.41	
2			5.37	
2′			12.46	

(A) 1.49%

(B) 1.55%

(C) 1.64%

(D) 1.79%

Problem II.53

Referring to the figure below, points A and B have been established in a previous survey. Later, a third point, C, was added to the survey. Since only a tape measure was at hand, no direction angles are available. Determine the grid coordinates of point C.

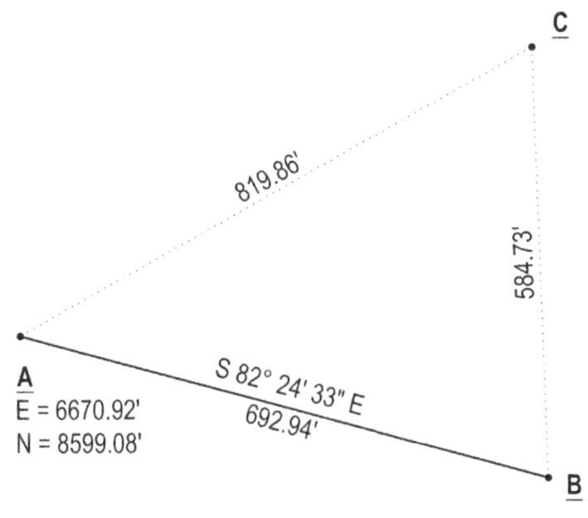

(A) $(E, N)_C = (7163.28, 9254.64)$[ft]

(B) $(E, N)_C = (7245.56, 9183.85)$[ft]

(C) $(E, N)_C = (7255.69, 9173.72)$[ft]

(D) $(E, N)_C = (7326.48, 9091.44)$[ft]

Problem II.54

A 415[ft] long $R = 330$[ft] curve is being staked out in the field. Starting at the beginning of curve, stakes are to be set at every station along the curve. For back-checking, what must be the chord distance between the last stake and the PT?

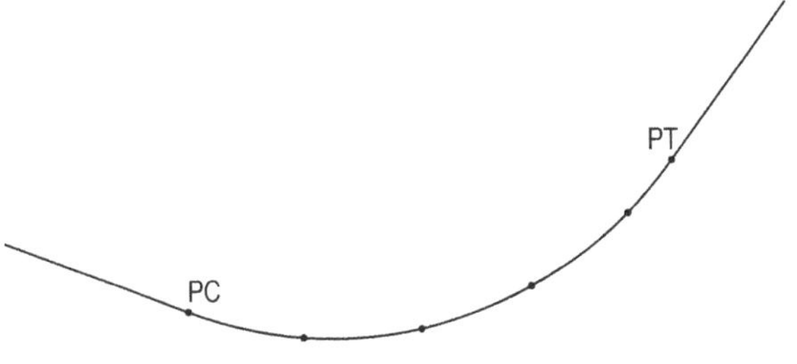

(A) 14.7998[ft]

(B) 14.8799[ft]

(C) 14.9879[ft]

(D) 14.9987[ft]

Problem II.55

Using the information provided in the figure below, determine the minimum vertical clearance between the riverbed and the top of the sewer pipe.

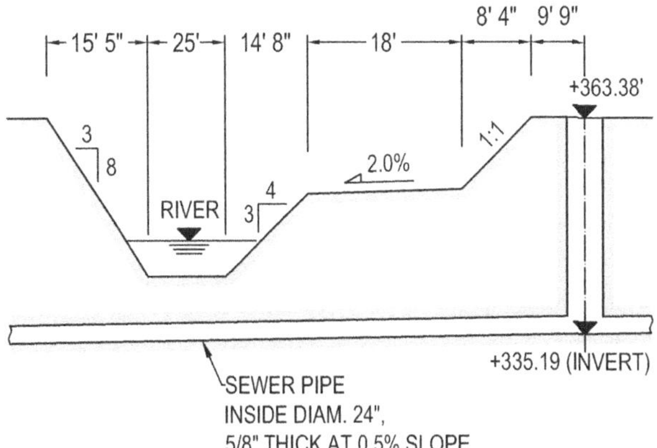

(A) 1.86′

(B) 6.65′

(C) 6.70′

(D) 6.80′

Chapter 6

Solutions to Practice Exam I

Answer Key to Practice Exam I

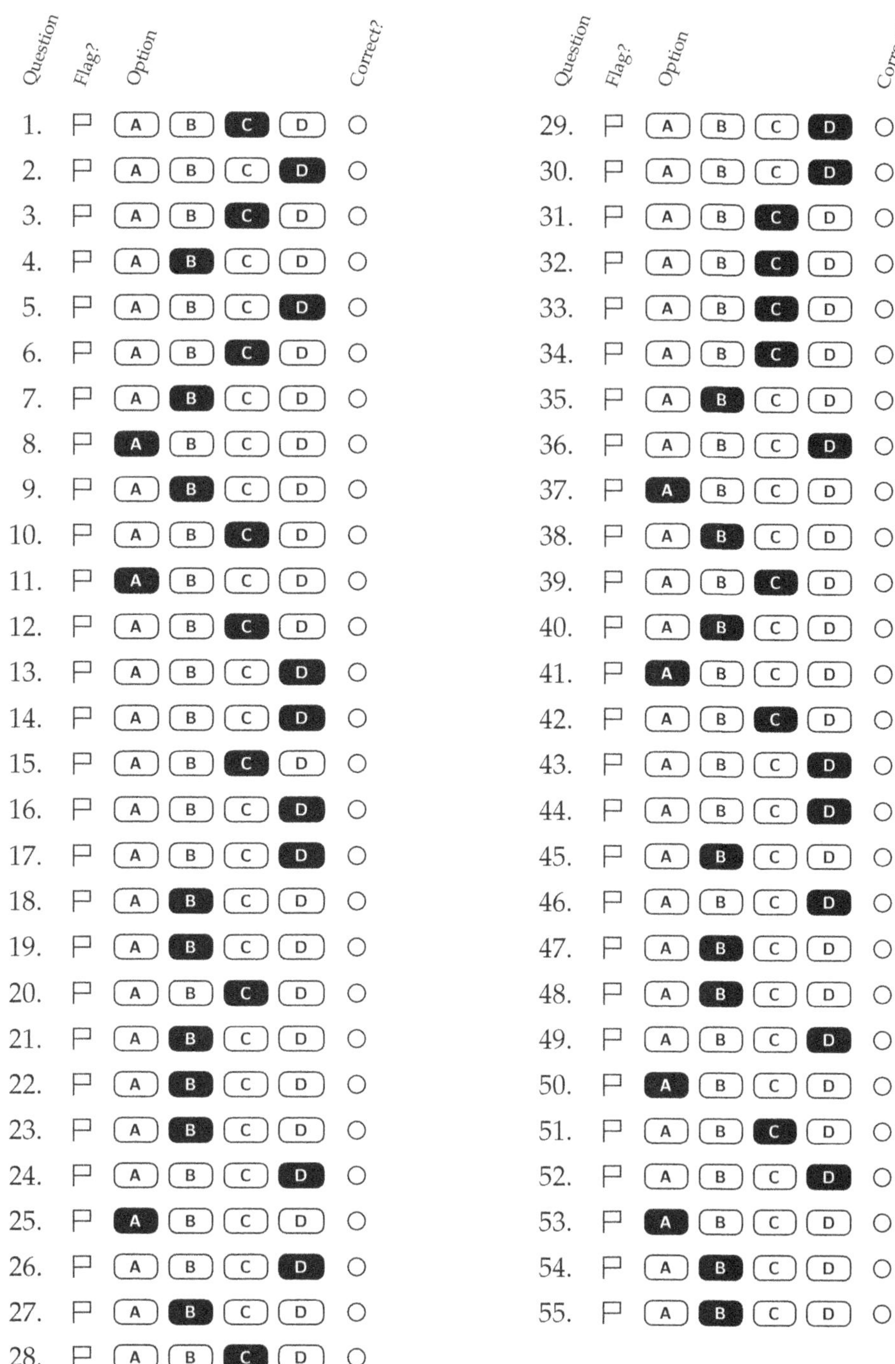

Question	Option	Question	Option
1.	C	29.	D
2.	D	30.	D
3.	C	31.	C
4.	B	32.	C
5.	D	33.	C
6.	C	34.	C
7.	B	35.	B
8.	A	36.	D
9.	B	37.	A
10.	C	38.	B
11.	A	39.	C
12.	C	40.	B
13.	D	41.	A
14.	D	42.	C
15.	C	43.	D
16.	D	44.	D
17.	D	45.	B
18.	B	46.	D
19.	B	47.	B
20.	C	48.	B
21.	B	49.	D
22.	B	50.	A
23.	B	51.	C
24.	D	52.	D
25.	A	53.	A
26.	D	54.	B
27.	B	55.	B
28.	C		

Tip: Overlay your printed out answer sheet for faster correction.

Problem I.01

The shaded area of an intersection is proposed to be repaved. Determine the area to be repaved. Assume a road width of 30′ and an 8′ curb radius.

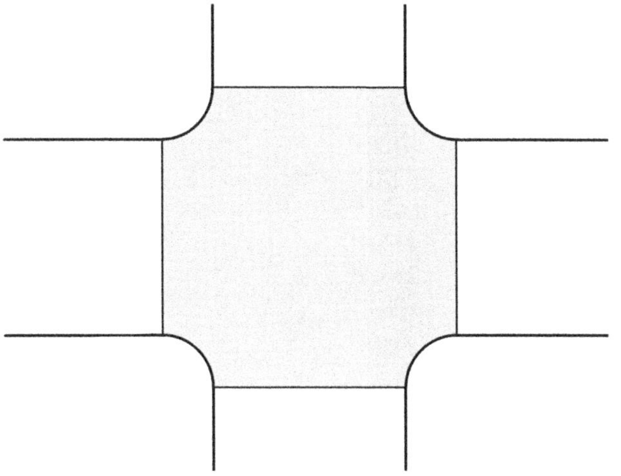

Solution to Problem I.01

The shaded area can be composed of a square that has 4 quarter circles chipped away from the corners. Therefore, compute the area of the square and subtract the 4 quarter circles.

$$\begin{aligned} A_{square} &= (W + 2 \cdot R)^2 \\ &= (30[\text{ft}] + 2 \cdot 8[\text{ft}])^2 \\ &= 2116[\text{ft}^2] \\ A_{circ} &= R^2 \cdot \pi \\ &= (8[\text{ft}])^2 \cdot \pi \\ &= 201[\text{ft}^2] \\ A &= A_{square} - A_{circ} \\ &= 2116[\text{ft}^2] - 201[\text{ft}^2] \\ &= \underline{\underline{1915[\text{ft}^2]}} \end{aligned}$$

(A) 699[ft²]

(B) 1243[ft²]

(C) 1915[ft²]

(D) 2066[ft²]

Problem I.02

To verify the intactness of the control points shown below the distance between the control points is being taped in the field. What is the expected distance between points B and D?

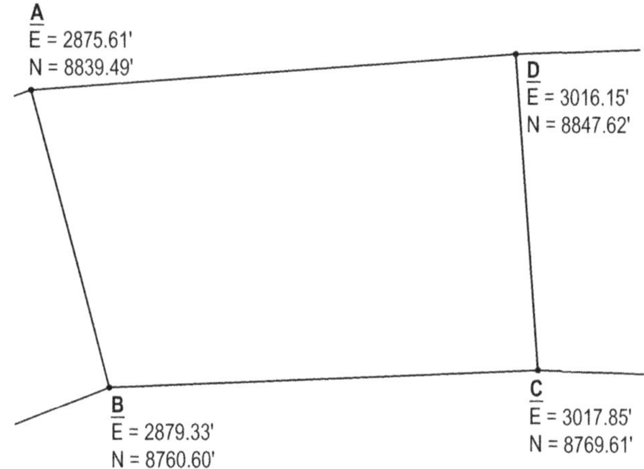

Solution to Problem I.02

Simply compute the distance between B and D based on their coordinates.

Differences in latitutes, departures:

$$\begin{aligned} \Delta N &= N_D - N_B \\ &= 8847.62[\text{ft}] - 8760.6[\text{ft}] \\ &= 87.02[\text{ft}] \\ \Delta E &= E_D - E_B \\ &= 3016.15[\text{ft}] - 2879.33[\text{ft}] \\ &= 136.82[\text{ft}] \end{aligned}$$

Expected distance between control points:

$$\begin{aligned} L_{BD} &= \sqrt{(\Delta N)^2 + (\Delta E)^2} \\ &= \sqrt{(87.02[\text{ft}])^2 + (136.82[\text{ft}])^2} \\ &= \underline{\underline{162.15[\text{ft}]}} \end{aligned}$$

(A) 87.02[ft]

(B) 123.06[ft]

(C) 136.82[ft]

(D) 162.15[ft]

Problem I.03

Referring to the curve shown below, the azimuth from PC to station (202+00.00) is?

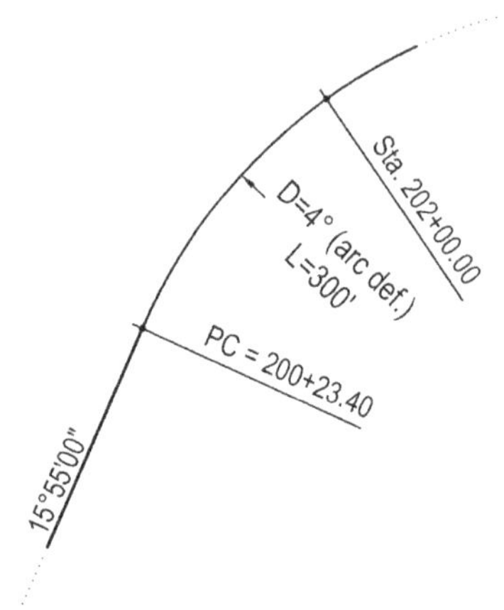

Solution to Problem I.03

Compute the deflection angle to the stake using the appropriate standard formula and add it to the bearing of the back tangent.

Arc length to stake:

$$\begin{aligned} x &= (202{+}00.00) - [\text{sta}]_{\text{PC}} \\ &= (202{+}00.00) - (200{+}23.40) \\ &= 176.60[\text{ft}] \end{aligned}$$

Deflection angle to stake:

$$\begin{aligned} d_x &= \frac{x}{100} \cdot \frac{1}{2} D \\ &= \frac{176.60[\text{ft}]}{100} \cdot \frac{1}{2} 4^\circ \\ &= 3.8852^\circ \end{aligned}$$

Deflection angle to stake:

$$\begin{aligned} \text{Az}_{(\text{stake})} &= \text{Az}_{(\text{PC})} + d_x \\ &= 15^\circ 55' 0'' + 3.8852^\circ \\ &= \underline{\underline{19^\circ 48' 7''}} \end{aligned}$$

(A) $8^\circ 8' 47''$

(B) $12^\circ 1' 53''$

(C) $\underline{\underline{19^\circ 48' 7''}}$

(D) $23^\circ 41' 13''$

Problem I.04

For a water reservoir, the water surface area for certain elevations was determined using GIS software. Determine the volume of water that can be stored between elevation 1500′ and 1375′. Use the contour area method.

Elevation [ft]	Surface Area [ac]
1500	1702.5
1450	957.6
1425	665.0
1400	425.6
1375	239.4
1350	106.4
1325	26.6

Solution to Problem I.04

Determine volume with contour area method:

$$\begin{aligned} V &= \text{CI} \cdot \left(\frac{A_{1500}}{2} + A_{1450} \right. \\ &\qquad \left. + A_{1425} + A_{1400} + \frac{A_{1375}}{2} \right) \\ &= 25[\text{ft}] \cdot \left(\frac{1702.5[\text{ac}]}{2} + 957.6[\text{ac}] + \right. \\ &\qquad \left. 665.0[\text{ac}] + 425.6[\text{ac}] + \frac{239.4[\text{ac}]}{2} \right) \\ &= \underline{\underline{75479[\text{ac ft}]}} \end{aligned}$$

(A) $33915[\text{ac ft}]$

(B) $\underline{\underline{75479[\text{ac ft}]}}$

(C) $96760[\text{ac ft}]$

(D) $99752[\text{ac ft}]$

Problem I.05

A cross section for a proposed road is shown below. In the figure, the row *Dist.* denotes the horizontal distance between dimensioned points, and *Cut* indicates the elevation difference between a proposed and the existing grade. Compute the total area of cut required in this section.

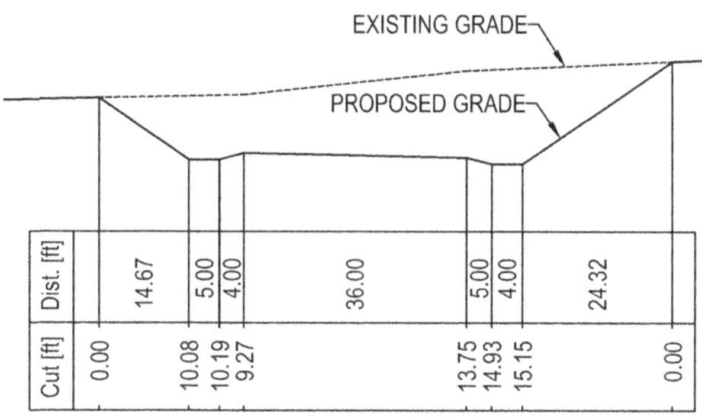

Solution to Problem I.05

Compute the total cross section area by summing up the trapezoidal areas between the dimensioned points. In the solution below, we use x_i for the horizontal distance between point i and the adjacent point to the left. Likewise, y_i is used for the cut depth at point i.

Trapeziodal areas:

$$A_1 = x_1 \cdot \frac{y_0 + y_1}{2} = 14.7 \cdot \frac{0.0 + 10.1}{2} = 73.9[\text{ft}^2]$$

$$A_2 = x_2 \cdot \frac{y_1 + y_2}{2} = 5 \cdot \frac{10.1 + 10.2}{2} = 50.7[\text{ft}^2]$$

$$A_3 = x_3 \cdot \frac{y_2 + y_3}{2} = 4.0 \cdot \frac{10.2 + 9.3}{2} = 38.9[\text{ft}^2]$$

$$A_4 = x_4 \cdot \frac{y_3 + y_4}{2} = 36.0 \cdot \frac{9.3 + 13.8}{2} = 414.4[\text{ft}^2]$$

$$A_5 = x_5 \cdot \frac{y_4 + y_5}{2} = 4.0 \cdot \frac{13.8 + 14.9}{2} = 57.4[\text{ft}^2]$$

$$A_6 = x_6 \cdot \frac{y_5 + y_6}{2} = 5.0 \cdot \frac{14.9 + 15.2}{2} = 75.2[\text{ft}^2]$$

$$A_7 = x_7 \cdot \frac{y_6 + y_7}{2} = 24.3 \cdot \frac{15.2 + 0}{2} = 184.2[\text{ft}^2]$$

Total area:

$$A = \sum_i A_i = 73.9 + 50.7 + 38.9 + 414.4 + 57.4 + 75.2 + 184.2 = \underline{\underline{894.7[\text{ft}^2]}}$$

(A) $429.3[\text{ft}^2]$

(B) $503.3[\text{ft}^2]$

(C) $687.5[\text{ft}^2]$

(D) $\underline{\underline{894.7[\text{ft}^2]}}$

Problem I.06

In order to determine the height of a building, a total station (height of instrument: 5′8″ above ground) was set up in front of the building and measurements to the top and base of the building were taken. See the table below. Determine the height of the building.

#	Zenith Angle	Sloped Distance
1	38°59′13″	111.26[ft]
2	94°37′42″	70.23[ft]

Solution to Problem I.06

Zenith angles measure the angle from a vertical line (0° pointing up). Therefore, use these angles to compute the corresponding vertical distances and sum them up to get the building's height. Because measurement #2 has a zenith angle greater than 90°, expect the probability that the resulting vertical distance be negative and consider this in your solution.

Vertical distance of measurement 1:

$$\begin{aligned} H_1 &= L_1 \cdot \cos(Z_1) \\ &= 111.26[\text{ft}] \cdot \cos(38°59'13'') \\ &= 86.48[\text{ft}] \end{aligned}$$

Vertical distance of measurement 2:

$$\begin{aligned} H_2 &= L_2 \cdot \cos(Z_2) \\ &= 70.23[\text{ft}] \cdot \cos(94°37'42'') \\ &= -5.67[\text{ft}] \end{aligned}$$

Height of building:

$$\begin{aligned} H &= H_1 - H_2 \\ &= 86.48[\text{ft}] - (-5.67[\text{ft}]) \\ &= \underline{\underline{92.15[\text{ft}]}} \end{aligned}$$

(A) 70.00[ft]

(B) 80.81[ft]

(C) 92.15[ft]

(D) 140.0[ft]

Problem I.07

The concrete pad for a bus stop is shown in the figure below. What is the required concrete volume if the pad thickness is 8″?

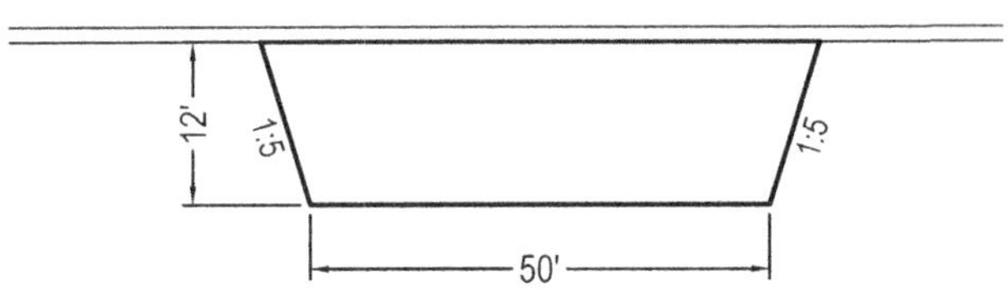

Solution to Problem I.07

Compute the curb-side length of the pad, then the pad area, finally the pad volume.

Length of pad on the curb side:

$$\begin{aligned} L_{\text{curbside}} &= L_{\text{roadside}} + 2 \cdot w \cdot (\text{taper}) \\ &= 50[\text{ft}] + 2 \cdot 12[\text{ft}] \cdot 1/5 \\ &= 54.8[\text{ft}] \end{aligned}$$

Pad area in the plan view:

$$\begin{aligned} A &= \frac{w}{2} \cdot (L_{\text{curbside}} + L_{\text{roadside}}) \\ &= \frac{12[\text{ft}]}{2} \cdot (54.8[\text{ft}] + 50[\text{ft}]) \\ &= 628.8[\text{ft}^2] \end{aligned}$$

Concrete pad volume:

$$\begin{aligned} V &= A \cdot t \\ &= 628.8[\text{ft}^2] \cdot 8'' \cdot 1/12[\text{ft/in}] \\ &= 419.2[\text{ft}^3] \\ &= \underline{\underline{15.5[\text{yd}^3]}} \end{aligned}$$

(A) 14.8[yd³]

(B) 15.5[yd³]

(C) 22.2[yd³]

(D) 32.6[yd³]

Problem I.08

Referring to the figure below, points A and B have been established in a previous survey. Later, a third point, C, was added to the survey. But, because only a tape measure was available, no direction angles are available. Determine the area enclosed by A, B, C.

Note: Storing the lengths a, b, c as variables in the calculator greatly improves your speed and reduces chances of typing mistakes.

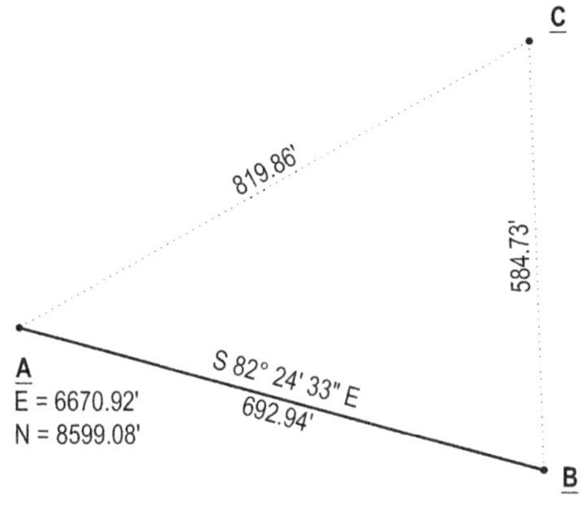

(A) $\underline{\underline{4.57[\text{ac}]}}$

(B) $13.1[\text{ac}]$

(C) $24.5[\text{ac}]$

(D) $54.2[\text{ac}]$

Solution to Problem I.08

The probably fastest way is to use the equation for area of an oblique triangle: $A = \sqrt{s\,(s-a)(s-b)(s-c)}$ with $s = a+b+c/2$.

Helper variables:

$$\begin{aligned} a &= L_{AB} = 692.94[\text{ft}] \\ b &= L_{BC} = 584.73[\text{ft}] \\ c &= L_{AC} = 819.86[\text{ft}] \\ s &= \frac{a+b+c}{2} \\ &= \frac{692.94 + 584.73 + 819.86}{2} \\ &= 1048.77[\text{ft}] \end{aligned}$$

Area:

$$\begin{aligned} A &= \sqrt{s \cdot (s-a) \cdot (s-b) \cdot (s-c)} \\ &= \sqrt{1048.77 \cdot (1048.77 - 692.94)} \\ &\quad \cdot \sqrt{(1048.77 - 584.73)} \\ &\quad \cdot \sqrt{(1048.77 - 819.86)} \\ &= 199095[\text{ft}^2] \\ &= \underline{\underline{4.57[\text{ac}]}} \end{aligned}$$

Problem I.09

The two construction stakes shown below were set for rough grading of a highway segment according to Caltrans' Surveys Manual. Determine the cross slope between the hinge points (assuming there is no additional grade point in between).

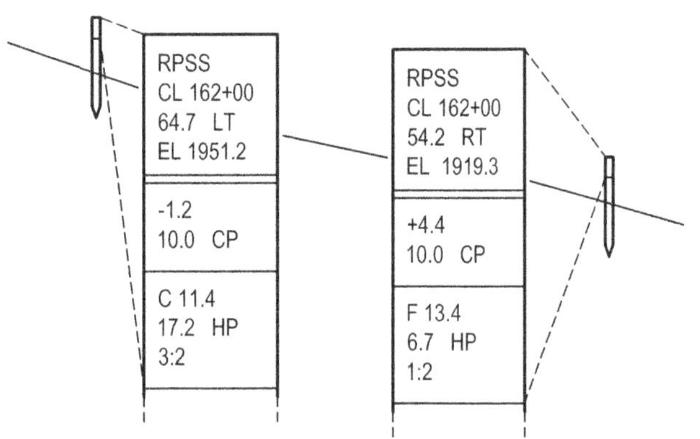

Solution to Problem I.09

Before solving this problem, it is recommended to sketch out the information shown on the stakes. Using this sketch, compute the sought quantity.

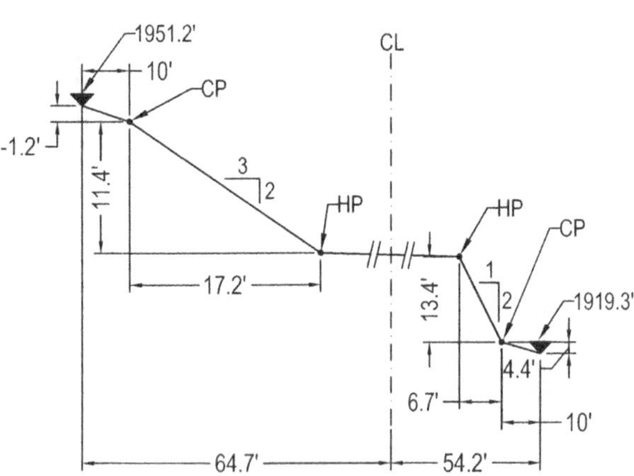

Elevations and offsets of hinge points:

$$\begin{aligned}\text{elev}_{\text{HP},L} &= \text{elev}_{\text{RPSS},L} - \Delta Y_{\text{CP},L} - \Delta Y_{\text{HP},L}\\ &= 1951.2 - 1.2 - 11.4\\ &= 1938.6[\text{ft}]\end{aligned}$$

$$\begin{aligned}\text{elev}_{\text{HP},R} &= \text{elev}_{\text{RPSS},R} + \Delta Y_{\text{CP},R} + \Delta Y_{\text{HP},R}\\ &= 1919.3 + 4.4 + 13.4\\ &= 1937.1[\text{ft}]\\ \text{offset}_{\text{HP},L} &= \text{offset}_{\text{RPSS},L} - \Delta X_{\text{CP},L} - \Delta X_{\text{HP},L}\\ &= 64.7 - 10 - 17.2\\ &= 37.5[\text{ft}]\\ \text{offset}_{\text{HP},R} &= \text{offset}_{\text{RPSS},R} - \Delta X_{\text{CP},R} - \Delta X_{\text{HP},R}\\ &= 54.2 - 10 - 6.7\\ &= 37.5[\text{ft}]\end{aligned}$$

Cross slope:

$$\begin{aligned}s &= \frac{\text{elev}_{\text{HP},L} - \text{elev}_{\text{HP},R}}{\text{offset}_{\text{HP},L} + \text{offset}_{\text{HP},R}}\\ &= \frac{1938.6[\text{ft}] - 1937.1[\text{ft}]}{37.5[\text{ft}] + 37.5[\text{ft}]}\\ &= 0.020\\ &= \underline{\underline{2.0\%}}\end{aligned}$$

(A) 0.5%

(B) <u>2.0%</u>

(C) 3.5%

(D) 5.0%

Problem I.10

A construction pit, shown below, is about to be excavated to an elevation of 234.40′. The construction pit is shored using pile sheet walls. The spot elevations shown in the figure represent existing soil elevations. Determine the excavation volume using the borrow pit method.

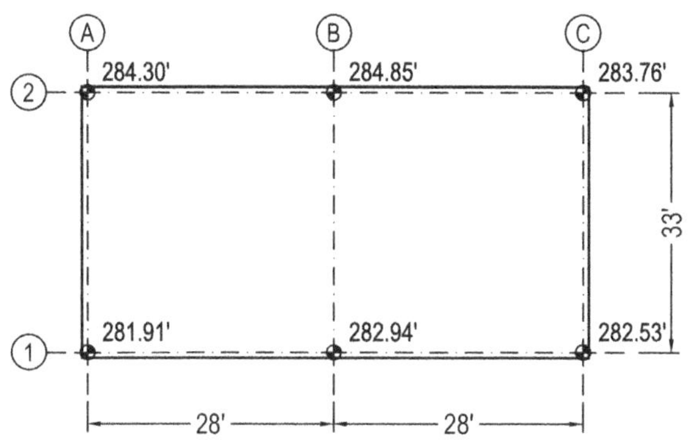

Solution to Problem I.10

Use the borrow pit method equation: $V = A/4\left(\sum_i n_i h_i\right)$; where A is the area of a grid square; h_i is the excavation depth at grid point i; and n_i is the number of areas joining at grid point i.

Area of a grid square:

$$\begin{aligned} A &= \Delta_x \cdot \Delta_y \\ &= 28[\text{ft}] \cdot 33[\text{ft}] \\ &= 924[\text{ft}^2] \end{aligned}$$

Excavation volume:

$$\begin{aligned} V = \frac{A}{4} \cdot \Big[& \\ & 1 \cdot (\text{elev}_{A1} - \text{elev}_{pit}) \\ & + 2 \cdot (\text{elev}_{B1} - \text{elev}_{pit}) \\ & + 1 \cdot (\text{elev}_{C1} - \text{elev}_{pit}) \\ & + 1 \cdot (\text{elev}_{A2} - \text{elev}_{pit}) \\ & + 2 \cdot (\text{elev}_{B2} - \text{elev}_{pit}) \\ & + 1 \cdot (\text{elev}_{C2} - \text{elev}_{pit}) \Big] \\ = \frac{924}{4} \cdot \Big[& \\ & 1 \cdot (281.91 - 234.40) \\ & + 2 \cdot (282.94 - 234.40) \\ & + 1 \cdot (282.53 - 234.40) \\ & + 1 \cdot (284.30 - 234.40) \\ & + 2 \cdot (284.85 - 234.40) \\ & + 1 \cdot (283.76 - 234.40) \Big] \\ = {} & 90755[\text{ft}^3] \\ = {} & \underline{\underline{3361[\text{yd}^3]}} \end{aligned}$$

Note: A few shortcuts can reduce the computation time in this example. You may simplify the expression above by pulling (elev_{pit}) out of the square brackets. You may also shift all spot elevations 200[ft] down. As an example 282.53[ft] reduces to 82.53[ft]. With this method you won't have to retype the leading 2 for each elevation anymore. Alternatively, since answer options are so far apart, simply use an average depth to get a close enough answer.

(A) 2514[yd^3]

(B) 2852[yd^3]

(C) $\underline{\underline{3361[\text{yd}^3]}}$

(D) 3962[yd^3]

Problem I.11

A two-lane urban street is to be extended to have a third lane. Based on the data in the figure below, what is the length L of the transition zone?

(A) 108.88[ft]

(B) 153.05[ft]

(C) 217.77[ft]

(D) 306.10[ft]

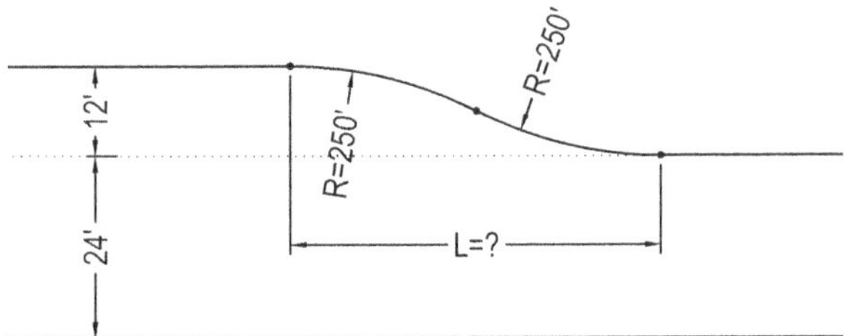

Solution to Problem I.11

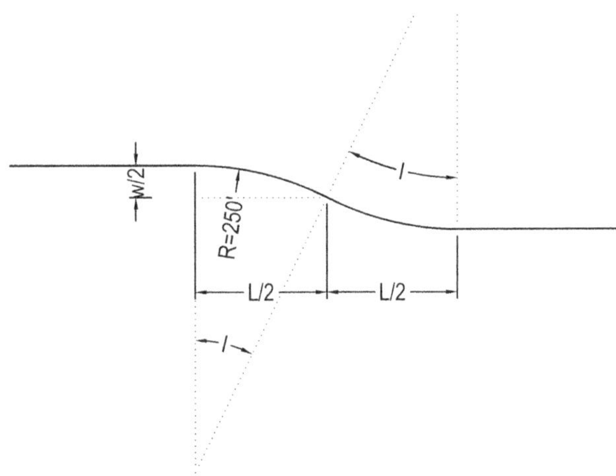

Sketch out the geometric relationship of the transition. Then you realize $L/2$ can be computed using Pythagoras' theorem:

$$\begin{aligned}\frac{L}{2} &= \sqrt{R^2 - \left(R - \frac{w}{2}\right)^2} \\ &= \sqrt{(250.00[\text{ft}])^2 - \left(250.00[\text{ft}] - \frac{12.00[\text{ft}]}{2}\right)^2} \\ &= 54.44[\text{ft}]\end{aligned}$$

$$\begin{aligned}L &= \frac{L}{2} \cdot 2 \\ &= 54.44[\text{ft}] \cdot 2 \\ &= \underline{\underline{108.88[\text{ft}]}}\end{aligned}$$

Problem I.12

A planned road has a stormwater drain running parallel, as depicted below: The flow line is $3'$ below center line of the road; except where the road has a sag vertical-curve, in which case the flow line follows the straight line extension of the vertical alignment. At the point of vertical intersection, the storm drain passes through a $2'6''$ diameter culvert.

Determine the required length L of the vertical curve such that the culvert has a $4'$ clearance between top of the culvert and center line of the road.

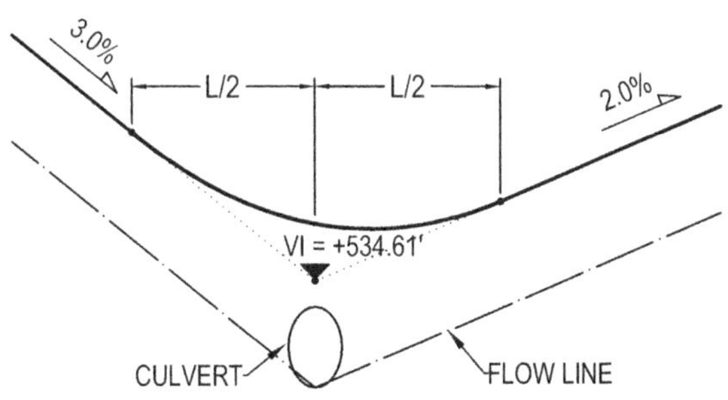

Solution to Problem I.12

This question is asking you to find the L that gives a certain road center-line elevation at VI. This elevation is determined by the culvert diameter and its required soil cover.

Required elevation at VI:

$$\begin{aligned} y &= y_{\mathrm{VI}} - \Delta y_{(\text{flow line})} + \varnothing_{\text{culvert}} + \Delta y_{(\text{soil cover})} \\ &= 534.61' - 3.0' + 2.5' + 4.0' \\ &= 538.11' \end{aligned}$$

Before L can be directly computed, the proper equation has to be transformed:

$$y = \mathcal{R}\frac{x^2}{2} + G_1 \cdot x + y_{\mathrm{BVC}}$$

with

$$\mathcal{R} = \frac{G_2 - G_1}{L}$$

$$x = \frac{L}{2}$$

$$y_{\mathrm{BVC}} = y_{\mathrm{VI}} - G_1\frac{L}{2}$$

gives

$$y = (G_2 - G_1) \cdot \frac{L}{8} + y_{\mathrm{VI}}$$

Solved for L:

$$\begin{aligned} L &= \frac{y - y_{\mathrm{VI}}}{G_2 - G_1} \cdot 8 \\ &= \frac{538.11' - 534.61'}{2\% - (-3)\%} \cdot 8 \\ &= \underline{\underline{5.6[\text{sta}]}} \end{aligned}$$

Note: In this example it is highly recommended to use the numerical solver function of your calculator to avoid rearranging $y = \mathcal{R}\frac{x^2}{2} + G_1 \cdot x + y_{\mathrm{BVC}}$ for x.

(A) 2.6[sta]

(B) 4.8[sta]

(C) 5.6[sta]

(D) 7.2[sta]

Problem I.13

A crest vertical curve, with 4.0[ft/sta] slope on both sides has its point of vertical intersection at elevation 2463.50′. Determine the required length of this vertical curve as such that the top turning point of the curve is at elevation 2450.00′.

Solution to Problem I.13

Having both grades (G_1, G_2) equal means the turning point of the curve will be at the same plan location as the point of vertical intersection. And elevations of the points BVC and EVC will also be the same. This allows us to use the equation for the middle ordinate, $M = \frac{1}{2}\left(Y_V - \frac{Y_{\text{BVC}}+Y_{\text{EVC}}}{2}\right)$, to compute the elevations of BVC/EVC. With this information, and together with the grades, we can calculate the length of the vertical curve. To speed things up, instead of computing the elevation of BVC/EVC, computing the elevation *differences* would suffice.

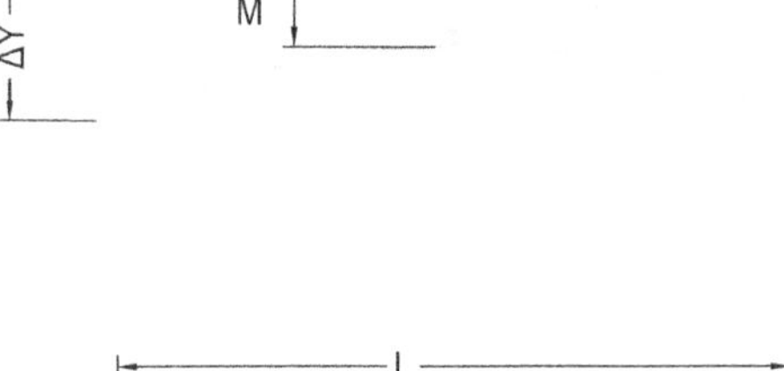

M is directly given as:

$$\begin{aligned} M &= Y_V - Y_{TP} \\ &= 2463.50' - 2450.00' \\ &= 13.5' \end{aligned}$$

Re-arrange M for Y_{VC} (or better ΔY):

$$M = \frac{1}{2}\left(Y_V - \underbrace{\frac{Y_{\text{BVC}} + Y_{\text{EVC}}}{2}}_{Y_{VC}}\right)$$

$$M = \frac{1}{2}\underbrace{(Y_V - Y_{VC})}_{\Delta Y}$$

$$\begin{aligned} \leadsto \Delta Y &= 2 \cdot M \\ &= 2 \cdot 13.5' \\ &= 27.0' \end{aligned}$$

Length of vertical curve:

$$\begin{aligned} \frac{L}{2} \cdot G &= \Delta Y \\ \leadsto L &= 2\frac{\Delta Y}{G} \\ &= 2 \cdot \frac{27.0'}{4[\text{ft/sta}]} \\ &= \underline{\underline{13.5[\text{sta}]}} \end{aligned}$$

(A) 1.7[sta]

(B) 3.4[sta]

(C) 6.8[sta]

(D) <u>13.5[sta]</u>

Problem I.14

A drain is running parallel to a road but keeps running straight as the road takes a turn, as shown below. Determine the required length of the culvert.

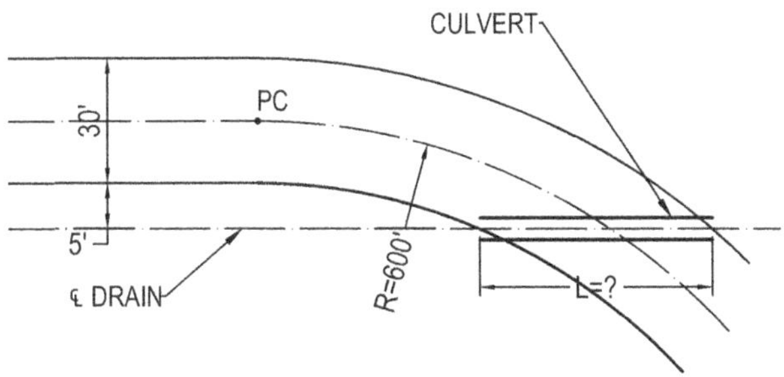

Solution to Problem I.14

As shown below, this problem boils down into two tangent offset problems that can be solved using Pythagoras' theorem. Solve the theorem for x_i, x_o to compute the culvert length: $L = x_o - x_i$.

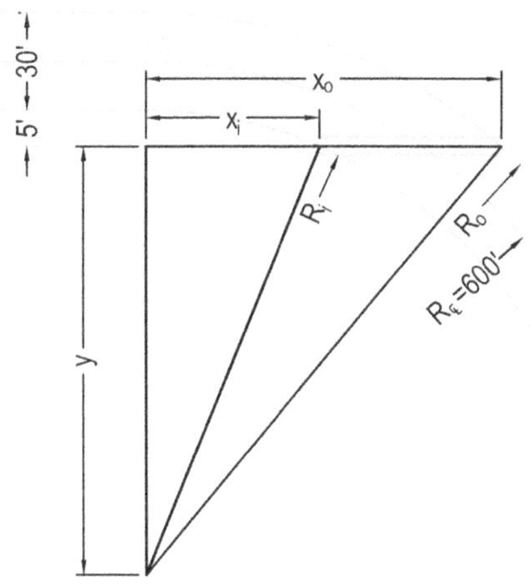

Determine x_i (the intersection of culvert with inner side of the road):

$$\begin{aligned} y &= R_{\text{CL}} - \frac{\text{(width of road)}}{2} - \text{(drain offset)} \\ &= 600[\text{ft}] - \frac{30[\text{ft}]}{2} - 5[\text{ft}] \\ &= 580[\text{ft}] \end{aligned}$$

$$\begin{aligned} R_i &= R_{\text{CL}} - \frac{\text{(width of road)}}{2} \\ &= 600[\text{ft}] - \frac{30[\text{ft}]}{2} \\ &= 585[\text{ft}] \end{aligned}$$

$$\begin{aligned} x_i &= \sqrt{R_i^2 - y^2} \\ &= \sqrt{585[\text{ft}]^2 - 580[\text{ft}]^2} \\ &= 76.32[\text{ft}] \end{aligned}$$

Determine x_o (the intersection of culvert with outer side of the road):

$$\begin{aligned} R_o &= R_{\text{CL}} + \frac{\text{(width of road)}}{2} \\ &= 600[\text{ft}] + \frac{30[\text{ft}]}{2} \\ &= 615[\text{ft}] \end{aligned}$$

$$\begin{aligned} x_o &= \sqrt{R_o^2 - y^2} \\ &= \sqrt{615[\text{ft}]^2 - 580[\text{ft}]^2} \\ &= 204.51[\text{ft}] \end{aligned}$$

Determine length of culvert:

$$\begin{aligned} L &= x_o - x_i \\ &= 204.51[\text{ft}] - 76.32[\text{ft}] \\ &= \underline{\underline{128.19[\text{ft}]}} \end{aligned}$$

(A) 71[ft]

(B) 91[ft]

(C) 99[ft]

(D) $\underline{\underline{128[\text{ft}]}}$

Problem I.15

A proposed power line is to run through an undivided, typical township section. The power line requires a 120[ft] wide right of way. Determine the required area for the power line's right of way within the township section.

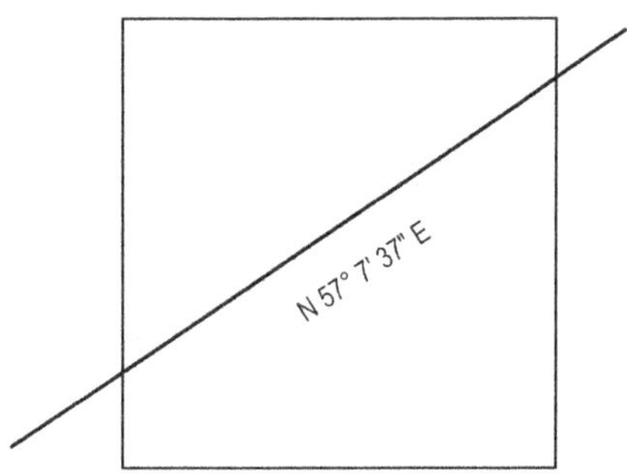

Problem I.16

A proposed, 32[ft] wide road is laid out to follow existing property lines. At a property line kink, the road takes a 500[ft] long curve, measured along the road center line. The area enclosed by the curve and property line, as shown in the exhibit, is to be greened. This area is most nearly?

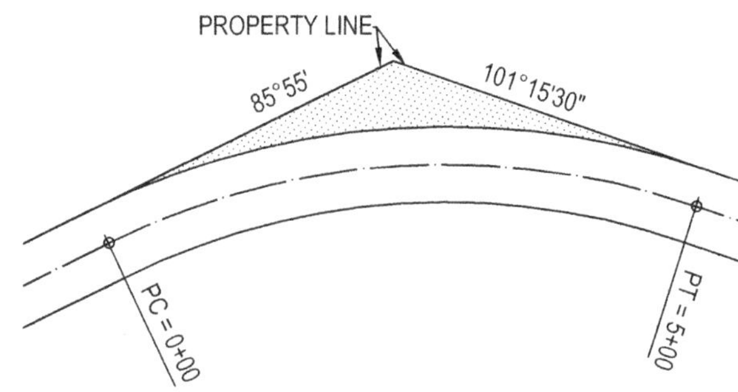

Solution to Problem I.15

A typical township section of the Public Land Survey System is 1[mi] wide. With this information, determine the length of the power line within this section.

Length of the power line:

$$\begin{aligned} L_{PL} &= \frac{L_{(\text{PLSS section})}}{\sin(\text{brg}_{PL})} \\ &= \frac{5280[\text{ft}]}{\sin(57°7'37'')} \\ &= 6287[\text{ft}] \end{aligned}$$

Right of way area:

$$\begin{aligned} A_{row} &= w_{RW} \cdot L_{PL} \\ &= 120[\text{ft}] \cdot 6287[\text{ft}] \\ &= 754440[\text{ft}^2] \\ &= \underline{\underline{17.3[\text{ac}]}} \end{aligned}$$

(A) 12.2[ac]

(B) 14.5[ac]

(C) 17.3[ac]

(D) 26.8[ac]

Solution to Problem I.16

Use the appropriate formula to determine this area:

$$A = TR - \frac{RL}{2}.$$

Keep in mind, the parameters T, R, L apply to the curve touching the property lines, not the road center lines.

Interior angle from property line azimuths:

$$\begin{aligned} I &= 101°15'30'' - 85°55' \\ &= 15°20'30'' \\ &= 15.3417° \end{aligned}$$

Center line radius:

$$\begin{aligned} R_{CL} &= \frac{L_{CL}}{I} \\ &= \frac{500[\text{ft}]}{15.3417° \frac{\pi}{180°}[\text{rad}/°]} \\ &= 1867.326[\text{ft}] \end{aligned}$$

Outer embankment radius:

$$R = R_{CL} + \frac{(\text{width of road})}{2}$$

$$= 1867.326[\text{ft}] + \frac{32[\text{ft}]}{2}$$
$$= 1883.326[\text{ft}]$$

Outer embankment length using similar triangles:

$$L = L_{CL}\frac{R}{R_{CL}}$$
$$= 500[\text{ft}]\frac{1883.326[\text{ft}]}{1867.326[\text{ft}]}$$
$$= 504.284[\text{ft}]$$

Outer embankment tangent length:

$$T = R\ \tan\left({}^{I}/_{2}\right)$$
$$= 1883.326[\text{ft}]\ \tan\left(\frac{15.3417^\circ}{2}\right)$$
$$= 253.659[\text{ft}]$$

Finally, compute area:

$$A = TR - \frac{RL}{2}$$
$$= (253.659[\text{ft}])(1883.326[\text{ft}]) - \frac{1883.326[\text{ft}] \cdot 504.284[\text{ft}]}{2}$$
$$= \underline{\underline{2857.687[\text{ft}^2]}}$$

(A) $2,713[\text{ft}^2]$

(B) $2,761[\text{ft}^2]$

(C) $2,809[\text{ft}^2]$

(D) $\underline{\underline{2,858[\text{ft}^2]}}$

Problem I.17

A 32[ft] wide road follows a property line, as shown below. At a property line kink, the road takes a 500[ft] curve (measured along the road centerline). Determine the minimum distance from the property line kink to the edge of the road.

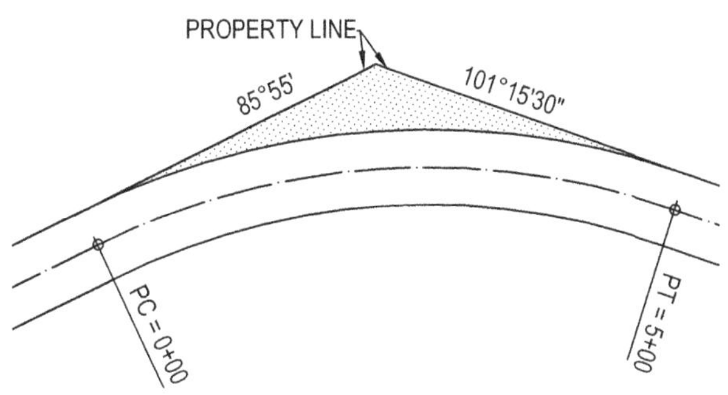

Solution to Problem I.17

The problem statement is asking for the *external distance* E, which is the shortest distance between the point of tangent intersection and the curve. Note that in this case we need to look at the curve of the outer edge of the road – not the curve of the centerline. The equation for the external distance is:

$$E = \frac{R}{\cos {}^{I}/_{2}} - R\,.$$

Deflection angle from azimuths:

$$I = \text{brg}_2 - \text{brg}_1$$
$$= 101^\circ 15' 30'' - 85^\circ 55' 0''$$
$$= 15^\circ 20' 30''$$

Centerline curve radius (from curve length):

$$R_{\text{CL}} = \frac{L}{I[\text{rad}]}$$
$$= \frac{500.00[\text{ft}]}{0.26776[\text{rad}]}$$
$$= 1867.33[\text{ft}]$$

Outer edge curve radius:

$$R_o = R_{\text{CL}} + \frac{(\text{road width})}{2}$$

$$= 1867.33[\text{ft}] + \frac{32.00[\text{ft}]}{2}$$
$$= 1883.33[\text{ft}]$$

Distance from kink to curve (ordinate M):

$$E = \frac{R_o}{\cos\left(\frac{I}{2}\right)} - R_o$$
$$= \frac{1883.33[\text{ft}]}{\cos\left(\frac{15°20'30''}{2}\right)} - 1883.33[\text{ft}]$$
$$= \underline{\underline{17.01[\text{ft}]}}$$

(A) 13.01[ft]

(B) 16.72[ft]

(C) 16.86[ft]

(D) 17.01[ft]

Problem I.18

A new pipeline is to be constructed, as shown below. Regulations require barriers for when the pipe line is closer than 200[ft] to the shoulder of the road. At what pipeline station may the special barriers end?

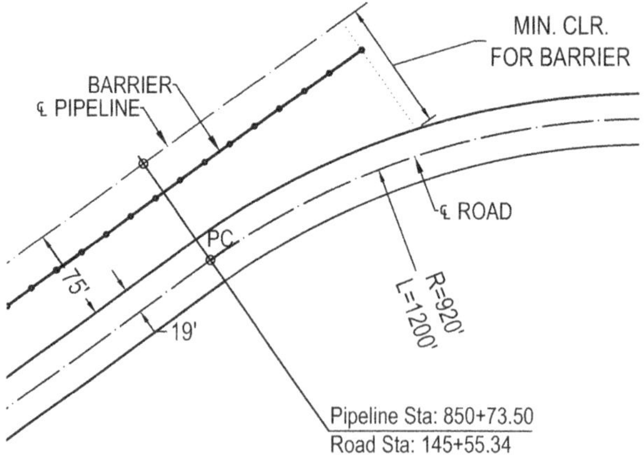

Solution to Problem I.18

The key is to recognize that the question is asking for the tangent distance $\Delta T = \overline{PT'\,POST'}$ at which a certain tangent offset $\Delta O = \overline{POC'\,POST'}$ is reached.

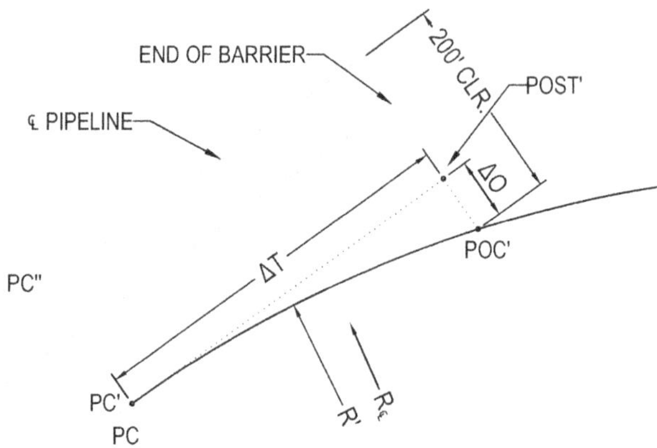

Required tangent offset:

$$\Delta O = \text{(req. clearance)} - \text{(typ. clearance)}$$
$$= 200[\text{ft}] - 75[\text{ft}]$$
$$= 125[\text{ft}]$$

Curve radius of left shoulder:

$$R' = R_{\text{CL}} + \text{(offset CL to left shoulder)}$$

$$= 920[\text{ft}] + 19[\text{ft}]$$
$$= 939[\text{ft}]$$

Re-arrange tangent offset equation for ΔT and solve:

$$\Delta O = R' - \sqrt{R'^2 - (\Delta T)^2}$$
$$\Delta T = \sqrt{R'^2 - (R'^2 - \Delta O)^2}$$
$$= \sqrt{(939[\text{ft}])^2 - ((939[\text{ft}])^2 - \Delta O)^2}$$
$$= 468.10[\text{ft}]$$

Finally, compute the pipeline station where barrier can end:

$$[\text{sta}]_{(\text{barrier end})} = [\text{sta}]_{PT''} + \Delta T$$
$$= (850{+}73.50) + 468.10[\text{ft}]$$
$$= \underline{\underline{(855{+}41.61)}}$$

Note: Instead of rearranging the tangent offset equation, use the numeric solver function on your calculator.

(A) Sta. (855+36.51)

(B) <u>Sta. (855+41.61)</u>

(C) Sta. (856+46.21)

(D) Sta. (856+52.81)

Problem I.19

For a construction project a temporary benchmark with elevation 591.63[ft] (project elevation: $-2.64'$) has been established.

If the excavation for a foundation needs to reach project elevation $-16'3''$, and the backsight rod reading is $4.61'$, what is the required foresight rod reading to verify the excavation elevation with a laser level?

Solution to Problem I.19

Rearrange the standard leveling equation, $\text{elev}_B = \text{elev}_A + \text{BS} - \text{FS}$, to solve FS.

$$\text{FS} = \text{elev}_{\text{TBM}} - \text{elev}_{\text{excavation}} + \text{BS}$$
$$= (-2.64') + 4.61' - (-16.25')$$
$$= \underline{\underline{18.22'}}$$

(A) 13.61′

(B) <u>18.22′</u>

(C) 18.89′

(D) 20.68′

Problem I.20

The underpass shown below requires an elevation difference of $\Delta H = 26[\text{ft}]$ using two vertical parabolic curves. If the maximum allowed slope is $G_{\text{max}} = 7.5\%$, what is the minimum length L of the transition?

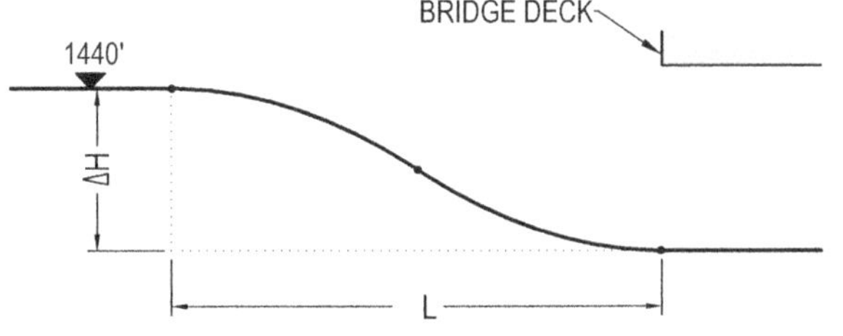

Solution to Problem I.20

By subdividing the vertical curves as shown below, the relation between the maximum slope (occurring at transition between the curves) and the required length of transition can be established.

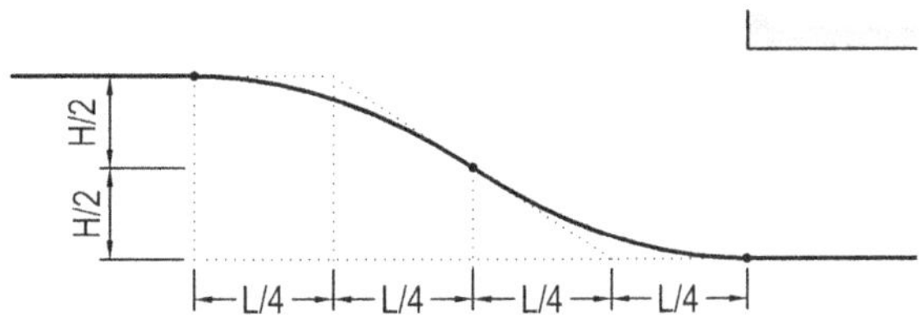

$$G_{\text{max}} = \frac{H/2}{L/4}$$

$$\leadsto L = \frac{2H}{G_{\text{max}}}$$

$$= \frac{2 \cdot 26[\text{ft}]}{7.5[\%]}$$

$$= \underline{\underline{6.93[\text{sta}]}}$$

(A) 1.73[sta]

(B) 3.47[sta]

(C) 6.93[sta]

(D) 13.86[sta]

Problem I.21

The same physical distance between two points is measured twice using the same metal tape. The first measurement was taken at a temperature of 72.6[°F]. The second measurement was taken at a temperature of 93.2[°F]. If the physical distance between the points did not change between the readings, which of the following statements can be made regarding the recorded lengths of the measurements?

Solution to Problem I.21

Because the first reading was taken at a lower temperature than the second reading, the metal tape was shorter than the second reading. If the tape is shorter, the length it reads is longer, because clearly more tick-marks would fit within the measured distance.

Therefore, the second measurement reads a lower distance than the first. (Answer B)

(A) The first measurement reads a lower distance.

(B) The second measurement reads a lower distance.

(C) Both measurements read the same value.

(D) None of the above statments can be made.

Problem I.22

A $D = 12°$ (arc definition) curve is being staked out in the field. If stakes are to be set every 100[ft] along the curve, what must be the corresponding chord length between the stakes?

Solution to Problem I.22

Use the appropriate equation to compute the chord length.

Curve radius:

$$\begin{aligned} R &= \frac{\text{(stake arc distance)}}{D} \\ &= \frac{100[\text{ft}]}{12} \\ &= 477.465[\text{ft}] \end{aligned}$$

Half the chord length:

$$\begin{aligned} c/2 &= R \sin \frac{D}{2} \\ &= 477.465[\text{ft}] \ \sin \frac{12°}{2} \\ &= 49.909[\text{ft}] \end{aligned}$$

Chord length c:

$$\begin{aligned} c &= (2)(49.909[\text{ft}]) \\ &= \underline{\underline{99.817[\text{ft}]}} \end{aligned}$$

(A) 99.635[ft]

(B) <u>99.817[ft]</u>

(C) 99.909[ft]

(D) 99.954[ft]

Problem I.23

The trapezoidal cross section of a riverbed shown below is being surveyed with 3-wire leveling. See the table below for field notes. The slope of the right riverbank is most nearly?

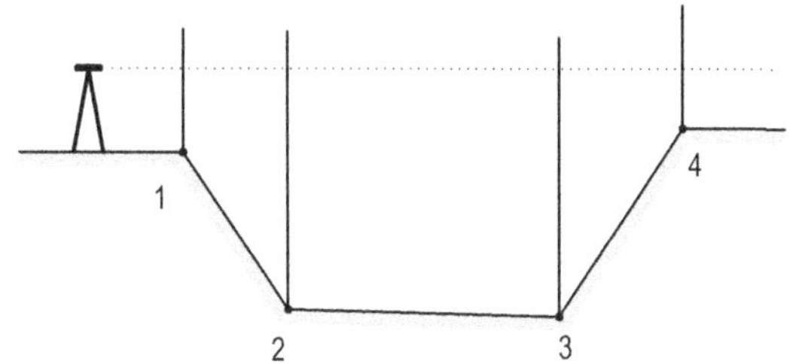

	FS	
1	5.67 5.64 5.61	
2	12.90 12.82 12.74	
3	13.72 13.57 13.42	
4	2.93 2.72 2.51	

Solution to Problem I.23

Start by deriving the distance of each reading. Calculate the differences of horizontal and vertical distances. Use the results to compute the slope. Because the stadia multiplier K is not given, use the default value of $K = 100$.

Distance to point 3:

$$\begin{aligned} d_3 &= ((\text{upper reading})_3 - (\text{lower reading})_3) \cdot 100 \\ &= (13.72[\text{ft}] - 13.42[\text{ft}]) \cdot 100 \\ &= 30[\text{ft}] \end{aligned}$$

Distance to point 4:

$$\begin{aligned} d_4 &= ((\text{upper reading})_4 - (\text{lower reading})_4) \cdot 100 \\ &= (2.93[\text{ft}] - 2.51[\text{ft}]) \cdot 100 \end{aligned}$$

$$= 42[\text{ft}]$$

Horizontal distance between point 3 and 4:

$$\begin{aligned}\Delta x &= d_4 - d_3\\ &= 42[\text{ft}] - 30[\text{ft}]\\ &= 12[\text{ft}]\end{aligned}$$

Vertical distance between point 3 and 4:

$$\begin{aligned}\Delta y &= (\text{mid reading})_3 - (\text{mid reading})_4\\ &= 13.57[\text{ft}] - 2.72[\text{ft}]\\ &= 10.85[\text{ft}]\end{aligned}$$

Slope between point 3 and 4:

$$\begin{aligned}G &= \frac{\Delta y}{\Delta x} \cdot 100\%\\ &= \frac{10.85[\text{ft}]}{12[\text{ft}]} \cdot 100\%\\ &= \underline{\underline{90.4\%}}\end{aligned}$$

(A) 89.6%

(B) 90.4%

(C) 99.3%

(D) 101.3%

Problem I.24

To verify the reflector constant of a newly bought EDM device, measurements of three points along a straight line were taken. See the table below for the measurement results, with *A* and *C* being the outer points. The reflector constant is most nearly?

Line	Distance [ft]
A–C	78.446
A–B	6.324
B–C	70.768

Solution to Problem I.24

Use the equation for the reflector constant to solve this problem.

$$\begin{aligned}c &= \overline{AC} - \overline{AB} - \overline{BC}\\ &= 78.446[\text{ft}] - 6.324[\text{ft}] - 70.768[\text{ft}]\\ &= \underline{\underline{1.354[\text{ft}]}}\end{aligned}$$

(A) 0.190[ft]

(B) 0.338[ft]

(C) 0.676[ft]

(D) 1.354[ft]

Problem I.25

In order to track the movement of an earthquake fault, the field measurements depicted below were taken. The azimuths noted are corrected for magnetic declination. Determine the magnitude of fault displacement based on the provided recordings.

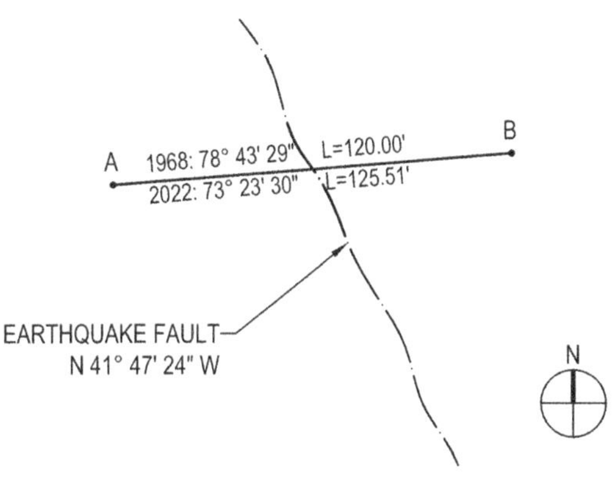

Solution to Problem I.25

The figure below sketches out the information provided in the problem statement. The sought fault displacement is denoted as δ_L.

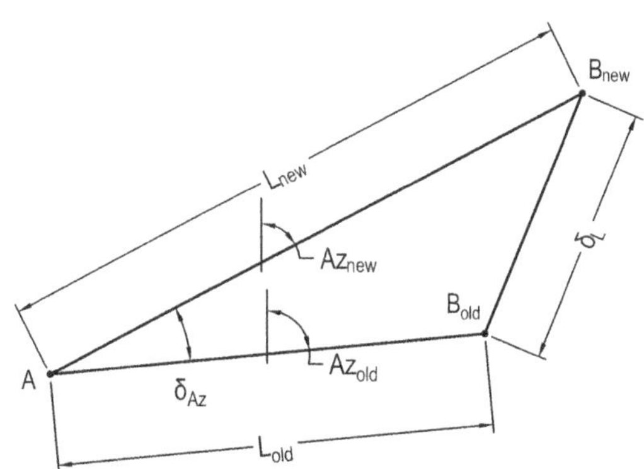

Change in azimuth angle:

$$\begin{aligned}\delta_{Az} &= |Az_{new} - Az_{old}| \\ &= (73°23'30'' - 78°43'29'') \\ &= 5°19'59''\end{aligned}$$

Fault displacement (using law of cosines):

$$\begin{aligned}a^2 &= b^2 + c^2 - 2\,b\,c\,\cos(\alpha) \\ \delta_L^2 &= (L_{new})^2 + (L_{old})^2 \\ &\quad - 2 \cdot L_{new} \cdot L_{old} \cdot \cos(\delta_{Az}) \\ &= (125.51)^2 + (120)^2 \\ &\quad - 2 \cdot 120 \cdot 125.51 \cdot \cos(5°19'59'') \\ &= 160.75[\text{ft}^2] \\ \delta_L &= \sqrt{\delta_L^2} \\ &= \sqrt{160.75} \\ &= \underline{\underline{2.7[\text{ft}]}}\end{aligned}$$

(A) $\underline{\underline{2.7[\text{ft}]}}$

(B) 5.5[ft]

(C) 11.2[ft]

(D) 11.7[ft]

Problem I.26

A cross section of a proposed highway is shown below. Determine the net amount of cut or fill for this cross section.

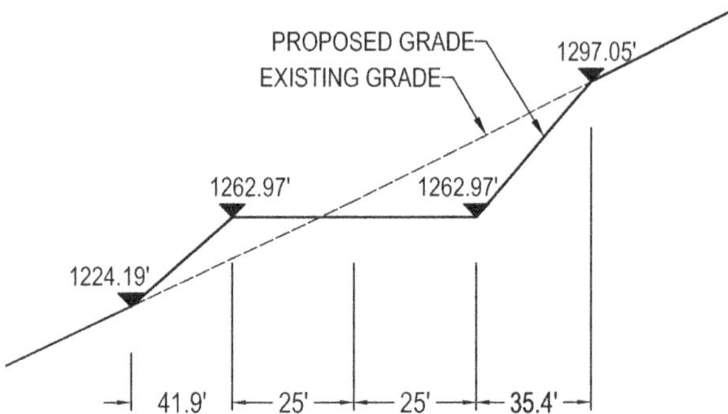

Solution to Problem I.26

Use the area of trapezium equation: $A = 1/2\ d\ h + 1/4\ b\ (h_L + h_R)$. Note, that this equation is written with *cut* sections in mind, but works for both cut and fill sections. Make sure to enter the heights with the appropriate sign.

Determine the required inputs for the equation:

$$
\begin{aligned}
h_L &= y_L - y_M \\
&= 1224.19 - 1262.97 \\
&= -38.78[\text{ft}] \\
h_R &= y_R - y_M \\
&= 1297.05 - 1262.97 \\
&= 34.08[\text{ft}] \\
b &= 50[\text{ft}] \\
d &= b + x_L + x_R \\
&= 50 + 41.9 + 35.4 \\
&= 127.3[\text{ft}]
\end{aligned}
$$

Interpolate height at mid profile:

$$
\begin{aligned}
h &= y_L + \frac{y_R - y_L}{d} \cdot \left(x_L + \frac{b}{2}\right) - y_M \\
&= 1224.19[\text{ft}] \\
&\quad + \frac{1297.05 - 1224.19}{127.3} \cdot \left(41.9 + \frac{50}{2}\right) \\
&\quad - 1262.97 \\
&= -0.49[\text{ft}]
\end{aligned}
$$

Compute the net cut area:

$$
\begin{aligned}
A &= \frac{1}{2} \cdot d \cdot h + \frac{1}{4} \cdot b \cdot (h_L + h_R) \\
&= \frac{1}{2} \cdot 127.3 \cdot (-0.49) + \frac{1}{4} \cdot 50 \cdot (-38.78 + 34.08) \\
&= \underline{\underline{-89.9[\text{ft}^2]}} \quad \text{(indicates } 89.9[\text{ft}^2] \textit{ fill} \text{ area)}
\end{aligned}
$$

(A) $27.6[\text{ft}^2]$ cut

(B) $27.6[\text{ft}^2]$ fill

(C) $89.9[\text{ft}^2]$ cut

(D) $\underline{\underline{89.9[\text{ft}^2]\text{ fill}}}$

Problem I.27

The results of a differential leveling exercise are depicted below. The linear misclosure was distributed equally to each measured elevation. Later on it was discovered that the actual elevation of BM 6281-05 is at 923.28′. Based on this, what is the actual, corrected elevation of point C?

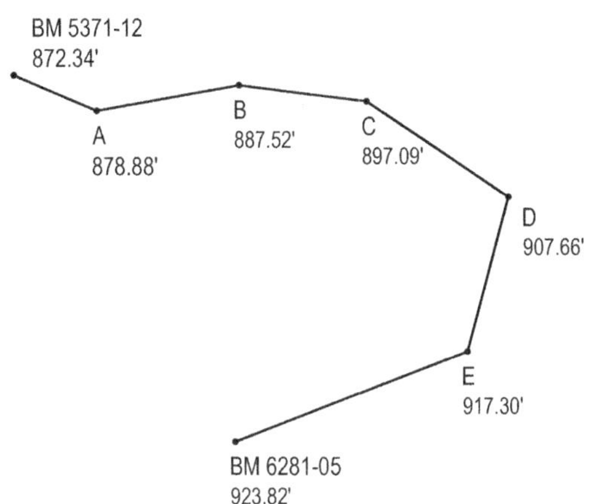

Solution to Problem I.27

Treat the elevation difference as a linear misclosure and distribute it equally to each elevation:

Elevation difference (total):

$$\begin{aligned} \Delta E_{tot} &= E_{new} - E_{old} \\ &= 923.28' - 923.82' \\ &= -0.54' \end{aligned}$$

Elevation difference (per setup):

$$\begin{aligned} \Delta E_{eql} &= \frac{\Delta E_{tot}}{\text{(number of setups)}} \\ &= \frac{-0.54'}{6} \\ &= -0.09' \end{aligned}$$

Elevation difference (for point C):

$$\begin{aligned} \Delta E_C &= \Delta E_{eql} \cdot \text{(number of setups to point } C) \\ &= (-0.09') \cdot 3 \\ &= -0.27' \end{aligned}$$

Adjusted elevation of point C:

$$\begin{aligned} C_{new} &= C_{old} + \Delta E_C \\ &= 897.09' + (-0.27') \\ &= \underline{\underline{896.82'}} \end{aligned}$$

(A) 896.69′

(B) $\underline{\underline{896.82'}}$

(C) 896.91′

(D) 897.00′

Problem I.28

Referring to the topographic map below, the average slope between which two points is the steepest? Assume the map is drawn to scale.

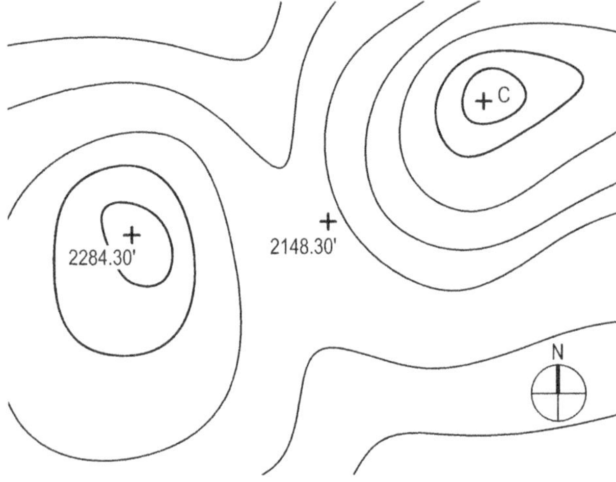

Solution to Problem I.28

Looking at the map, the horizontal distance between the point at elevation 2284.30′ (point A) and the point at elevation 2148.30′ (point M) is the same as between the point M and point C. Because between A and M there are only 3 contour lines, but 5 contour lines between M and C, the average slope must be the highest between these two points.

(A) Between point at elevation 2284.30′ and point at elevation 2148.30′

(B) Between point at elevation 2284.30′ and point C

(C) Between point at elevation 2148.30′ and point C

(D) None of the above can be concluded without additional information.

Problem I.29

To demolish an existing concrete building, a temporary 22[ft] tall and 15[ft] wide ramp needs to be built. If the maximum allowed slope is 12%, what is the minimum required ramp length?

Solution to Problem I.29

Compute the required ramp length based on the ramp slope and height:

$$L = \frac{\text{(ramp height)}}{\text{(slope)}} = \frac{22[\text{ft}]}{12\%S} = 183[\text{ft}]$$

(A) 100[ft]

(B) 125[ft]

(C) 147[ft]

(D) 183[ft]

Problem I.30

A 260′ long and 3′ wide ditch with 2.5[ft/sta] slope along the flow line is being excavated. A dumpy level is used to verify the excavation depths. If the rod reading at beginning of the ditch is 6.54[ft], what should be the rod reading at the end of the ditch?

Solution to Problem I.30

First, compute the elevation difference:

$$\begin{aligned}\Delta H &= (\text{length of ditch}) \frac{(\text{slope of ditch})[\text{ft/sta}]}{100} \\ &= 260[\text{ft}] \frac{2.5[\text{ft/sta}]}{100} \\ &= 6.50[\text{ft}]\end{aligned}$$

Finally, calculate the required rod reading at the ditch end:

$$\begin{aligned}\text{FS} &= \text{BS} + \Delta H \\ &= 6.54[\text{ft}] + 6.50[\text{ft}] \\ &= \underline{\underline{13.04[\text{ft}]}}\end{aligned}$$

(A) 0.04[ft]

(B) 6.50[ft]

(C) 12.74[ft]

(D) <u>13.04[ft]</u>

Problem I.31

The construction drawings for the existing horizontal curve shown below were destroyed in a wild fire. Based on the conducted field survey, which is shown below, determine the centerline radius of the curve.

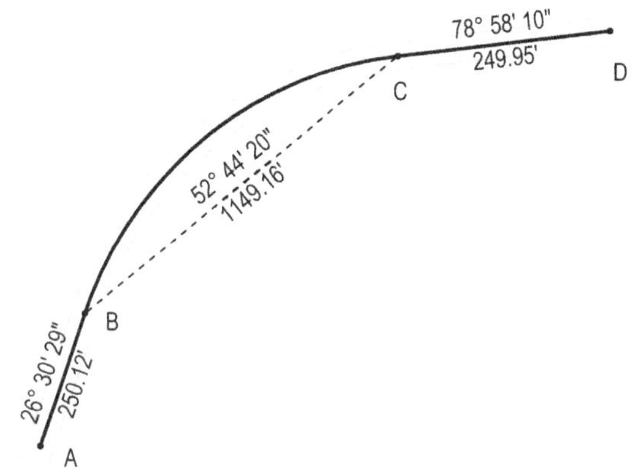

Solution to Problem I.31

Backcalculate the radius from the chord-length equation: $C = 2\,R\,\sin {}^{I}/_{2}$.

Interior angle:

$$\begin{aligned}I &= \text{Az}_{CD} - \text{Az}_{AB} \\ &= 78°58'10'' - 26°30'29'' \\ &= 52°27'41''\end{aligned}$$

Chord length:

$$\begin{aligned}C &= L_{BC} \\ &= 1149.16[\text{ft}]\end{aligned}$$

Curve radius:

$$\begin{aligned}R &= \frac{C}{2 \cdot \sin\left(\frac{I}{2}\right)} \\ &= \frac{1149.16}{2 \cdot \sin\left(\frac{52°27'41''}{2}\right)} \\ &= \underline{\underline{1300[\text{ft}]}}\end{aligned}$$

(A) 1130[ft]

(B) 1200[ft]

(C) <u>1300[ft]</u>

(D) 1450[ft]

Problem I.32

For a horizontal curve with $R = 600[\text{ft}]$, the azimuths of the forward and backward tangent are $89°40'0''$ and $32°30'15''$, respectively. With the coordinates of PI being $(N = 15884.23[\text{ft}], E = 416.55[\text{ft}])$, determine coordinates of the point of PC.

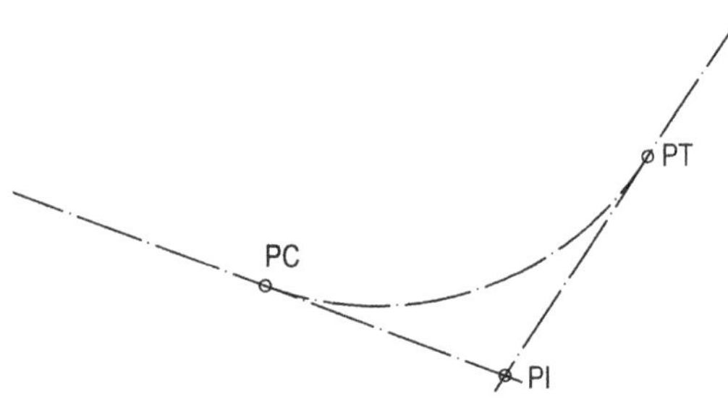

Solution to Problem I.32

Determine tangent length:

$$\begin{aligned} I &= \text{Az}_{(\text{forward tangent})} - \text{Az}_{(\text{backward tangent})} \\ &= 89°40'0'' - 32°30'15'' \\ &= 57.1625° \\ T &= R \cdot \tan\left({}^{I}/_{2}\right) \\ &= 600[\text{ft}] \cdot \tan\left(\frac{57.1625°}{2}\right) \\ &= 326.876[\text{ft}] \end{aligned}$$

Determine PC coordinates based on bearing and tangent length:

$$\begin{aligned} \text{Az}_{PI,PC} &= \text{Az}_{(\text{backward tangent})} + 180° \\ &= 32°30'15'' + 180° \\ &= 212.5041° \\ N_{PC} &= N_{PI} + T \cdot \sin(\text{Az}_{PI,PC}) \\ &= 15884.23[\text{ft}] + 326.876[\text{ft}] \cdot \sin(212.5041°) \\ &= \underline{\underline{15608.558[\text{ft}]}} \\ E_{PC} &= E_{PI} + T \cdot \cos(\text{Az}_{PI,PC}) \\ &= 416.55[\text{ft}] + 326.876[\text{ft}] \cdot \cos(212.5041°) \\ &= \underline{\underline{240.900[\text{ft}]}} \end{aligned}$$

(A) (15100.181[ft], -83.024[ft])

(B) (15100.181[ft], 240.900[ft])

(C) <u>(15608.558[ft], 240.900[ft])</u>

(D) (16159.902[ft], 592.200[ft])

Problem I.33

An existing railway fork, as shown in the figure below, is to be extended with an additional turn. Determine the distance between point PC_1 and PT_2.

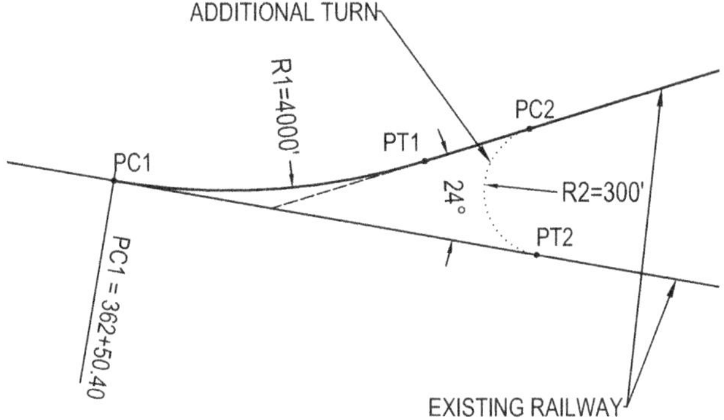

Solution to Problem I.33

The distance to be determined, L, comprises tangent lengths of both curves.

First tangent length:

$$\begin{aligned} T_1 &= R_1 \tan\left(\frac{I}{2}\right) \\ &= 4000[\text{ft}] \tan\left(\frac{24°}{2}\right) \\ &= 850.226[\text{ft}] \end{aligned}$$

Interior angle of second curve:

$$\begin{aligned} I_2 &= 180° - I \\ &= 180° - 24° \\ &= 156° \end{aligned}$$

Second tangent length:

$$\begin{aligned} T_2 &= R_2 \tan\left(\frac{I_2}{2}\right) \\ &= 300[\text{ft}] \tan\left(\frac{156°}{2}\right) \\ &= 1411.389[\text{ft}] \end{aligned}$$

Distance between PC_1 and PT_2:

$$\begin{aligned} L &= T_1 + T_2 \\ &= 850.226[\text{ft}] + 1411.389[\text{ft}] \end{aligned}$$

$= \underline{\underline{2261.62[\text{ft}]}}$

(A) 1045.05[ft]

(B) 1647.35[ft]

(C) 2261.62[ft]

(D) 2454.73[ft]

Problem I.34

A proposed road network was staked out in the field. The construction drawings specify the curves through coordinates of their end-points and the degree of curvature using chord basis. However, the surveyor mistakenly staked out using the arc basis definition for degree of curvature.

How do the proposed curve radii (R_{plan}) compare to the staked out(R_{field})?

Solution to Problem I.34

Try out using $D = 4°$:

arc basis:

$$R_{\text{arc}} = \frac{180° 100[\text{ft}]}{\pi[\text{rad}]D} \tag{6.1}$$

$$= \frac{180° 100[\text{ft}]}{\pi[\text{rad}]4°} \tag{6.2}$$

$$= 1432.39[\text{ft}] \tag{6.3}$$

chord basis:

$$R_{\text{chord}} = \frac{50}{\sin\frac{D}{2}} \tag{6.4}$$

$$= \frac{50}{\sin\frac{4°}{2}} \tag{6.5}$$

$$= 1432.69[\text{ft}] \tag{6.6}$$

Because $R_{\text{plan}} = R_{\text{chord}}$ and $R_{\text{field}} = R_{\text{arc}}$, it follows that $\underline{\underline{R_{\text{plan}} > R_{\text{field}}}}$.

(A) $R_{\text{plan}} < R_{\text{field}}$

(B) $R_{\text{plan}} = R_{\text{field}}$

(C) $\underline{\underline{R_{\text{plan}} > R_{\text{field}}}}$

(D) Cannot be determined without further information.

Problem I.35

Consider the curve of a 32[ft] wide road with deflection angle $I = 23°52'14''$. Project specific regulations require that PT_i remains visible from PC_i. This is enforced by defining a setback distance of $S = 15[\text{ft}]$ in which no obstructions may be built. What is the minimum possible centerline radius of this curve?

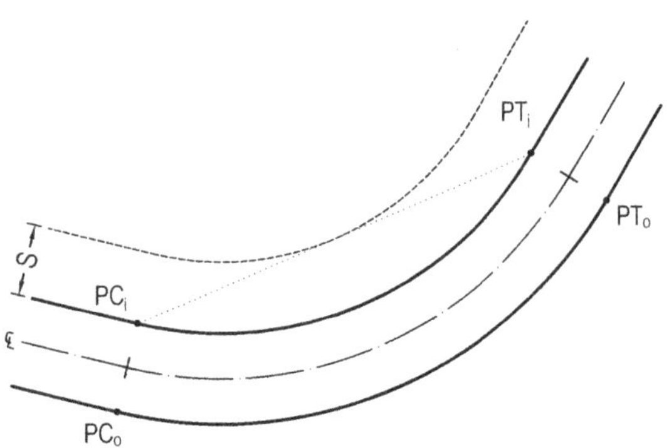

Solution to Problem I.35

For this question, the equation for the middle ordinate $M = 1(R - \cos {}^{I}/_{2})$ comes in useful. Specifically, it is being used to backcalculate the allowable radius, at which the middle ordinate M equals the required setback S.

Re-arrange equation:

$$M = R(1 - \cos {}^{I}/_{2})$$
$$\rightsquigarrow R = \frac{S}{1 - \cos {}^{I}/_{2}} \quad \text{(with } M = S\text{)}$$

Inner curve radius:

$$\begin{aligned} R_i &= \frac{S}{1 - \cos\left(\frac{I}{2}\right)} \\ &= \frac{15.00[\text{ft}]}{1 - \cos\left(\frac{23°52'14''}{2}\right)} \\ &= 693.86[\text{ft}] \end{aligned}$$

Centerline radius:

$$\begin{aligned} R_{\text{CL}} &= R_i + \frac{w}{2} \\ &= 693.86[\text{ft}] + \frac{32.00[\text{ft}]}{2} \\ &= \underline{\underline{709.86[\text{ft}]}} \end{aligned}$$

Note: Use the numeric solver function on your calculator to solve R_i without re-arranging the equation.

(A) 191.36[ft]

(B) <u>709.86[ft]</u>

(C) 756.12[ft]

(D) 1496.24[ft]

Problem I.36

A storm drain—currently starting at point E—is to be extended to start at point A. It is planned to use a 48″ (inside diameter) reinforced concrete pipe with 5″ wall thickness. At point E, the invert elevation is 950.04′. The storm drain requires a minimum cover of 4′6″ above the pipe top. The maximum slope is 6.0% and can change at every full station.

Determine the highest possible pipe invert elevation at point A.

(A) 963.81′

(B) 964.64′

(C) 966.12′

(D) <u>968.23′</u>

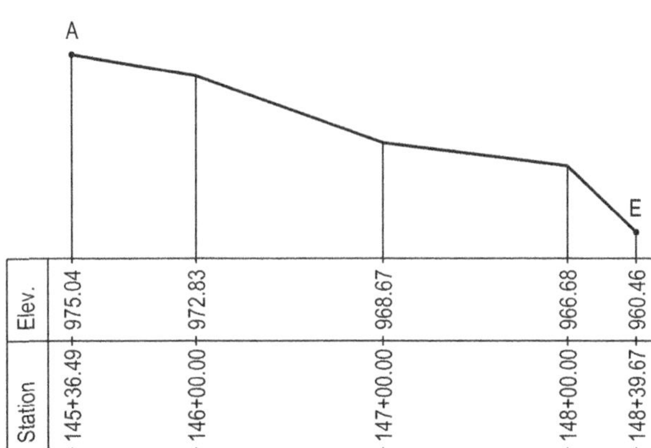

Solution to Problem I.36

The highest possible pipe invert elevation at point A may be limited by either constraint: 1) minimum soil cover, or 2) maximum slope of the pipe. Test both constraints.

Elevation from min. soil cover:

$$\begin{aligned} \text{elev}_{A,d} &= y_A - d_{min} - \varnothing_{pipe} - t_{pipe} \\ &= 975.04' - 4.5' - 48'' \cdot 1/12[\text{in/ft}] \\ &\qquad - 5'' \cdot 1/12[\text{in/ft}] \\ &= 966.12' \end{aligned}$$

Elevation from max. pipe slope:

$$\begin{aligned} \text{elev}_{A,s} &= \text{elev}_E + s_{max} \cdot (x_E - x_A) \\ &= 950.04' \\ &\quad + 6.0[\text{ft/sta}] \cdot \begin{pmatrix} 148.3967[\text{sta}] \\ \quad - 145.3649[\text{sta}] \end{pmatrix} \\ &= 968.23' \end{aligned}$$

Governing criterion

$$e_A = \min\left(\text{elev}_{A,d},\ \text{elev}_{A,s}\right)$$

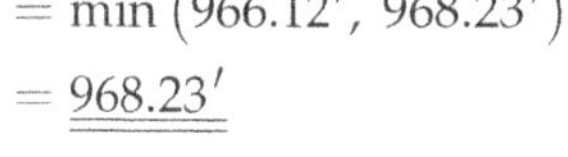

$$\begin{aligned} &= \min\left(966.12',\ 968.23'\right) \\ &= \underline{\underline{968.23'}} \end{aligned}$$

Problem I.37

In order to track the movement of an earthquake fault, the field measurements depicted below were taken. The azimuths noted are *not* corrected for magnetic declination. Determine the magnitude of fault-parallel displacement based on the provided recordings. Assume the line $B - C$ is initially perpendicular to the fault and points A, B were not displaced relative to each other.

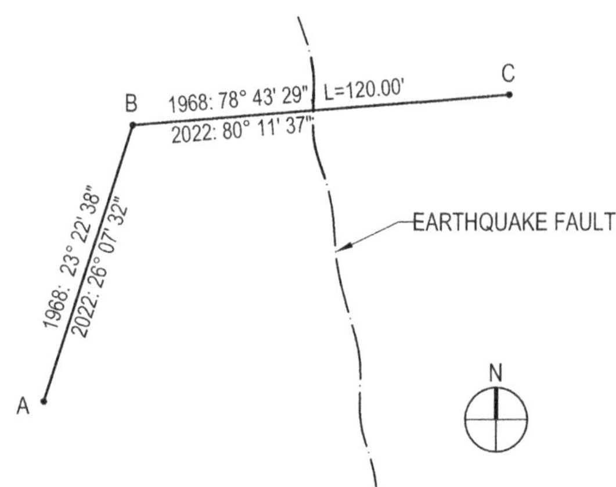

Solution to Problem I.37

Start by recognizing that the fault displacement is to be determined based on the change of azimuth $A - C$, corrected by the change in magnetic declination. Determine the change in magnetic declination using azimuth reading for $A - B$.

Magnetic deviation:

$$\begin{aligned}\delta_{magn} &= Az_{AB,22} - Az_{AB,68} \\ &= (26°7'32'') - (23°22'38'') \\ &= 2°44'54''\end{aligned}$$

Angular change for $B - C$

$$\begin{aligned}\delta &= Az_{BC,22} - Az_{BC,68} - \delta_{magn} \\ &= 80°11'37'' - 78°43'29'' - 2°44'54'' \\ &= -2°43'14''\end{aligned}$$

Fault-parallel displacement:

$$\begin{aligned}\Delta &= \ell_{BC,68} \cdot \tan\delta \\ &= 120.00[\text{ft}] \tan\left(-2°43'14''\right) \\ &= \underline{\underline{-2.68[\text{ft}]}}\end{aligned}$$

The way the equation was set up, a negative δ corresponds to a counter-clockwise rotation, a negative Δ corresponds to a northward movement of point C.

(A) <u>East side moving 2.68[ft] northwards.</u>

(B) East side moving 3.08[ft] northwards.

(C) East side moving 8.85[ft] northwards.

(D) East side moving 14.66[ft] northwards.

Problem I.38

The excavation plan for a construction pit is shown below. Determine the excavation volume using the average end formula. For determination of excavation depth, assume an existing elevation of 342.50′ and a final grade of 321.40′ for the excavation.

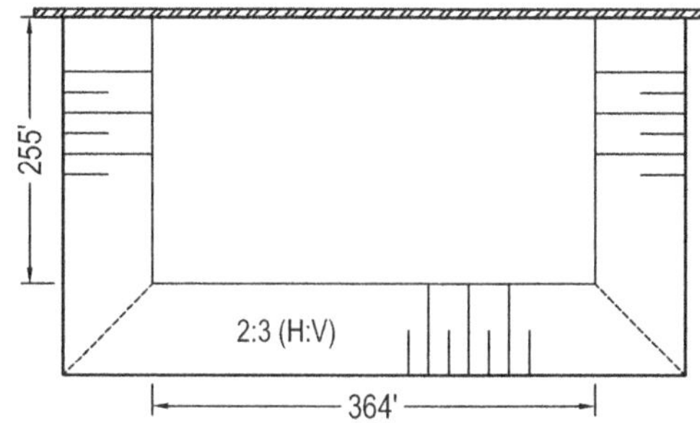

Solution to Problem I.38

Use the equation for the average end area: $A = {}^{h}/_{2}\,(A_1 + A_2)$. The dimensions of the lower area can be read directly from the figure. The upper area dimensions are found by adding the width of the slope.

Excavation depth:

$$\begin{aligned} h &= \text{elev}_{(E)} - \text{elev}_{pit} \\ &= 342.50[\text{ft}] - 321.40[\text{ft}] \\ &= 21.1[\text{ft}] \end{aligned}$$

Lower area:

$$\begin{aligned} A_1 &= x_1 \cdot y_1 \\ &= 364[\text{ft}] \cdot 255[\text{ft}] \\ &= 92820[\text{ft}^2] \end{aligned}$$

Upper area:

$$\begin{aligned} A_2 &= (x_1 + 2 \cdot h \cdot \text{slope}) \cdot (y_1 + h \cdot \text{slope}) \\ &= (364[\text{ft}] + 2 \cdot 21.1[\text{ft}] \cdot {}^{2}/_{3}) \\ &\quad \cdot (255[\text{ft}] + 21.1[\text{ft}] \cdot {}^{2}/_{3}) \\ &= 105510[\text{ft}^2] \end{aligned}$$

Excavation volume

$$\begin{aligned} V &= \frac{h}{2} \cdot (A_1 + A_2) \\ &= \frac{21.1[\text{ft}]}{2} \cdot (92820[\text{ft}] + 105510[\text{ft}]) \\ &= 2092382[\text{ft}^3] \\ &= \underline{\underline{77500[\text{yd}^3]}} \end{aligned}$$

(A) $76000[\text{yd}^3]$

(B) $\underline{\underline{77500[\text{yd}^3]}}$

(C) $79700[\text{yd}^3]$

(D) $84100[\text{yd}^3]$

Problem I.39

A curve with radius $R = 1800[\text{ft}]$ and deflection angle $\delta = 28°$ is to be laid out in the field using stakes at 100[ft] chord distance. The number of stakes between PC and PT is:

Solution to Problem I.39

In essence, compute the interior angle between stakes. Use the formula for chord length of a curve and solve it for the deflection angle:

$$C = 2R\sin(I/2) \rightsquigarrow I = 2\arcsin\left(\frac{C}{2R}\right)$$

Also, note that the deflection angle equals the curve's interior angle.

Interior angle between stakes:

$$\begin{aligned} I' &= 2\arcsin\left(\frac{C'}{2R}\right) \\ &= 2\arcsin\left(\frac{100[\text{ft}]}{2(1800[\text{ft}])}\right) \\ &= 3.1835° \end{aligned}$$

Number of stakes *between* PC and PT:

$$\begin{aligned} n &= \frac{I}{I'} \\ &= \frac{28°}{3.1835°} \\ &= 8.79 \rightsquigarrow \underline{\underline{8[\text{intermediate stakes}]}} \end{aligned}$$

(A) 4

(B) 5

(C) 8

(D) 9

Problem I.40

Determine the slope of the ramp shown below.

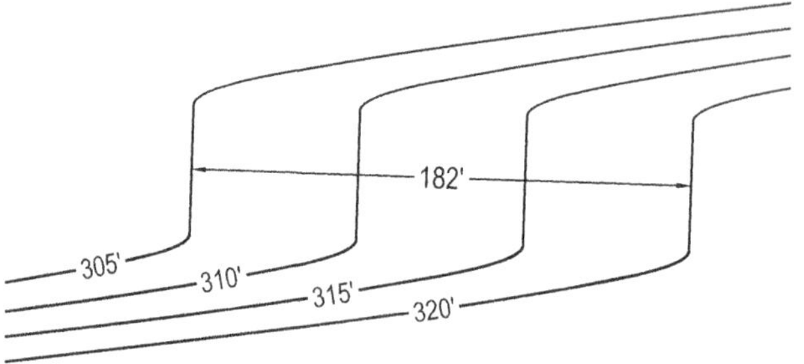

Solution to Problem I.40

Compute the slope:

$$\begin{aligned} H &= \frac{L}{\text{elev}_T - \text{elev}_B} \\ &= \frac{182[\text{ft}]}{320[\text{ft}] - 305[\text{ft}]} \\ &= \underline{\underline{12.13}} \end{aligned}$$

(A) 8 : 1 (H : V)

(B) 12 : 1 (H : V)

(C) 15 : 1 (H : V)

(D) 18 : 1 (H : V)

Problem I.41

The underpass shown below realizes an elevation difference of $\Delta H = 28[\text{ft}]$ using two vertical parabolic curves. If the horizontal length of the two horizontal curves is 12.5[sta], what is the maximum grade in the transition?

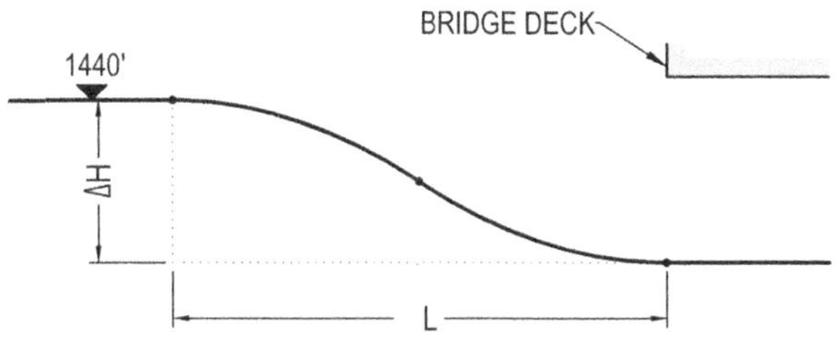

Solution to Problem I.41

By subdividing the vertical curves as shown below and adding the tangent lines, the relation between the maximum slope length of the transition can be established. From the figure it is clear that the maximum slope is the slope of the tangent lines and occurs at the transition from one curve to the next.

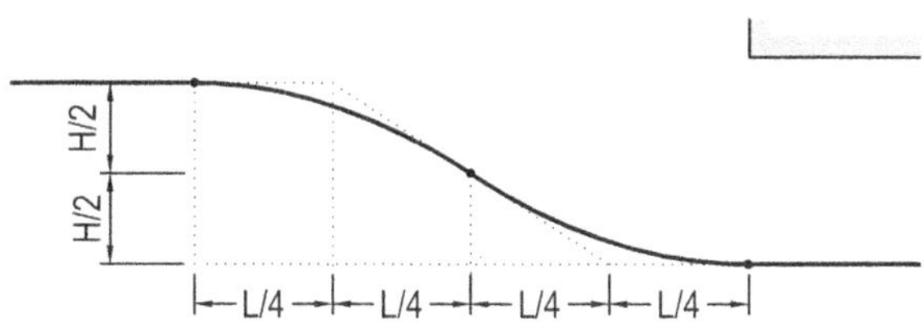

$$G = \frac{\Delta H/2}{L/4}$$
$$= \frac{28[\text{ft}]/2}{12.5[\text{sta}]/4}$$
$$= \underline{\underline{4.5[\text{ft}/\text{sta}]}}$$

(A) $\underline{\underline{4.5[\text{ft}/\text{sta}]}}$

(B) 9.0[ft/sta]

(C) 13.0[ft/sta]

(D) 18.0[ft/sta]

Problem I.42

Measurements were taken from point C to points A and B, as shown below. What is the distance between points A and B?

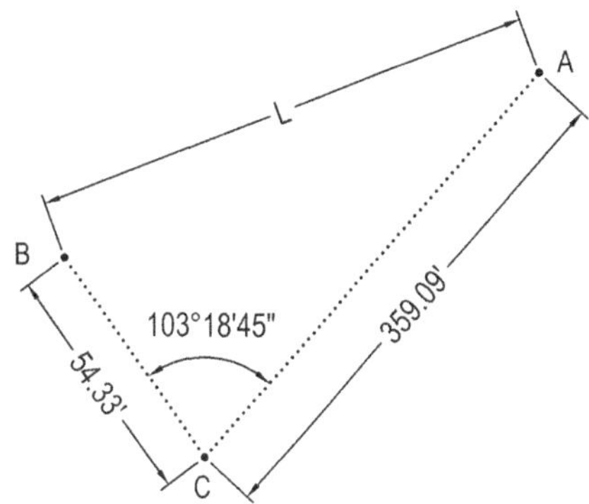

Solution to Problem I.42

Use law of cosines:

$$\begin{aligned} L_c^2 &= L_A^2 + L_B^2 - 2\,L_A\,L_B\,\cos(c) \\ &= (54.33[\text{ft}])^2 + (359.09[\text{ft}])^2 \\ &\quad - 2\,(54.33[\text{ft}])\,(359.09[\text{ft}])\,\cos(103°18'45'') \\ &= 140881.91[\text{ft}]^2 \\ L_c &= \underline{\underline{375.34[\text{ft}]}} \end{aligned}$$

(A) 306.47[ft]

(B) 350.58[ft]

(C) $\underline{\underline{375.34[\text{ft}]}}$

(D) 359.09[ft]

Problem I.43

Flight planning for a photogrammetry flight mission: The plan is to shoot with a 6[in]-focal length lens on 9 × 9[in] photos. The altitude above ground will be 3000[ft] and the plane will fly with a speed of 105[mph]. What is the required timing between photos to achieve a forward overlap of 50%?

Solution to Problem I.43

To answer such questions calculate the photo scale first. With that, compute the length of a photo on ground. Use the result to compute the ground distance between photos. Together with the velocity of the plane, this gives the required timing between photo exposures.

Photo scale:

$$\begin{aligned} S &= \frac{f}{H} \\ &= \frac{6[\text{in}]\ {}^{1}/_{12}[\text{ft/in}]}{3000[\text{ft}]} \\ &= 1.667 \times 10^{-4} \end{aligned}$$

Length of photo on ground:

$$\begin{aligned} L_{ground} &= \frac{L_{photo}}{S} \\ &= \frac{9[\text{in}]}{1.667 \times 10^{-4}} \\ &= 53999[\text{in}] \cdot {}^{1}/_{12}[\text{ft/in}] \cdot {}^{1}/_{5280}[\text{mi/ft}] \\ &= 0.85227[\text{mi}] \end{aligned}$$

Length on ground between photo centers:

$$\begin{aligned} L_{snap} &= \frac{L_{ground}}{2} \\ &= \frac{0.85227[\text{mi}]}{2} \\ &= 0.42613[\text{mi}] \end{aligned}$$

Timing between photos:

$$\begin{aligned} T_{snap} &= \frac{L_{snap}}{V} \\ &= \frac{0.42613[\text{mi}]}{105[\text{mph}]} \cdot 3600[\text{sec/hr}] \\ &= \underline{\underline{14.6[\text{sec}]}} \end{aligned}$$

(A) 1.2[sec]

(B) 3.6[sec]

(C) 7.3[sec]

(D) <u>14.6[sec]</u>

Problem I.44

The open traverse shown below represents centerline points of a natural creek. The creek is to be streamlined from A to D in a straight line. Determine the bearing from A to D.

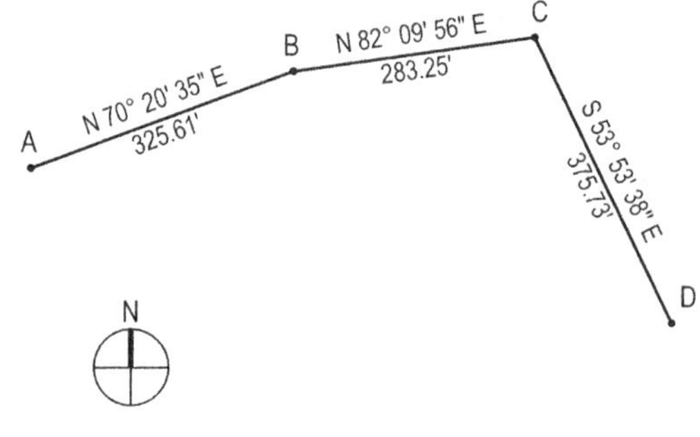

Solution to Problem I.44

Solve this problem by determining the total departure and latitude from A to D, then compute azimuth or bearing.

Convert bearing BC to azimuth angle:

$$\begin{aligned} \text{Az}_{CD} &= 180^\circ - \text{brg}_{CD} \\ &= 180^\circ - 53^\circ 53' 38'' \\ &= 126^\circ 6' 22'' \end{aligned}$$

Latitude:

$$\begin{aligned} \Delta N &= L_{AB} \cdot \cos(\text{Az}_{AB}) \\ &\quad + L_{BC} \cdot \cos(\text{Az}_{BC}) \\ &\quad + L_{CD} \cdot \cos(\text{Az}_{CD}) \\ &= 325.61 \cdot \cos(70^\circ 20' 35'') \\ &\quad + 283.25 \cdot \cos(82^\circ 9' 56'') \\ &\quad + 375.73 \cdot \cos(126^\circ 6' 22'') \\ &= -73.270[\text{ft}] \end{aligned}$$

Departure:

$$\begin{aligned} \Delta E &= L_{AB} \cdot \sin(\text{Az}_{AB}) \\ &\quad + L_{BC} \cdot \sin(\text{Az}_{BC}) \\ &\quad + L_{CD} \cdot \sin(\text{Az}_{CD}) \\ &= 325.61 \cdot \sin(70^\circ 20' 35'') \\ &\quad + 283.25 \cdot \sin(82^\circ 9' 56'') \end{aligned}$$

$$+375.73 \cdot \sin\left(126°6'22''\right)$$
$$= 890.803[\text{ft}]$$

Direction angle from A to D:

$$\beta_{AD} = \arctan\left(\frac{\Delta E}{\Delta N}\right)$$
$$= \arctan\left(\frac{890.803}{-73.27}\right)$$
$$= -86°42'7''$$

Based on ΔE, ΔN, AD lies in the south east quadrant, hence:

$$\text{brg}_{AD} = \underline{\underline{S\,86°42'7''\,E}}$$

Note: Instead of the explicit consideration of quadrants when using arctan(), consider using `atan2(y,x)`, which takes care of the quadrants and directly gives the azimuth. On TI calculators, this function is called $R \blacktriangleright P\Theta$.

(A) N 4°42′7″ E

(B) N 86°42′7″ W

(C) S 4°42′7″ E

(D) S 86°42′7″ E

Problem I.45

Using the differential leveling field notes below, determine the elevation of the lowest surveyed point (out of A,B,C,D,E).

	BS	HI	FS	Elev
BM 574-5	5.34			875.36
TP 1	3.92		7.38	
A			7.54	
B			7.61	
C			7.83	
TP 2	10.55		8.54	
D			5.84	
E			6.04	
TP 3	5.64		3.5	
BM 574-5			6.13	

Solution to Problem I.45

Out of the five points of interest, only C or D may be the ones with the lowest elevation, because these two have the highest values for the FS reading per instrument setup.

Elevation of TP1:

$$\begin{aligned}\text{elev}_{\text{TP1}} &= \text{elev}_{\text{BM}} + \text{BS}_{\text{BM}} - \text{FS}_{\text{TP1}}\\ &= 875.36 + 5.34 - 7.38\\ &= 873.32[\text{ft}]\end{aligned}$$

Elevation of C:

$$\begin{aligned}\text{elev}_{C} &= \text{elev}_{\text{TP1}} + \text{BS}_{\text{TP1}} - \text{FS}_{C}\\ &= 873.32 + 3.92 - 7.83\\ &= 869.41[\text{ft}]\end{aligned}$$

Elevation of E:

$$\begin{aligned}\text{elev}_{E} &= \text{elev}_{\text{TP1}} + \text{BS}_{\text{TP1}} - \text{FS}_{\text{TP2}}\\ &\quad + \text{BS}_{\text{TP2}} - \text{FS}_{E}\\ &= 873.32 + 3.92 - 8.54 + 10.55 - 6.04\\ &= 873.21[\text{ft}]\end{aligned}$$

Because $\text{elev}_C < \text{elev}_E$, point C is the correct answer.

(A) 868.31[ft]

(B) 869.41[ft]

(C) 873.21[ft]

(D) 868.7[ft]

Problem I.46

For the traverse shown below, determine the bearing angle of the segment $D-E$.

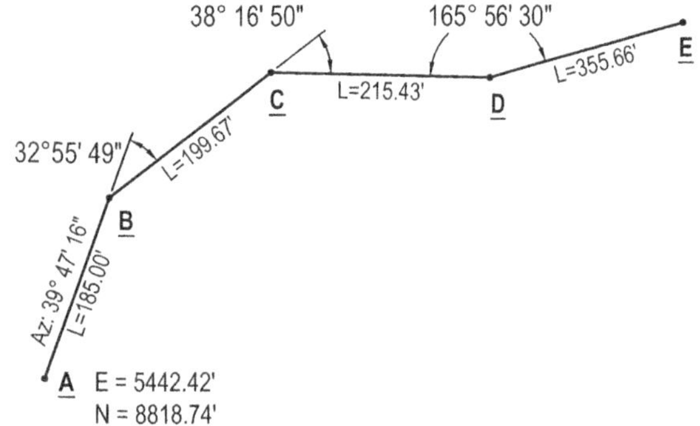

Solution to Problem I.46

Determine azimuth angle for $D-E$:

$$\begin{aligned} Az_{(DE)} &= Az_{(AB)} + d_B + d_C - 180^\circ + i_D \\ &= 39^\circ 47'16'' + 32^\circ 55'49'' + 38^\circ 16'50'' \\ &\quad - 180^\circ + 165^\circ 56'30'' \\ &= 96^\circ 56'25'' \end{aligned}$$

Convert azimuth to bearing:

$$\begin{aligned} brg_{(DE)} &= 180^\circ - Az_{(DE)} \\ &= 180^\circ - 96^\circ 56'25'' \\ &= \underline{\underline{S\ 83^\circ 3'35''\ E}} \end{aligned}$$

(A) S 7°3′35″ E

(B) S 21°0′5″ E

(C) S 54°56′35″ E

(D) S 83°3′35″ E

Problem I.47

Using the leveling field notes and the sketch below, determine the misclosure for point 2′.

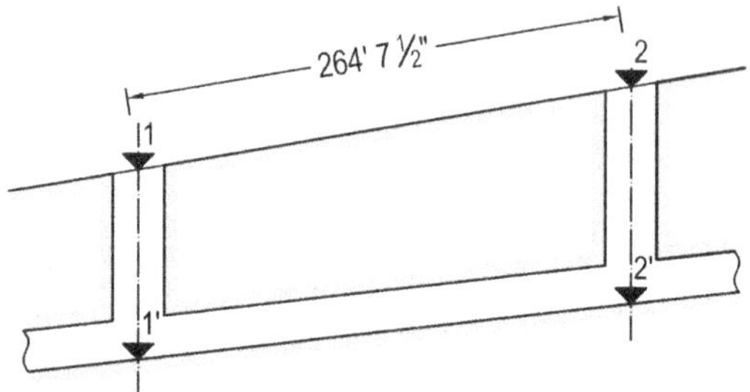

	BS	HI	FS	Elev
BM 12-06431	5.54			263.383
1			10.54	
1′			16.41	
2			5.37	
2′			12.46	256.472

Solution to Problem I.47

Use the equation for the misclosure: $\varepsilon = x_{obs} - x_{actual}$. In this case, x_{obs} is computed from the field notes and x_{actual} is read from the field notes.

Compute elevation from field notes:

$$\begin{aligned} elev_{observed} &= elev_{BM} + BS_{BM} - FS_{2'} \\ &= 263.383[ft] + 5.54[ft] - 12.46[ft] \\ &= 256.463[ft] \end{aligned}$$

Compute misclosure:

$$\begin{aligned} \varepsilon &= elev_{observed} - elev_{actual} \\ &= 256.463[ft] - 256.472[ft] \\ &= \underline{\underline{-0.009[ft]}} \end{aligned}$$

(A) −0.015[ft]

(B) −0.009[ft]

(C) ±0.000[ft]

(D) 0.015[ft]

Problem I.48

The intersections in a residential neighborhood are to be changed to have raised cross walks. For the typical intersection shown below, determine the area of asphalt to be replaced (shaded area). For determining the north ramp length, assume a 6″ height difference between the road and cross walk.

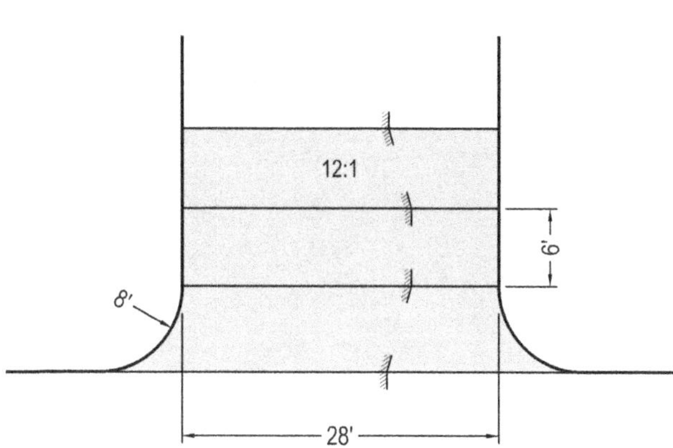

Solution to Problem I.48

Compute the length of the north ramp. Note that the length of the south ramp is given by the curb radius.

Length of ramp:

$$L_{ramp} = R + W_{crossing} + \frac{h_{curb}}{\text{(ramp slope)}}$$
$$= 8' + 6' + \frac{0.5'}{1/12}$$
$$= 20.0'$$

Area of ramp excluding curved areas:

$$A_{rect} = L_{ramp} \cdot W_{road}$$
$$= 20' \cdot 28'$$
$$= 560[\text{ft}^2]$$

Curved areas:

$$A_{radius} = \frac{(2 \cdot R)^2 - R^2 \cdot \pi}{4}$$
$$= \frac{(2 \cdot 8')^2 - (8')^2 \cdot \pi}{4}$$
$$= 13.7[\text{ft}^2]$$

Total ramp area:

$$A_{ramp} = A_{rect} + 2 \cdot A_{radius}$$
$$= 560[\text{ft}^2] + 2 \cdot 13.7[\text{ft}^2]$$
$$= \underline{\underline{587.4[\text{ft}^2]}}$$

(A) $573.7[\text{ft}^2]$

(B) $\underline{\underline{587.4[\text{ft}^2]}}$

(C) $610.3[\text{ft}^2]$

(D) $660.5[\text{ft}^2]$

Problem I.49

The figure below shows field notes of a closed traverse. Determine the enclosed area.

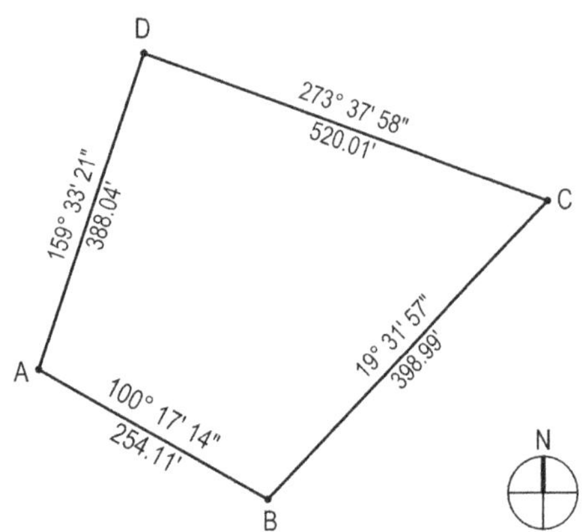

Solution to Problem I.49

Decompose the area into two triangles $\triangle ABC$ and $\triangle CDA$, then compute the area of each using the general formula: $A = \frac{1}{2}\, b\, c\, \sin(\alpha)$ where b and c are the lengths of two sides adjacent to the corner with interior angle α.

Enclosing angle at B:

$$\begin{aligned} \beta_B &= 180^\circ + \mathrm{Az}_{BC} - \mathrm{Az}_{AB} \\ &= 180^\circ + 19^\circ 31' 57'' - 100^\circ 17' 14'' \\ &= 99^\circ 14' 43'' \end{aligned}$$

Area of $\triangle ABC$:

$$\begin{aligned} A_{ABC} &= 1/2\; L_{AB}\; L_{BC}\; \sin(\beta_B) \\ &= 1/2\; (254.11[\mathrm{ft}])\; (398.99[\mathrm{ft}])\; \sin(99^\circ 14' 43'') \\ &= 50,035[\mathrm{ft}^2] \end{aligned}$$

Enclosing angle at D:

$$\begin{aligned} \beta_D &= 180^\circ + \mathrm{Az}_{DA} - \mathrm{Az}_{CD} \\ &= 159^\circ 33' 21'' - 273^\circ 37' 58'' \\ &= 65^\circ 55' 23'' \end{aligned}$$

Area of $\triangle CDA$:

$$\begin{aligned} A_{CDA} &= 1/2\; L_{CD}\; L_{DA}\; \sin(\beta_D) \\ &= 1/2\; (520.01[\mathrm{ft}])\; (388.04[\mathrm{ft}])\; \sin(65^\circ 55' 23'') \\ &= 92,115[\mathrm{ft}^2] \end{aligned}$$

Total area:

$$\begin{aligned} A &= A_{ABC} + A_{CDA} \\ &= 50,035[\mathrm{ft}^2] + 92,115[\mathrm{ft}^2] \\ &= 142,150[\mathrm{ft}^2] \\ &= \underline{\underline{3.26[\mathrm{ac}]}} \end{aligned}$$

(A) 0.76[ac]

(B) 1.93[ac]

(C) 2.09[ac]

(D) $\underline{\underline{3.26[\mathrm{ac}]}}$

Problem I.50

Determine the shaded area of the turnaround shown below. The incoming road is 50[ft] wide and the radius of the turnaround is 45[ft].

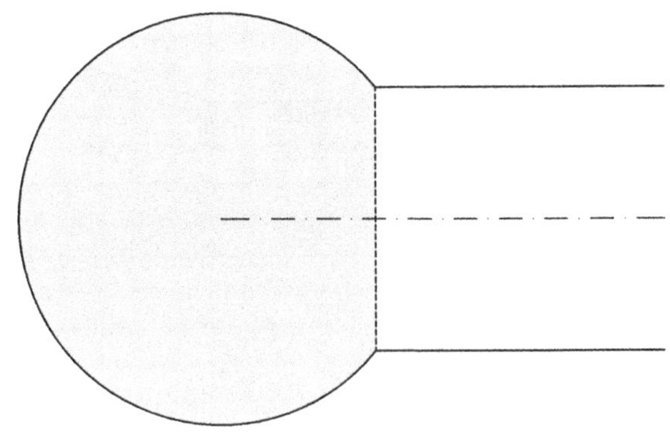

Solution to Problem I.50

Compute the turnaround area as the full circle area minus the circular segment shaded in the figure below.

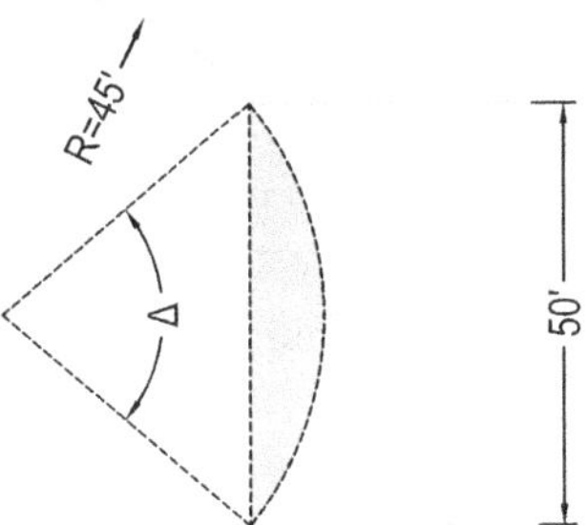

Area of full circle:

$$\begin{aligned} A_O &= (R)^2 \cdot \pi \\ &= (45)^2 \cdot 3.14 \\ &= 6362[\text{ft}^2] \end{aligned}$$

Enclosing angle of circular segment:

$$\sin\frac{\Delta}{2} = \frac{w/2}{R} \quad \rightsquigarrow \quad \frac{\Delta}{2} = \arcsin\frac{w/2}{R}$$

$$\begin{aligned} \Delta &= 2 \cdot \arcsin\left(\frac{w/2}{R}\right) \\ &= 2 \cdot \arcsin\left(\frac{50/2}{45}\right) \\ &= 1.18[\text{rad}] \end{aligned}$$

Area of circular segment:

$$\begin{aligned} A_D &= \frac{R^2}{2} \cdot (\Delta - \sin(\Delta)) \\ &= \frac{(45[\text{ft}])^2}{2} \cdot (1.18[\text{rad}] - \sin(1.18[\text{rad}])) \\ &= 257[\text{ft}^2] \end{aligned}$$

Net area:

$$\begin{aligned} A &= A_O - A_D \\ &= 6362[\text{ft}^2] - 257[\text{ft}^2] \\ &= \underline{\underline{6104[\text{ft}^2]}} \end{aligned}$$

(A) $\underline{\underline{6104[\text{ft}^2]}}$

(B) $6328[\text{ft}^2]$

(C) $6357[\text{ft}^2]$

(D) $6396[\text{ft}^2]$

Problem I.51

For the storm drain shown below, determine the amount of water in the cross section if freeboard f is 3[ft].

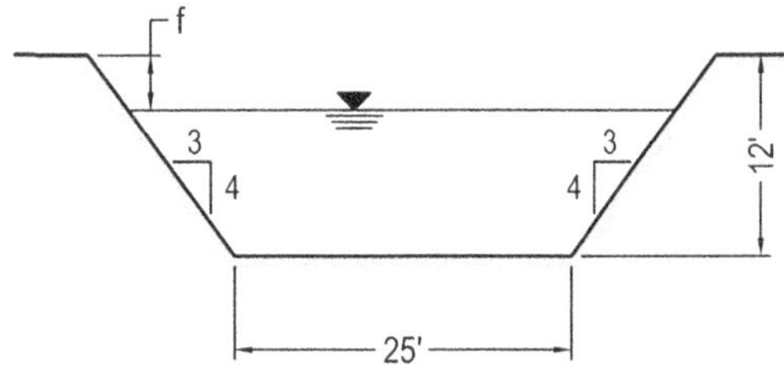

Solution to Problem I.51

Determine the water depth and the width of the channel at mid-depth to compute the area.

Depth of water:

$$\begin{aligned} d &= h - f \\ &= 12[\text{ft}] - 3[\text{ft}] \\ &= 9.0[\text{ft}] \end{aligned}$$

Width of water table at mid-depth:

$$\begin{aligned} w_{mid} &= b + 2 \cdot \left(\frac{d}{2} \cdot \frac{H}{V} \right) \\ &= 25[\text{ft}] + 2 \cdot \left(\frac{9[\text{ft}]}{2} \cdot \frac{3}{4} \right) \\ &= 31.75[\text{ft}] \end{aligned}$$

Water filled area:

$$\begin{aligned} A_{filled} &= w_{mid} \cdot d \\ &= 31.75[\text{ft}] \cdot 9.0[\text{ft}] \\ &= \underline{\underline{286[\text{ft}^2]}} \end{aligned}$$

(A) $255[\text{ft}^2]$

(B) $279[\text{ft}^2]$

(C) $\underline{\underline{286[\text{ft}^2]}}$

(D) $333[\text{ft}^2]$

Problem I.52

For the traverse shown below, determine the bearing angle of the segment $A - D$.

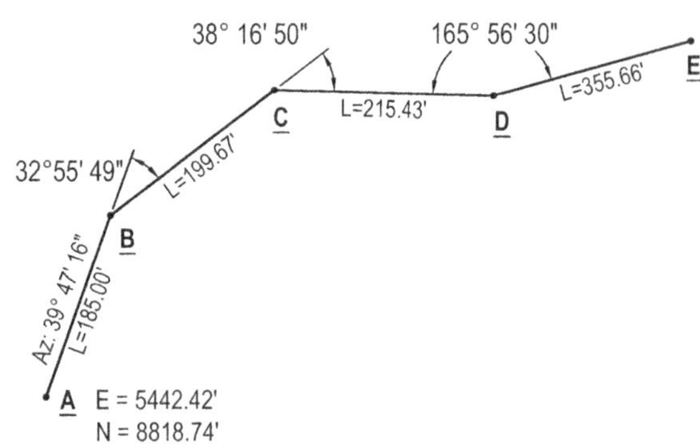

Solution to Problem I.52

Start by computing the missing azimuth angles. Then proceed with computing departure and latitude between the mentioned points.

$$\begin{aligned} \text{Az}_{BC} &= \text{Az}_{AB} + \delta_B \\ &= 39°47'16'' + 32°55'49'' \\ &= 72°43'5'' \end{aligned}$$

$$\begin{aligned} \text{Az}_{CD} &= \text{Az}_{BC} + \delta_C \\ &= 72°43'5'' + 38°16'50'' \\ &= 110°59'55'' \end{aligned}$$

$$\begin{aligned} \Delta E_{AD} &= L_{AB} \cdot \sin(\text{Az}_{AB}) \\ &\quad + L_{BC} \cdot \sin(\text{Az}_{BC}) \\ &\quad + L_{CD} \cdot \sin(\text{Az}_{CD}) \\ &= 185.00 \cdot \sin(39°47'16'') \\ &\quad + 199.67 \cdot \sin(72°43'5'') \\ &\quad + 215.43 \cdot \sin(110°59'55'') \\ &= 510.17[\text{ft}] \end{aligned}$$

$$\begin{aligned} \Delta N_{AD} &= L_{AB} \cdot \cos(\text{Az}_{AB}) \\ &\quad + L_{BC} \cdot \cos(\text{Az}_{BC}) \\ &\quad + L_{CD} \cdot \cos(\text{Az}_{CD}) \\ &= 185.0 \cdot \cos(39°47'16'') \\ &\quad + 199.67 \cdot \cos(72°43'5'') \\ &\quad + 215.43 \cdot \cos(110°59'55'') \\ &= 124.28[\text{ft}] \end{aligned}$$

$$
\begin{aligned}
E_D &= E_A + \Delta E_{AD} \\
&= 5442.42[\text{ft}] + 510.17[\text{ft}] \\
&= \underline{\underline{5952.59[\text{ft}]}}
\end{aligned}
$$

$$
\begin{aligned}
N_D &= N_A + \Delta N_{AD} \\
&= 8818.74[\text{ft}] + 124.28[\text{ft}] \\
&= \underline{\underline{8943.02[\text{ft}]}}
\end{aligned}
$$

(A) $(E, N)_D = (5566.7, 9328.91)[\text{ft}]$

(B) $(E, N)_D = (5629.64, 8842.54)[\text{ft}]$

(C) $(E, N)_D = (5873.29, 9197.89)[\text{ft}]$

(D) $\underline{\underline{(E, N)_D = (5952.59, 8943.02)[\text{ft}]}}$

Problem I.53

A cross section of a proposed highway is shown below. Determine the net amount of cut or fill for this cross section.

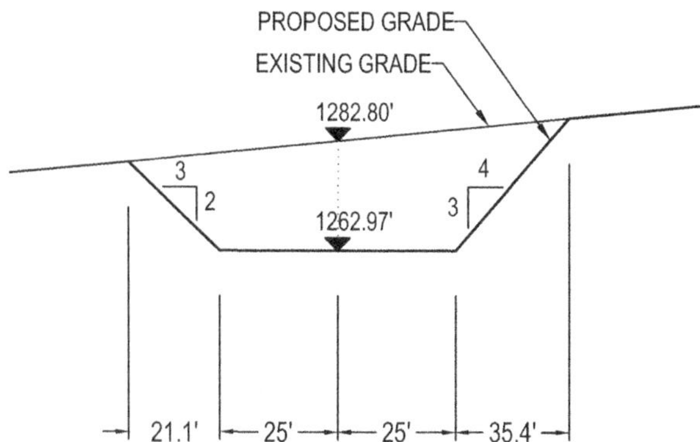

Solution to Problem I.53

Use the area of trapezium formula: $A = 1/2\ d\ h + 1/4\ b\ (h_L + h_R)$.

Determine equation inputs:

$$
\begin{aligned}
h &= y_E - y_P \\
&= 1282.8 - 1262.97 \\
&= 19.83[\text{ft}] \\
h_L &= x_L \cdot g_L \\
&= 21.1 \cdot 2/3 \\
&= 14.07[\text{ft}] \\
h_R &= x_R \cdot g_R \\
&= 35.4 \cdot 3/4 \\
&= 26.55[\text{ft}] \\
b &= x_M \\
&= 50.0[\text{ft}] \\
d &= x_L + x_M + x_R \\
&= 21.1 + 50 + 35.4 \\
&= 106.50[\text{ft}]
\end{aligned}
$$

Compute the net cut area:

$$
\begin{aligned}
A &= \frac{1}{2} \cdot d \cdot h + \frac{1}{4} \cdot b \cdot (h_L + h_R) \\
&= \frac{1}{2} \cdot 106.5 \cdot 19.83 + \frac{1}{4} \cdot 50 \cdot (14.07 + 26.55) \\
&= \underline{\underline{1564[\text{ft}^2]}}
\end{aligned}
$$

(A) 1564[ft^2] cut

(B) 1783[ft^2] cut

(C) 1821[ft^2] cut

(D) 2042[ft^2] cut

Problem I.54

A hillside sewer pipe is daylighting after a landslide. To asses its continued functionality, the measurements given below were taken. Determine the current slope of the sewer pipe using the information provided.

Point	BS	HI	FS	Notes
A			5.67	to manhole cover
B			27.18	to top of pipe

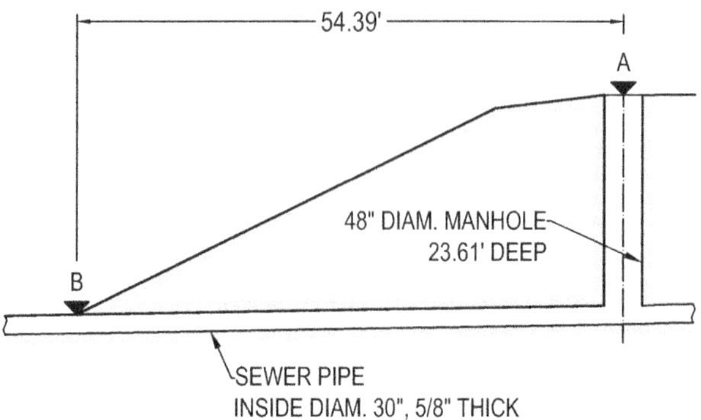

Solution to Problem I.54

The strategy is to compute pipe elevations (in this case the elevation of invert) at the manhole and the location where the pipe daylights. For simplicity, use the height of instrument as a common reference datum. From elevation differences and the measured horizontal length, the slope can then be computed.

Height at daylight location:

$$\begin{aligned} H_{DL} &= \text{FS}_{\text{top of pipe}} + (\text{pipe diam.}) + (\text{pipe thk.}) \\ &= 27.18' + \frac{30''}{12[\text{ft/in}]} + \frac{(5/8)''}{12[\text{ft/in}]} \\ &= 29.73' \end{aligned}$$

Height at manhole:

$$\begin{aligned} H_{MH} &= \text{FS}_{\text{manhole}} + (\text{manhole depth}) \\ &= 5.67' + 23.61' \\ &= 29.28' \end{aligned}$$

Sewer pipe slope:

$$
\begin{aligned}
g &= \frac{\Delta H}{\Delta L} \\
&= \frac{H_{DL} - H_{MH}}{L} \\
&= \frac{29.73' - 29.28'}{54.39'} \\
&= \underline{\underline{0.83\%}}
\end{aligned}
$$

(A) 0.64%

(B) 0.83%

(C) 3.86%

(D) 3.96%

Problem I.55

A certain typical section in the Public Land Surveying System is occupied by a 128[ac]-lake. What percentage of this section is occupied by the lake?

Solution to Problem I.55

A typical section in the Public Land Surveying System is 640[ac], hence the lake occupies

$$\frac{128[\text{ac}]}{640[\text{ac}]} = 0.2 = \underline{\underline{20\%}}$$

of this section.

(A) 10%

(B) 20%

(C) 25%

(D) 33%

Chapter 7

Solutions to Practice Exam II

Answer Key to Practice Exam II

Question	Flag?	Option	Correct?
1.		C	
2.		B	
3.		C	
4.		B	
5.		C	
6.		C	
7.		A	
8.		B	
9.		C	
10.		A	
11.		B	
12.		A	
13.		A	
14.		D	
15.		B	
16.		A	
17.		B	
18.		D	
19.		D	
20.		B	
21.		A	
22.		D	
23.		A	
24.		A	
25.		C	
26.		B	
27.		B	
28.		D	

Question	Flag?	Option	Correct?
29.		D	
30.		D	
31.		D	
32.		D	
33.		B	
34.		D	
35.		D	
36.		B	
37.		A	
38.		D	
39.		B	
40.		A	
41.		A	
42.		B	
43.		A	
44.		C	
45.		C	
46.		A	
47.		A	
48.		A	
49.		D	
50.		C	
51.		B	
52.		A	
53.		D	
54.		D	
55.		C	

Tip: Overlay your printed out answer sheet for faster correction.

Problem II.01

A 1800[ft] long, 5[ft] deep utility trench as shown below is to be built. Determine the volume of sand bedding required.

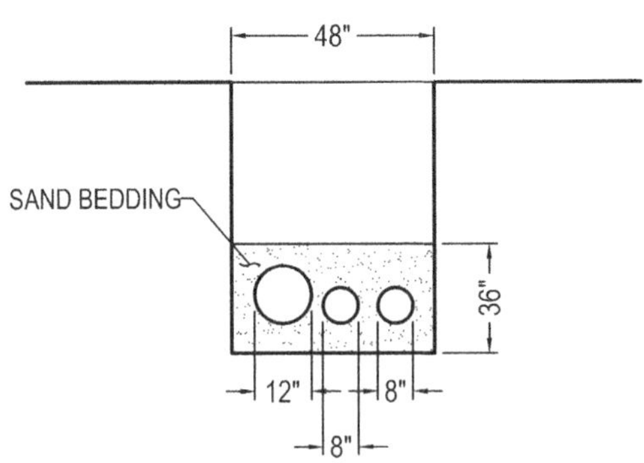

Solution to Problem II.01

Simply compute the net area of sand bedding in the cross section shown and multiply it by the length of the trench.

Cross sectional area of sand bedding:

$$\begin{aligned} A_{net} &= w \cdot h - (D_1)^2 \cdot \frac{\pi}{4} - (D_2)^2 \cdot \frac{\pi}{4} - (D_3)^2 \cdot \frac{\pi}{4} \\ &= 48 \cdot 36 - (12)^2 \cdot \frac{\pi}{4} - (8)^2 \cdot \frac{\pi}{4} - (8)^2 \cdot \frac{\pi}{4} \\ &= 1514[\text{in}^2] \end{aligned}$$

Volume of sand bedding:

$$\begin{aligned} V &= A_{net} \cdot L \\ &= \frac{1514[\text{in}^2]}{12^2[(\text{in}/\text{ft})^2]} \cdot 1800[\text{ft}] \\ &= 18930[\text{ft}^3] \\ &= \underline{\underline{701[\text{yd}^3]}} \end{aligned}$$

(A) $643[\text{yd}^3]$

(B) $672[\text{yd}^3]$

(C) $\underline{\underline{701[\text{yd}^3]}}$

(D) $730[\text{yd}^3]$

Problem II.02

What is most likely the elevation of point C shown in the topographic map below?

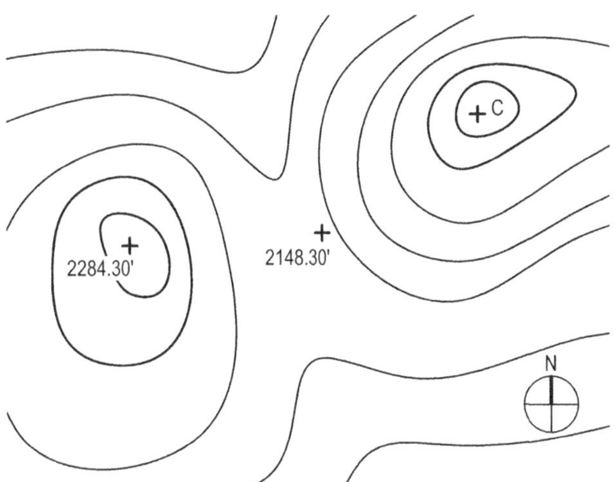

Solution to Problem II.02

Because there are no contour intervals (CIs) printed, we can either guess reasonable contour intervals, check our assumptions and estimate point C's elevation. Or, we may estimate the elevation of point C simply based on the *number* of contour intervals between the three points:

Height difference between the known points:

$$\begin{aligned} \Delta H_1 &= 2284.30' - 2148.30' \\ &= 136' \end{aligned}$$

Height difference to point C:

$$\begin{aligned} \Delta H_C &= \Delta H_1 \cdot \frac{(\#\text{ of CIs to point } C)}{(\#\text{ of CIs between known points})} \\ &= 136' \cdot \frac{5}{3} \\ &= 227' \end{aligned}$$

Estimated elevation of C:

$$\begin{aligned} \text{elev}_C &= 2148.30' + \Delta H_C \\ &= 2148.30' + 227' \\ &= 2375.3' \quad \rightsquigarrow \quad \underline{\underline{2382'}} \end{aligned}$$

The other answer options are out of the range of possible elevations based on theoretically possible contour intervals.

(A) 2282′

(B) 2382′

(C) 2557′

(D) 2588′

Problem II.03

A new tunnel, as shown below, requires a 7[ft] clearance to the vertical curve crossing it. Determine the required length L of the vertical curve to keep the required clearance.

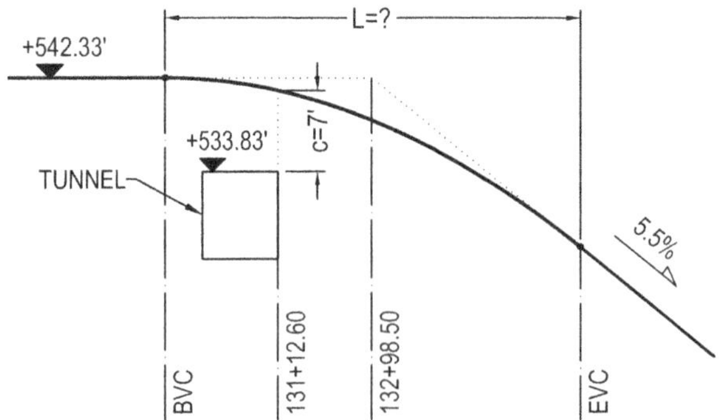

Solution to Problem II.03

This problem asks for the length of the vertical curve, such that it passes through a certain point (The point that is 7[ft] above the right edge of the tunnel.) Use the equation $L = 2m\frac{1+\sqrt{o_1/o_2}}{1-\sqrt{o_1/o_2}}$.

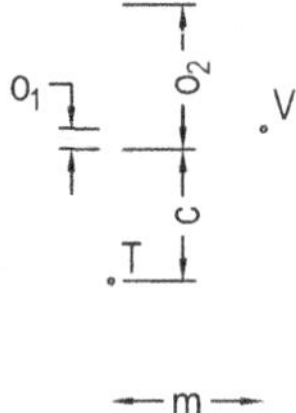

Compute the required inputs for equation:

$$\begin{aligned} m &= X_V - X_T \\ &= 132.9850[\text{sta}] - 131.1260[\text{sta}] \\ &= 1.8590[\text{sta}] \end{aligned}$$

$$
\begin{aligned}
o_1 &= Y_V - Y_T - c \\
&= 542.33[\text{ft}] - 533.83[\text{ft}] - 7[\text{ft}] \\
&= 1.5[\text{ft}]
\end{aligned}
$$

$$
\begin{aligned}
o_2 &= o_1 + m \cdot (-G_2) \\
&= 1.5[\text{ft}] + 1.8590[\text{ft}] \cdot (-5.5[\%]) \\
&= 11.72[\text{ft}]
\end{aligned}
$$

$$
\begin{aligned}
\sqrt{o_1/o_2} &= \sqrt{1.5[\text{ft}]/11.72[\text{ft}]} \\
&= 0.3577[-]
\end{aligned}
$$

Substitute into equation:

$$
\begin{aligned}
L &= 2m\frac{1+\sqrt{o_1/o_2}}{1-\sqrt{o_1/o_2}} \\
&= 2 \cdot 1.8590[\text{sta}] \cdot \frac{1+0.3577}{1-0.3577} \\
&= \underline{\underline{7.8588[\text{sta}]}}
\end{aligned}
$$

(A) 1.7589[sta]

(B) 3.9294[sta]

(C) 7.8588[sta]

(D) 8.9853[sta]

Problem II.04

The top of a retaining wall is continuously monitored for creeping deflections. The table below shows raw tape measurements taken between a stable point and the top of the retaining wall. After applying temperature corrections, what is the top-of-wall movement between 01/01 and 07/01?

Date	$T[°\text{F}]$	$L[\text{ft}]$
01/01	9	88.53
03/01	36	88.96
05/02	64	90.12
07/01	83	90.57
09/01	71	90.62
11/01	23	91.57

Solution to Problem II.04

Determine the corrected distances for both dates, then take the difference.

Corrected distance for 01/01:

$$
\begin{aligned}
\overline{L}_{01} &= L_{01}\left(1+\alpha_t\left(T_{01/01}-T_0\right)\right) \\
&= 88.53\left(1+(6.45\times10^{-6})[°\text{F}^{-1}]\,(9-68)[°\text{F}]\right) \\
&= 88.496[\text{ft}]
\end{aligned}
$$

Corrected distance for 07/01:

$$
\begin{aligned}
\overline{L}_{07} &= L_{07}\left(1+\alpha_t\left(T_{01/01}-T_0\right)\right) \\
&= 90.57\left(1+(6.45\times10^{-6})[°\text{F}^{-1}]\,(83-68)[°\text{F}]\right) \\
&= 90.579[\text{ft}]
\end{aligned}
$$

Wall movement between 01/01 and 07/01:

$$
\begin{aligned}
\Delta\overline{L} &= \overline{L}_{07} - \overline{L}_{01} \\
&= 90.579[\text{ft}] - 88.496[\text{ft}] \\
&= \underline{\underline{2.08[\text{ft}]}}
\end{aligned}
$$

(A) 2.01[ft]

(B) 2.08[ft]

(C) 2.33[ft]

(D) 2.64[ft]

Problem II.05

A road alignment is passing through a bridge, as shown in the figure below. Determine the minimum clearance between the road and the underside of the bridge deck at the left side of the bridge deck.

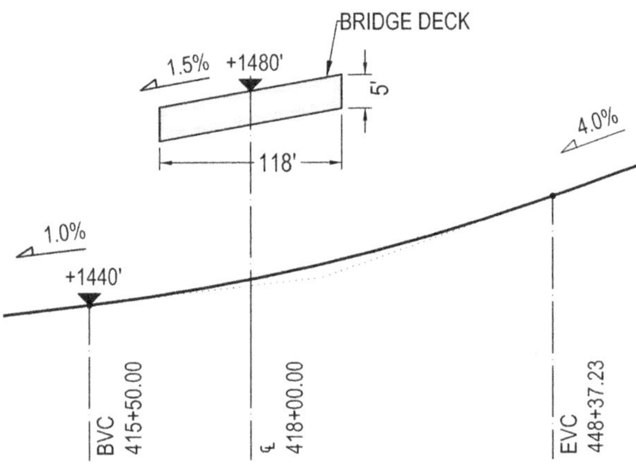

Solution to Problem II.05

Compute the elevation of the lower left bridge deck (BD) point and the elevation of the vertical curve at that same station. Then subtract the difference from these elevations.

Elevation of lower left point:

$$\begin{aligned} \text{elev}_{\text{BD}} &= \text{elev}_{\text{BD CL}} - \frac{w_{\text{BD}}}{2} \cdot \frac{\text{slope}_{\text{BD}}}{100} - d_{\text{BD}} \\ &= 1480[\text{ft}] - \frac{118[\text{ft}]}{2} \cdot \frac{1.5\%}{100\%} - 5[\text{ft}] \\ &= 1474.12[\text{ft}] \end{aligned}$$

Rate of grade change:

$$\begin{aligned} R &= \frac{G_2 - G_1}{\text{sta}_{EVC} - \text{sta}_{\text{BVC}}} \\ &= \frac{4\% - 1\%}{448.37[\text{ft}] - 415.5[\text{ft}]} \\ &= 9.13 \times 10^{-2}[\%/\text{sta}] \end{aligned}$$

Distance from BVC to left end of bridge BD:

$$\begin{aligned} x_{\text{VC}} &= \text{sta}_{\text{BD CL}} - \frac{w_{\text{BD}}}{100} \cdot \frac{1}{2} - \text{sta}_{\text{BVC}} \\ &= 418.0[\text{sta}] - \frac{118[\text{ft}]}{100[\text{ft}/\text{sta}]} \cdot \frac{1}{2} - 415.5[\text{sta}] \\ &= 1.91[\text{sta}] \end{aligned}$$

Elevation of the vertical curve at left end of the bridge deck:

$$\begin{aligned} \text{elev}_{\text{VC}} &= R \cdot \frac{(x_{\text{VC}})^2}{2} + G_1 \cdot x_{\text{VC}} + \text{elev}_{\text{BVC}} \\ &= 9.13 \times 10^{-2}[\%/\text{sta}] \cdot \frac{(1.91[\text{sta}])^2}{2} \\ &\quad + 1.0\% \cdot 1.91[\text{sta}] + 1440[\text{ft}] \\ &= 1442.08[\text{ft}] \end{aligned}$$

Vertical clearance:

$$\begin{aligned} \text{clr} &= \text{elev}_{\text{BD}} - \text{elev}_{\text{VC}} \\ &= 1474.12[\text{ft}] - 1442.08[\text{ft}] \\ &= \underline{\underline{32.04[\text{ft}]}} \end{aligned}$$

(A) 29.30[ft]

(B) 31.42[ft]

(C) $\underline{\underline{32.04[\text{ft}]}}$

(D) 34.30[ft]

Problem II.06

A theodolite, set up above a point A, was used to determine the height of a point B. The height of instrument was 5′9″ above point A and the foresight reading to point B was $5.34'$ under an elevation angle of $\alpha = 48°13'54''$ and a sloped distance of $L = 52.75'$. Determine the elevation of point B if the elevation of point A is $1252.48'$ above datum.

Solution to Problem II.06

First, compute the vertical distance from theodolite reading:

$$\begin{aligned} \Delta Y &= L \cdot \sin \alpha \\ &= 52.75' \cdot \sin(48°13'54'') \\ &= 39.34' \end{aligned}$$

Then determine the elevation of point B:

$$\begin{aligned} \text{elev}_B &= \text{elev}_A + (\text{H.I.}) + \Delta Y - \text{FS}_B \\ &= 1252.48' + 5.75' + 39.34' - 5.34' \\ &= \underline{\underline{1292.23'}} \end{aligned}$$

(A) 1224.23′

(B) 1252.89′

(C) <u>1292.23′</u>

(D) 1297.16′

Problem II.07

For the given river channel cross section shown below, determine the required slope of the storm sewer pipe, such that the pipe daylights 1 feet above the mean river elevation.

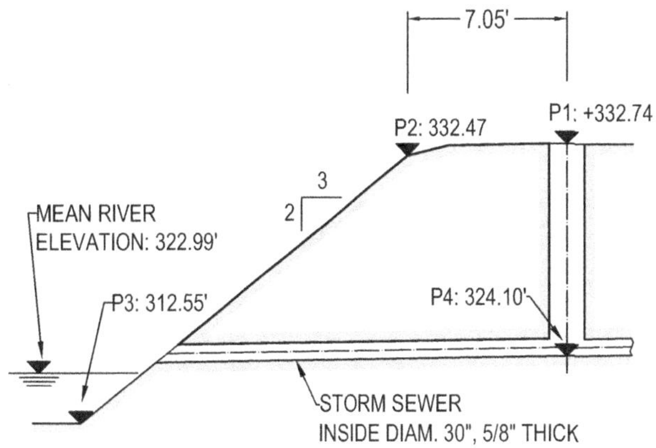

Solution to Problem II.07

First, determine the location (elevation and distance) where the pipe invert hits the river bank. From there, compute the required pipe slope.

The point where the pipe hits the surface:

$$\begin{aligned} y_5 &= (\text{mean river elevation}) + 1[\text{ft}] \\ &= 322.99' + 1' \\ &= 323.99' \\ x_{25} &= (\text{distance from } P2) \\ &= (y_2 - y_5) \cdot 1/(\text{river bank slope}) \\ &= (332.47' - 323.99') \cdot \frac{3}{2} \\ &= 12.72' \end{aligned}$$

The required slope:

$$\begin{aligned} g_{req} &= \frac{y_4 - y_5}{x_{12} + x_{25}} \\ &= \frac{324.10' - 323.99'}{7.05' + 12.72'} \\ &= 5.564 \times 10^{-3} \\ &= \underline{\underline{0.6\%}} \end{aligned}$$

(A) <u>0.6%</u>

(B) 1.5%

(C) 5.2%

(D) 7.9%

Problem II.08

Referring to the curve shown below, the bearing of the curve tangent at station (202+00.00) is?

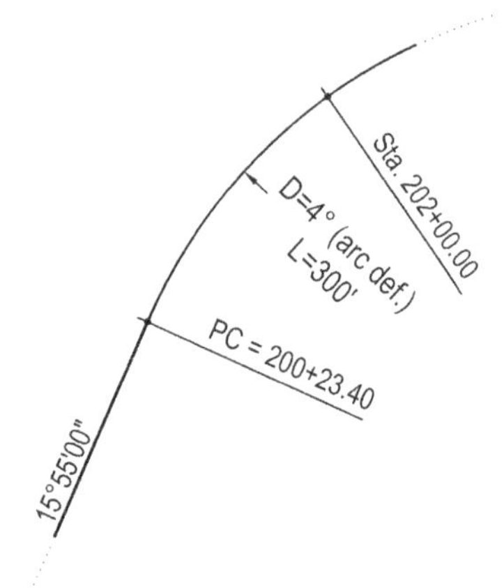

Solution to Problem II.08

Compute the arc length to station 202, then scale the enclosing angle-based arc length definition of the curve.

Arc length between PC and station (202+00):

$$\begin{aligned} L &= \text{sta}_{(202)} - \text{sta}_{(\text{PC})} \\ &= (202{+}00) - (200{+}23.40) \\ &= 176.6[\text{ft}] \end{aligned}$$

Enclosing angle between PC and station (202+00):

$$\begin{aligned} \delta &= D \cdot \frac{L}{100[\text{ft}]} \\ &= 4^\circ \cdot \frac{176.6[\text{ft}]}{100[\text{ft}]} \\ &= 7.064^\circ \\ &= 7^\circ 3' 50'' \end{aligned}$$

Azimuth angle of curve tangent at station (202+00):

$$\begin{aligned} \text{Az}_{(202)} &= \text{Az}_{(\text{PC})} + \delta \\ &= 15^\circ 55' 0'' + 7^\circ 3' 50'' \\ &= \underline{\underline{22^\circ 58' 50''}} \end{aligned}$$

(A) $22^\circ 51' 10''$

(B) $\underline{\underline{22^\circ 58' 50''}}$

(C) $27^\circ 3' 50''$

(D) $28^\circ 51' 10''$

Problem II.09

The traverse shown below contains uncorrected field notes. Determine the linear misclosure of the traverse.

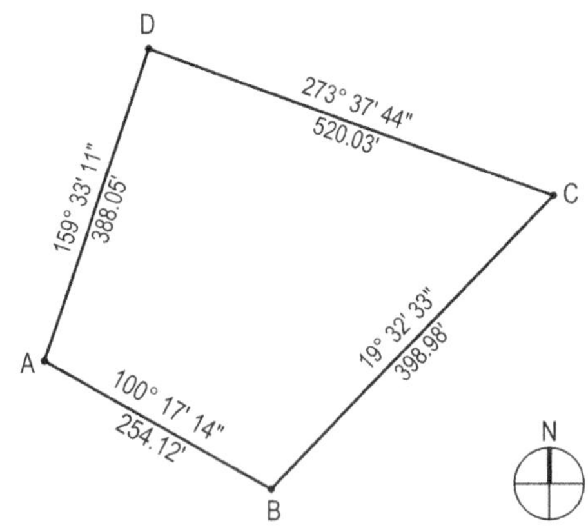

Solution to Problem II.09

Determine departures and latitudes for each segment, sum them up, and take the vectorial length.

For segment $A-B$:

$$\begin{aligned} \Delta N_{A-B} &= L_{A-B} \cdot \cos(\alpha_{A-B}) \\ &= 254.12' \cdot \cos(100^\circ 17' 14'') \\ &= -45.39' \\ \Delta E_{A-B} &= L_{A-B} \cdot \sin(\alpha_{A-B}) \\ &= 254.12' \cdot \sin(100^\circ 17' 14'') \\ &= 250.03' \end{aligned}$$

For all segments:

	ΔE	ΔN
A-B	250.03	-45.39
B-C	133.46	376.00
C-D	-518.99	32.92
D-A	135.56	-363.60

Sum of departures, latitudes:

$$\begin{aligned} \sum \Delta E &= 250.03 + 133.46 + (-518.99) + 135.56 \\ &= 0.06 \\ \sum \Delta N &= (-45.39) + 376.00 + 32.92 + (-363.60) \\ &= -0.07 \end{aligned}$$

Linear Misclosure:

$$\begin{aligned}\varepsilon &= \sqrt{(\sum \Delta E)^2 + (\sum \Delta N)^2}\\ &= \sqrt{(0.06)^2 + (-0.07)^2}\\ &= \underline{\underline{0.09'}}\end{aligned}$$

(A) $-0.19'$

(B) $-0.09'$

(C) $\underline{\underline{0.09'}}$

(D) $0.19'$

Problem II.10

For a tapered precast concrete manhole, determine the amount of concrete required, while neglecting the geometry around the joints.

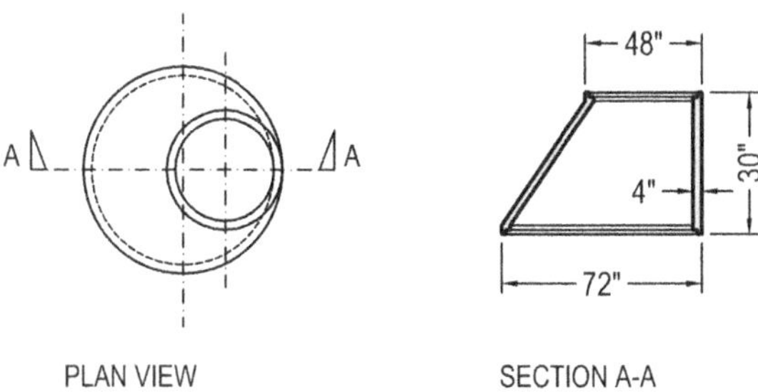

Solution to Problem II.10

Determine the needed volume by first computing the cross-sectional areas at the top and bottom sections. Then calculate the volume using the average end formula. For the area of each ring, use $A = (D_o^2 - D_i^2)\frac{\pi}{4}$.

Area of upper section:

$$\begin{aligned}A_u &= \left((D_{ou})^2 - (D_{ou} - 2\cdot t)^2\right)\cdot\frac{\pi}{4}\\ &= \left((48)^2 - (48 - 2\cdot 4)^2\right)\cdot\frac{3.14}{4}\\ &= 552.92[\text{in}^2]\end{aligned}$$

Area of lower section:

$$\begin{aligned}A_l &= \left((D_{ol})^2 - (D_{ol} - 2\cdot t)^2\right)\cdot\frac{\pi}{4}\\ &= \left((72)^2 - (72 - 2\cdot 4)^2\right)\cdot\frac{3.14}{4}\\ &= 854.51[\text{in}^2]\end{aligned}$$

Volume of part:

$$\begin{aligned}V &= \frac{d}{2}\cdot(A_u + A_l)\\ &= \frac{30}{6}\cdot(552.92 + 854.51)\\ &= 21112[\text{in}^3]\\ &= \underline{\underline{12.2[\text{ft}^3]}}\end{aligned}$$

(A) $\underline{\underline{12.2[\text{ft}^3]}}$

(B) $13.1[\text{ft}^3]$

(C) $14.0[\text{ft}^3]$

(D) $14.9[\text{ft}^3]$

Problem II.11

The ramp of the excavation pit shown below is to be removed. The slope angle of the ramp side was constructed at 35°. Assuming the construction pit is 18[ft] deep, determine the excavation volume to remove the ramp.

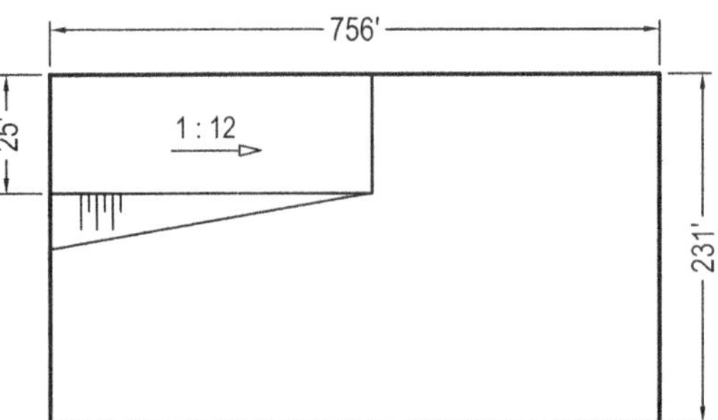

Solution to Problem II.11

The problem statement is asking for the volume of the ramp. Because the ramp is *not* a pyramid, decompose the ramp geometry into a 3-sided pyramid (the side slope) and a wedge (the main part of the ramp).

Length of ramp:

$$\begin{aligned} L_{ramp} &= \frac{h}{(\text{ramp slope})} \\ &= \frac{18[\text{ft}]}{1/12} \\ &= 216.0[\text{ft}] \end{aligned}$$

Volume of ramp main section (wedge):

$$\begin{aligned} V_{wedge} &= A_{base} \cdot \frac{L}{2} \\ &= h \cdot (\text{width})_{ramp} \cdot \frac{L_{ramp}}{2} \\ &= 18[\text{ft}] \cdot 25[\text{ft}] \cdot \frac{216.0[\text{ft}]}{2} \\ &= 48600[\text{ft}^3] \end{aligned}$$

Volume of ramp side (pyramid):

$$\begin{aligned} V_{pyramid} &= A_{base} \cdot \frac{L}{3} \\ &= h \cdot \frac{h}{\tan(\alpha_{side})} \cdot \frac{1}{2} \cdot \frac{L_{ramp}}{3} \end{aligned}$$

$$= 18[\text{ft}] \cdot \frac{18[\text{ft}]}{\tan(35°)} \cdot \frac{1}{2} \cdot \frac{216.0[\text{ft}]}{3}$$
$$= 16658[\text{ft}^3]$$

Total ramp volume:

$$\begin{aligned} V_{ramp} &= V_{wedge} + V_{pyramid} \\ &= 48600 + 16658 \\ &= 65258[\text{ft}^3] \\ &= \underline{\underline{2417[\text{yd}^3]}} \end{aligned}$$

Note: Alternatively, the prismoidal formula would also lead to the same result.

(A) $2033[\text{yd}^3]$

(B) $\underline{\underline{2417[\text{yd}^3]}}$

(C) $2725[\text{yd}^3]$

(D) $3651[\text{yd}^3]$

Problem II.12

The leveling field notes below were taken to survey the corner points of the parcel shown beneath. Based on the leveling notes, determine the direction in which water flows toward.

	BS	HI	FS	Elev.
BM 627-95	8.54			746.37
TP1	14.59		2.66	
A			10.26	
B			10.77	
TP2	6.15		9.54	
C			9.42	
D			9.86	

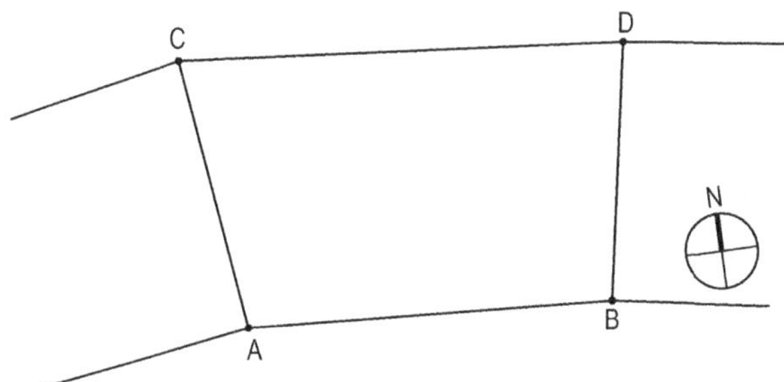

Solution to Problem II.12

The best strategy to solve this problem is to look at the elevation differences along the property lines. For this, use $\Delta = \sum \text{BS} - \sum \text{FS}$.

Elevation difference along $A - B$:

Note: In this case the reading FS_A is used with a positive sign, indicating that A acts as the known elevation.

$$\begin{aligned} \Delta_{AB} &= \text{FS}_A - \text{FS}_B \\ &= 10.26 - 10.77 \\ &= -0.51[\text{ft}] \end{aligned}$$

Elevation difference along $C - B$:

$$\begin{aligned} \Delta_{AC} &= \text{FS}_C - \text{FS}_B \\ &= 9.42 - 9.86 \\ &= -0.44[\text{ft}] \end{aligned}$$

Elevation difference along $A - C$:

> **Note:** Because points A, C are not read from the same level position (i.e., with different instrument heights), the turning point connecting the two readings (TP2) needs to be taken into account.

$$
\begin{aligned}
\Delta_{AC} &= FS_A - FS_{TP2} + BS_{TP2} - FS_C \\
&= 10.26 - 9.54 + 6.15 - 9.42 \\
&= -2.55[\text{ft}]
\end{aligned}
$$

Elevation difference along $B - D$:

$$
\begin{aligned}
\Delta_{BD} &= FS_B - FS_{TP2} + BS_{TP2} - FS_D \\
&= 10.77 - 9.54 + 6.15 - 9.86 \\
&= -2.48[\text{ft}]
\end{aligned}
$$

0.44'

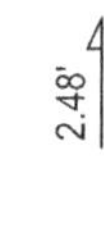

0.51'

When sketching up the elevation differences, it is clear that the property sheds water mostly in the north direction.

(A) North

(B) East

(C) South

(D) West

Problem II.13

For the traverse shown below, determine the length of a straight line connecting A and C.

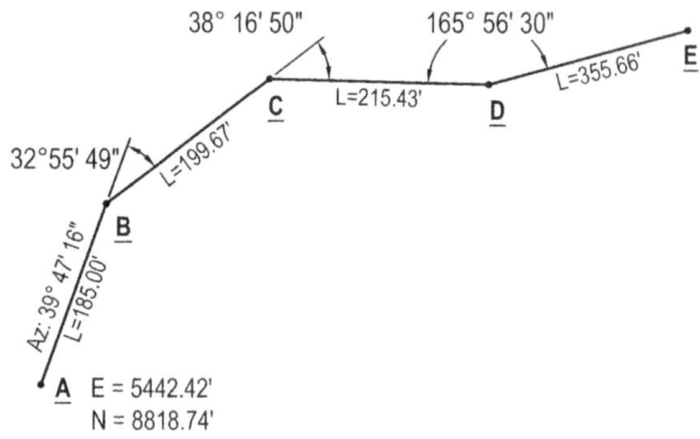

Solution to Problem II.13

Compute latitude and departure for each segment, then use Pythagoras to compute the final answer.

Departure, latitude for $\overline{AB}$:

$$
\begin{aligned}
\Delta N_{AB} &= L_{AB} \cdot \cos\left(\text{Az}_{AB}\right) \\
&= 185[\text{ft}] \cdot \cos\left(39^\circ 47' 16''\right) \\
&= 142.16[\text{ft}] \\
\Delta E_{AB} &= L_{AB} \cdot \sin\left(\text{Az}_{AB}\right) \\
&= 185[\text{ft}] \cdot \sin\left(39^\circ 47' 16''\right) \\
&= 118.39[\text{ft}]
\end{aligned}
$$

Departure, latitude for $\overline{BC}$:

$$
\begin{aligned}
\text{Az}_{BC} &= \text{Az}_{AB} + \delta_B \\
&= 39^\circ 47' 16'' + 32^\circ 55' 49'' \\
&= 72^\circ 43' 5'' \\
\Delta N_{BC} &= L_{BC} \cdot \cos\left(\text{Az}_{BC}\right) \\
&= 199.67[\text{ft}] \cdot \cos\left(72^\circ 43' 5''\right) \\
&= 59.32[\text{ft}] \\
\Delta E_{BC} &= L_{BC} \cdot \sin\left(\text{Az}_{BC}\right) \\
&= 199.67[\text{ft}] \cdot \sin\left(72^\circ 43' 5''\right) \\
&= 190.66[\text{ft}]
\end{aligned}
$$

Distance $\overline{AC}$:

$$
\begin{aligned}
L_{AC} &= \sqrt{\left(\Delta N_{AB} + \Delta N_{BC}\right)^2 + \left(\Delta E_{AB} + \Delta E_{BC}\right)^2} \\
&= \sqrt{(142.16 + 59.32)^2 + (118.39 + 190.66)^2}
\end{aligned}
$$

$$= \underline{\underline{368.92[\text{ft}]}}$$

(A) $\underline{\underline{368.92[\text{ft}]}}$

(B) $383.08[\text{ft}]$

(C) $383.98[\text{ft}]$

(D) $384.67[\text{ft}]$

Problem II.14

In the survey shown below, point C was surveyed from both points A and point B. Determine the linear misclosure in grid coordinates when grid coordinates are computed based on point A and point B respectively.

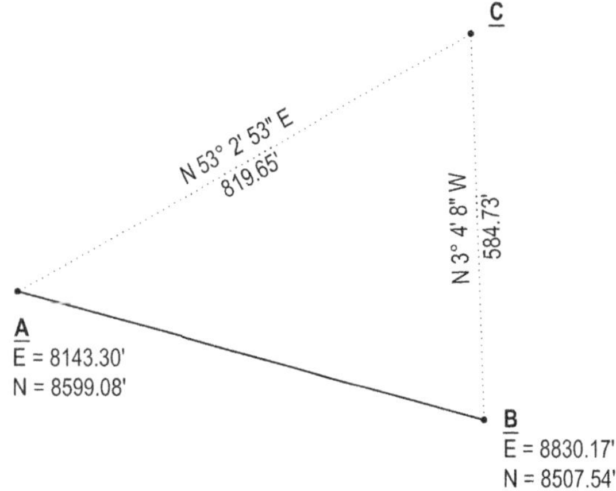

Solution to Problem II.14

First compute grid coordinates of point C. Once based on point A, and once based on point B. Then compute the linear misclosure between the two computed coordinates.

Point C coordinates from A:

$$\begin{aligned}
E_{C_A} &= E_A + L_{AC} \cdot \sin\left(\text{Az}_{AC}\right) \\
&= 8143.3 + 819.65 \cdot \sin\left(53°2'53''\right) \\
&= 8798.32[\text{ft}] \\
N_{C_A} &= N_A + L_{AC} \cdot \cos\left(\text{Az}_{AC}\right) \\
&= 8599.08 + 819.65 \cdot \cos\left(53°2'53''\right) \\
&= 9091.81[\text{ft}]
\end{aligned}$$

Point C coordinates from B:

$$\begin{aligned}
\text{Az}_{BC} &= -\text{brg}_{BC} = -3°4'8'' \\
E_{C_B} &= E_B + L_{BC} \cdot \sin\left(\text{Az}_{BC}\right) \\
&= 8830.17 + 584.73 \cdot \sin\left(-3°4'8''\right) \\
&= 8798.87[\text{ft}] \\
N_{C_B} &= N_B + L_{BC} \cdot \cos\left(\text{Az}_{BC}\right) \\
&= 8507.54 + 584.73 \cdot \cos\left(-3°4'8''\right) \\
&= 9091.43[\text{ft}]
\end{aligned}$$

Linear misclosure:

$$\epsilon = \sqrt{\left(E_{C_A} - E_{C_B}\right)^2 + \left(N_{C_A} - N_{C_B}\right)^2}$$

$$= \sqrt{\begin{aligned}&(8798.32 - 8798.87)^2\\&+ (9091.81 - 9091.43)^2\end{aligned}}$$
$$= \underline{\underline{0.667[\text{ft}]}}$$

(A) 0.037[ft]

(B) 0.377[ft]

(C) 0.550[ft]

(D) 0.667[ft]

Problem II.15

Which of the following Public Land Surveying System sections might measure 5076[ft] along the south edge and 5215[ft] along the east edge?

Solution to Problem II.15

The Public Land Surveying System (PLSS) section sought in the problem statement is curtailed in both the north-south and east-west directions, because the typical edge length would be 5280[ft] (1 mile) long.

In a township of the PLSS, the sections along the north and the west edges are smaller. Section 6 is the section in the north-west corner of a township, and hence is shortened in both north-south and east-west directions.

(A) Section 1

(B) Section 6

(C) Section 31

(D) Section 36

Problem II.16

An excavation for a pad foundation needs to be dug 3[ft] deep from existing soil. To regularly check the progress of the excavation, a level is used. If the rod reading to existing soil is 5.56′ and to current excavation depth 7.18′, how much deeper the excavation needs to go to reach the required depth?

Solution to Problem II.16

To solve this problem, first compute the current depth, by subtracting the rod reading to current excavation depth from the reading to existing soil. Then subtract the current excavation depth from the required depth.

Current depth:

$$\begin{aligned}H_{curr} &= 7.18' - 5.56'\\&= 1.62'\end{aligned}$$

Remaining depth:

$$\begin{aligned}\Delta H &= H_{req} - H_{curr}\\&= 3' - 1.62'\\&= \underline{\underline{1.38'}}\end{aligned}$$

(A) 1.38′

(B) 1.62′

(C) 2.22′

(D) 2.56′

Problem II.17

Using the surveying records below, determine the distance from B to the closest point on the line $\overline{AC}$.

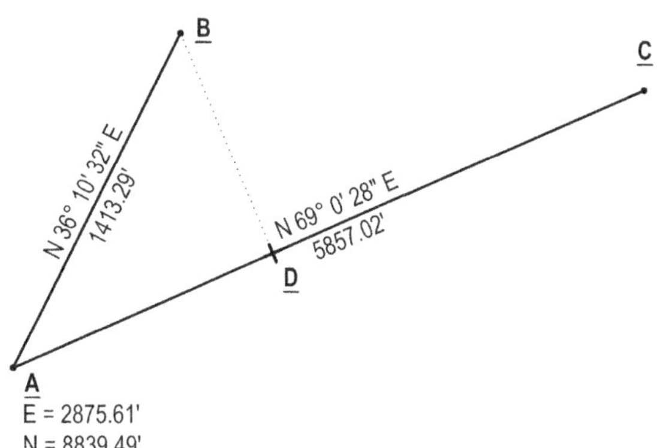

Solution to Problem II.17

Point D—which is the closest point to B on $\overline{AC}$—forms a right triangle with A and B, as shown below. With this the closest distance can be computed directly:

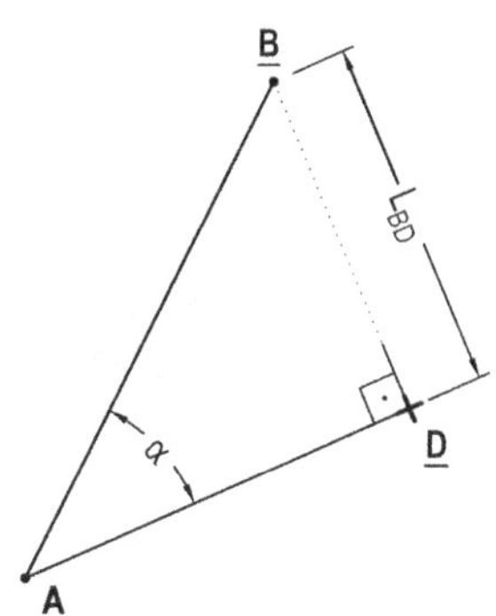

Enclosing angle:

$$\begin{aligned}\alpha &= \mathrm{Az}_{AC} - \mathrm{Az}_{AB} \\ &= 69°0'28'' - 36°10'32'' \\ &= 32°49'56''\end{aligned}$$

$$\begin{aligned}L_{BD} &= L_{AB} \cdot \sin(\alpha) \\ &= 1413.29[\text{ft}] \cdot \sin(32°49'56'') \\ &= \underline{\underline{766.26[\text{ft}]}}\end{aligned}$$

(A) 370.15[ft]

(B) 766.26[ft]

(C) 1187.53[ft]

(D) 1363.96[ft]

Problem II.18

Based on the field notes shown below, determine the vertical clearance between the road and the bottom of the bridge.

	BS	FS	Elev
BM 12-06431	5.54		263.383
TP 1	4.38	13.69	
CL Road @ edge of bridge		6.87	
Bottom of bridge [1]		10.62	

[1] *Rod was held upside down.*

Solution to Problem II.18

Compute the clearance directly from the rod readings.

Determine clearance:

$$\begin{aligned}(\text{clearance}) &= \mathrm{FS}_{\text{road}} + \mathrm{FS}_{\text{bridge}} \\ &= 6.87[\text{ft}] + 10.62[\text{ft}] \\ &= \underline{\underline{17.49[\text{ft}]}}\end{aligned}$$

(A) 3.75[ft]

(B) 6.87[ft]

(C) 10.62[ft]

(D) 17.49[ft]

Problem II.19

The pile cap shown below couples six cast-in-place piles. Determine the total concrete volume for pouring the six piles and the pile cap. Assume the length of each pile starts at the bottom of pile cap. Neglect the volume of reinforcement.

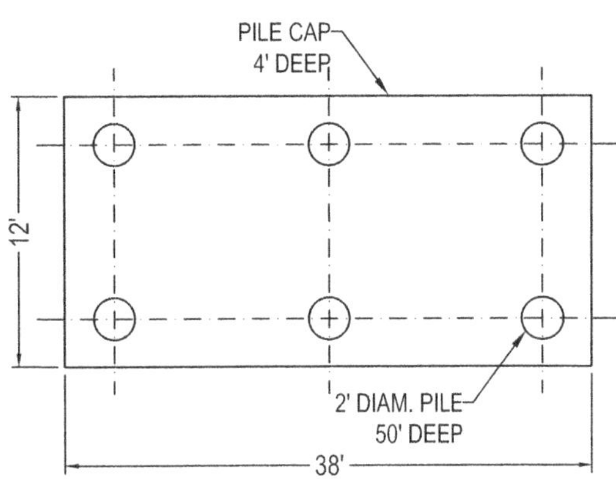

Solution to Problem II.19

Simply compute the volume of the pile cap as if it was a box and the piles as if they were cylinders.

$$\begin{aligned} V_{pile} &= \left(d_{pile}\right)^2 \cdot \frac{\pi}{4} \cdot L_{pile} \\ &= (2[\text{ft}])^2 \cdot \frac{3.14}{4} \cdot 50[\text{ft}] \\ &= 157.08[\text{ft}^3] \end{aligned}$$

$$\begin{aligned} V_{pc} &= L_{pc} \cdot W_{pc} \cdot d_{pc} \\ &= 38[\text{ft}] \cdot 12[\text{ft}] \cdot 4[\text{ft}] \\ &= 1824[\text{ft}^3] \end{aligned}$$

$$\begin{aligned} V_{tot} &= V_{pc} + 6 \cdot V_{pile} \\ &= 1824[\text{ft}^3] + 6 \cdot 157.08[\text{ft}^3] \\ &= 2766[\text{ft}^3] \\ &= \underline{\underline{102.5[\text{yd}^3]}} \end{aligned}$$

(A) $65.9[\text{yd}^3]$

(B) $71.5[\text{yd}^3]$

(C) $99.7[\text{yd}^3]$

(D) $\underline{\underline{102.5[\text{yd}^3]}}$

Problem II.20

For the rectangular parcel shown below, determine the coordinates of point C.

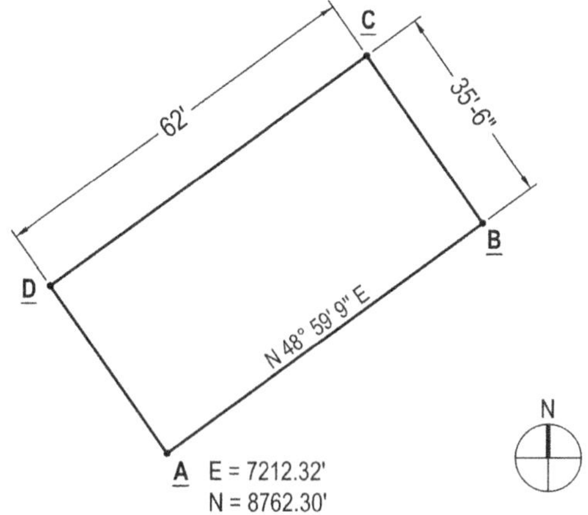

Solution to Problem II.20

Compute the coordinates of C by determining departure, latitude. Note that the azimuth for $\overline{BC}$ is indirectly given by knowing the parcel is rectangular.

Easting:

$$\begin{aligned} E_C &= E_A + L_{AB} \cdot \sin(\text{Az}_{BC}) - L_{BC} \cdot \cos(\text{Az}_{BC}) \\ &= 7212.32 + 62 \cdot \sin(48°59'9'') \\ &\quad - 35.5 \cdot \cos(48°59'9'') \\ &= \underline{\underline{7235.81[\text{ft}]}} \end{aligned}$$

Northing:

$$\begin{aligned} N_C &= N_A + L_{AB} \cdot \cos(\text{Az}_{BC}) + L_{BC} \cdot \sin(\text{Az}_{BC}) \\ &= 8762.3 + 62 \cdot \cos(48°59'9'') \\ &\quad + 35.5 \cdot \sin(48°59'9'') \\ &= \underline{\underline{8829.77[\text{ft}]}} \end{aligned}$$

Note: Instead of using the azimuth of $\overline{BC}$ ($\text{Az}_{BC} = \text{Az}_{AB} - 90°$), the example was solved by using the fact that $\sin(\alpha) = \cos(\alpha + 90°)$.

(A) $(E, N)_C = (7226.22, 8832.38)[\text{ft}]$

(B) $\underline{\underline{(E, N)_C = (7235.81, 8829.77)[\text{ft}]}}$

(C) $(E, N)_C = (7253.01, 8809.08)[\text{ft}]$

(D) $(E, N)_C = (7282.40, 8776.20)[\text{ft}]$

Problem II.21

An existing railway fork, as shown in the figure below, is to be extended with an additional turn. Determine the distance between point PT_1 and PC_2.

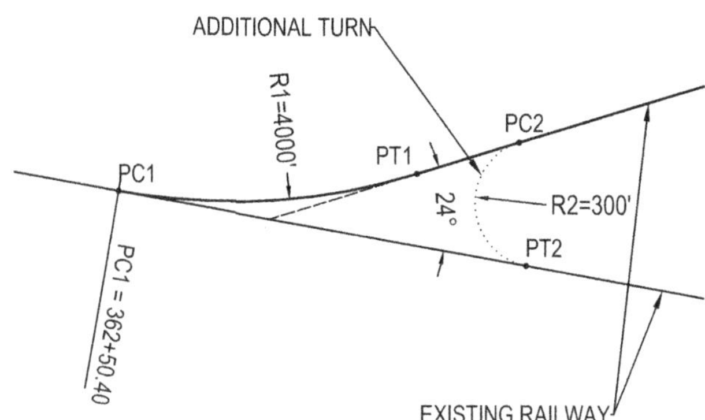

Solution to Problem II.21

The distance L to be determined is the tangent length of the additional curve minus the tangent length of the existing curve.

Tangent length of curve 1:

$$\begin{aligned} T_1 &= R_1 \cdot \tan\left(\frac{I_1}{2}\right) \\ &= 4000.00[\text{ft}] \cdot \tan\left(\frac{24°0'0''}{2}\right) \\ &= 850.23[\text{ft}] \end{aligned}$$

Interior angle of curve 2:

$$\begin{aligned} I_2 &= 180° - I_1 \\ &= 180° - 24°0'0'' \\ &= 156°0'0'' \end{aligned}$$

Tangent length of curve 2:

$$\begin{aligned} T_2 &= R_2 \cdot \tan\left(\frac{I_2}{2}\right) \\ &= 300.00[\text{ft}] \cdot \tan\left(\frac{156°0'0''}{2}\right) \\ &= 1411.39[\text{ft}] \end{aligned}$$

Distance $PT_1 - PC_2$:

$$L = T_2 - T_1$$

$$= 1411.39[\text{ft}] - 850.23[\text{ft}]$$
$$= \underline{\underline{561.16[\text{ft}]}}$$

(A) 561.16[ft]

(B) 786.46[ft]

(C) 913.99[ft]

(D) 2261.62[ft]

Problem II.22

A solar power plant is to be built on the semi-circular lot shown below. Determine the area of the lot.

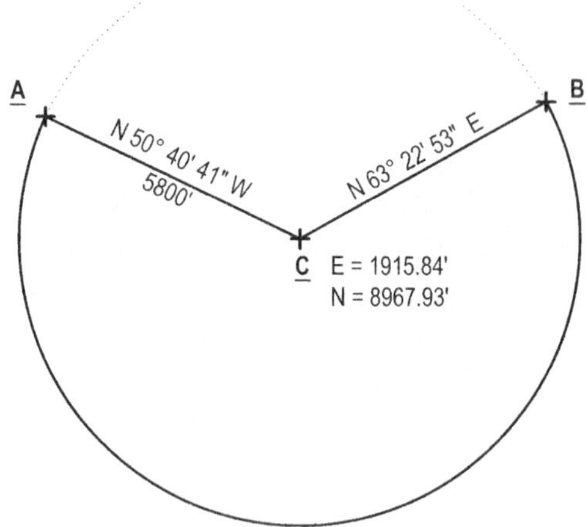

Solution to Problem II.22

The problem statement boils down to computing the area of a semicircle.

Interior angle of semicircle:

$$\begin{aligned}\alpha &= 360° - (\text{brg}_{CB} + \text{brg}_{CA}) \\ &= 360° - (63°22'53'' + 50°40'41'') \\ &= 245°56'26''\end{aligned}$$

Area of semicircle:

$$\begin{aligned}A &= (L_{CA})^2 \cdot \pi \cdot \frac{\alpha}{360°} \\ &= (5800[\text{ft}])^2 \cdot \pi \cdot \frac{245°56'26''}{360°} \\ &= 72199387[\text{ft}^2] \\ &= \underline{\underline{1657[\text{ac}]}}\end{aligned}$$

(A) 161[ac]

(B) 769[ac]

(C) 1375[ac]

(D) 1657[ac]

Problem II.23

The parcel shown below is to be refurbished. Currently, the lot (excluding the building) is paved with concrete. Determine the area of concrete that needs to be removed (assuming all concrete will be removed).

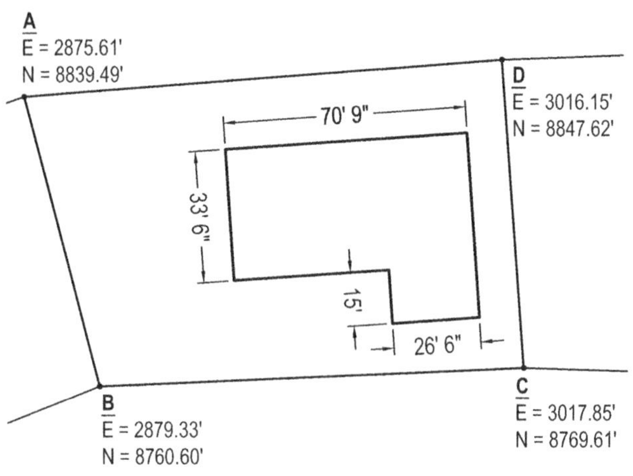

Solution to Problem II.23

Determine the area of the lot and subtract the area of the building. As for the lot area, the coordinate method seems most efficient: $A = \frac{1}{2}\left|\sum x_i \cdot y_{i+1} - \sum x_{i+1} \cdot y_i\right|$.

Lot Area:

$$\begin{aligned}\sum x_i \cdot y_{i+1} &= E_A\, N_B + E_B\, N_C + E_C\, N_D + E_D\, N_A \\ &= 2875.61 \cdot 8760.60 + 2879.33 \cdot 8769.61 \\ &\quad + 3017.85 \cdot 8847.62 + 3016.15 \cdot 8839.49 \\ &= 103804688[\text{ft}^2]\end{aligned}$$

$$\begin{aligned}\sum y_i \cdot x_{i+1} &= N_A\, E_B + N_B\, E_C + N_C\, E_D + N_D\, E_A \\ &= 8839.49 \cdot 2879.33 + 8760.60 \cdot 3017.85 \\ &\quad + 8769.61 \cdot 3016.15 + 8847.62 \cdot 2875.61 \\ &= 103782749[\text{ft}^2]\end{aligned}$$

$$\begin{aligned}A_{lot} &= \frac{1}{2}\left|\sum x_i \cdot y_{i+1} - \sum x_{i+1} \cdot y_i\right| \\ &= \frac{1}{2}\left|103804688 - 103782749\right| \\ &= 10969[\text{ft}^2]\end{aligned}$$

Building Area:

$$\begin{aligned}A_{blg} &= (70'9'')\,(33'6'') + (26'6'')\,(15') \\ &= 2767[\text{ft}^2]\end{aligned}$$

Concrete Area:

$$\begin{aligned}A &= A_{lot} - A_{blg} \\ &= 10969[\text{ft}^2] - 2767[\text{ft}^2] \\ &= \underline{\underline{8202[\text{ft}^2]}}\end{aligned}$$

(A) $\underline{\underline{8202[\text{ft}^2]}}$

(B) $8996[\text{ft}^2]$

(C) $19171[\text{ft}^2]$

(D) $19966[\text{ft}^2]$

Problem II.24

Using the differential leveling field notes below, compute the misclosure for BM 574-5.

	BS	HI	FS	Elev
BM 574-5	5.34			875.364
TP 1	3.92		7.38	
A			7.54	
B			7.61	
C			7.83	
TP 2	10.55		8.54	
D			5.84	
E			6.04	
TP 3	5.64		3.5	
BM 574-5			6.13	

Solution to Problem II.24

Compute the misclosure between the observed and the known elevation of the given benchmark.

Obeserved elevation for BM 574-5:

$$\begin{aligned} \text{elev}_{\text{BM,observed}} &= \text{elev}_{\text{BM,actual}} + \sum \text{BS} - \sum \text{FS} \\ &= 875.364 \\ &\quad + (5.34 + 3.92 + 10.55 + 5.64) \\ &\quad - (7.38 + 8.54 + 3.5 + 6.13) \\ &= 875.264[\text{ft}] \end{aligned}$$

Misclosure:

$$\begin{aligned} \varepsilon &= x_{\text{observed}} - x_{\text{actual}} \\ &= \text{elev}_{\text{BM,observed}} - \text{elev}_{\text{BM,actual}} \\ &= 875.264[\text{ft}] - 875.364[\text{ft}] \\ &= \underline{\underline{-0.10[\text{ft}]}} \end{aligned}$$

(A) $\underline{\underline{-0.10[\text{ft}]}}$

(B) $-0.01[\text{ft}]$

(C) $+0.01[\text{ft}]$

(D) $+0.10[\text{ft}]$

Problem II.25

A drainage ditch is to be dug along the stations shown in the table; starting at point 0, ending at point 5. The ditch requires a minimum depth of 4[ft] at each point. Assume the ditch starts with a 4[ft] depth and the ditch slope doesn't change. What is the minimum ditch slope required to maintain the minimum depth along its length?

Point	Station [sta]	Elevation (existing) [ft]
0	(145+36.49)	975.04
1	(146+00.00)	972.83
2	(147+00.00)	968.67
3	(148+00.00)	966.68
4	(149+00.00)	932.05
5	(149+39.67)	929.46

Solution to Problem II.25

To test the minimum required slope, check the slope between project start and each subsequent point. Because the ditch starts with 4[ft] deep, which is also the minimum required depth, these two cancel each other out and thus can be ignored.

Check slope to station 1:

$$\begin{aligned} s_1 &= \frac{(y_1 - y_0)[\text{ft}]}{(x_1 - x_0)[\text{sta}]} \\ &= \frac{(972.83 - 975.04)[\text{ft}]}{(146.0 - 145.36)[\text{sta}]} \\ &= -3.48\% \end{aligned}$$

Check slope to station 2:

$$\begin{aligned} s_2 &= \frac{(y_2 - y_0)[\text{ft}]}{(x_2 - x_0)[\text{sta}]} \\ &= \frac{(968.67 - 975.04)[\text{ft}]}{(147.0 - 145.36)[\text{sta}]} \\ &= -3.90\% \end{aligned}$$

Check slope to station 3:

$$\begin{aligned} s_3 &= \frac{(y_3 - y_0)[\text{ft}]}{(x_3 - x_0)[\text{sta}]} \\ &= \frac{(966.68 - 975.04)[\text{ft}]}{(148.0 - 145.36)[\text{sta}]} \\ &= -3.17\% \end{aligned}$$

Check slope to station 4:

$$s_4 = \frac{(y_4 - y_0)[\text{ft}]}{(x_4 - x_0)[\text{sta}]}$$

$$= \frac{(932.05 - 975.04)[\text{ft}]}{(149.0 - 145.36)[\text{sta}]}$$
$$= -11.83\%$$

Check slope to station 5:

$$s_5 = \frac{(y_5 - y_0)[\text{ft}]}{(x_5 - x_0)[\text{sta}]}$$
$$= \frac{(929.46 - 975.04)[\text{ft}]}{(149.4 - 145.36)[\text{sta}]}$$
$$= -11.31\%$$

Find the governing slope:

$$s_{min} = \min(s_1,\ s_2,\ s_3,\ s_4)$$
$$= \min(-3.48,\ -3.90,\ -3.17,\ -11.83)$$
$$= \underline{\underline{-11.83\%}} \rightsquigarrow 11.83\% \text{ downward slope}$$

Note: You could reduce computation time, by studying the elevations provided in the table beforehand. You will notice a sudden drop in elevation at point 4 (while stations are equally spaced), so the ditch slope will likely be only controlled by either point 4 or 5.

(A) 10.72%

(B) 11.31%

(C) 11.83%

(D) 12.93%

Problem II.26

For the flared sidewalk ramp shown below, determine its area (the shaded portion). Assume a height difference of 6″ between sidewalk and road.

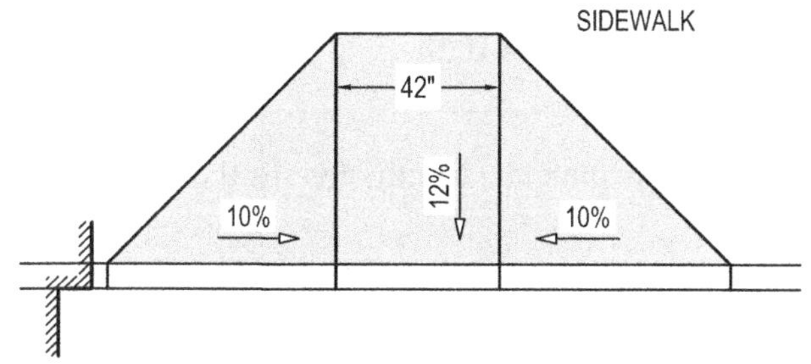

Solution to Problem II.26

Ramp dimensions:

$$w_{\text{flare}} = \frac{(\text{sidewalk height})}{(\text{flare grade})}$$
$$= \frac{6''}{10\%}$$
$$= 5.00[\text{ft}]$$

$$d_{\text{flare}} = \frac{(\text{sidewalk height})}{(\text{main grade})}$$
$$= \frac{6''}{12\%}$$
$$= 4.17[\text{ft}]$$

Ramp area:

$$A = 2 \cdot \left(\frac{w_{\text{flare}} \cdot d_{\text{flare}}}{2}\right) + (w \cdot d_{\text{flare}})$$
$$= 2 \cdot \left(\frac{5.00[\text{ft}] \cdot 4.17[\text{ft}]}{2}\right) + (3.5[\text{ft}] \cdot 4.17[\text{ft}])$$
$$= \underline{\underline{35.4[\text{ft}^2]}}$$

(A) $31.9[\text{ft}^2]$

(B) $35.4[\text{ft}^2]$

(C) $39.6[\text{ft}^2]$

(D) $56.3[\text{ft}^2]$

Problem II.27

The vertical grade of a highway changes from $G_1 = 3.5\%$ to $G_2 = -0.5\%$ with a rate of change of grade of -0.1627 percent per station. Determine the station at the end of the vertical curve, assuming the beginning of vertical curve is at station (1034+71.16).

Solution to Problem II.27

First backcalculate the length of vertical curve:

$$\begin{aligned} L &= \frac{G_2 - G_1}{R} \\ &= \frac{-0.5\% - 3.5\%}{-0.1627[\%/\text{sta}]} \\ &= 24.59[\text{sta}] \end{aligned}$$

Then compute the station of EVC:

$$\begin{aligned} \text{sta}_{EVC} &= \text{sta}_{BVC} + L \\ &= 1034.7116[\text{sta}] + 24.59[\text{sta}] \\ &= 1059.2967[\text{sta}] \\ &= \underline{\underline{(1059+29.67)}} \end{aligned}$$

(A) (1053+15.04)

(B) (1059+29.67)

(C) (1071+58.93)

(D) (1083+88.19)

Problem II.28

The two construction stakes shown below were set for rough grading of a highway segment according to Caltrans' Surveys Manual. Determine the rough grading elevation of the centerline. Assume a constant slope of the proposed grade between the catch points.

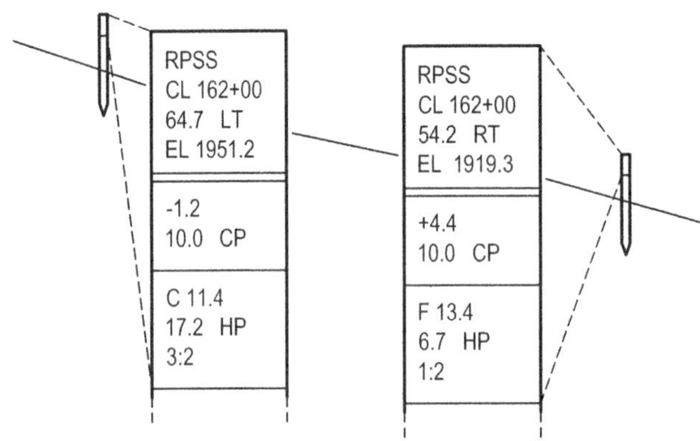

Solution to Problem II.28

Before solving this problem, it is recommended to sketch out the information shown on the stakes. With that sketch, compute the sought quantity.

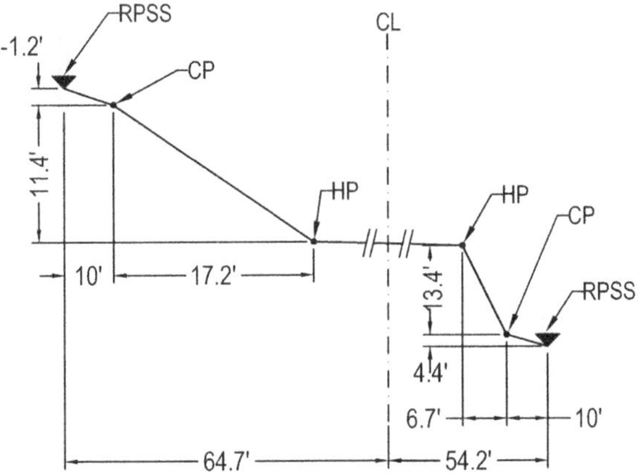

From this sketch the offsets of the hinge points can be computed easily:

$$\begin{aligned} \text{offset}_{HP,L} &= \text{offset}_{RPSS,L} - \Delta X_{CP,L} - \Delta X_{HP,L} \\ &= 64.7 - 10 - 17.2 \\ &= 37.5[\text{ft}] \end{aligned}$$

$$\text{offset}_{HP,R} = \text{offset}_{RPSS,R} - \Delta X_{CP,R} - \Delta X_{HP,R}$$

$$= 54.2 - 10 - 6.7$$
$$= 37.5[\text{ft}]$$

Because both offsets are equal, the centerline lies exactly in the middle and its elevation can be taken as the average of the hinge point elevations. Therefore, compute the hinge point elevations:

$$\begin{aligned} \text{elev}_{\text{HP},L} &= \text{elev}_{\text{RPSS},L} - \Delta Y_{\text{CP},L} - \Delta_{Y_{\text{HP},L}} \\ &= 1951.2 - 1.2 - 11.4 \\ &= 1938.6[\text{ft}] \\ \text{elev}_{\text{HP},R} &= \text{elev}_{\text{RPSS},R} + \Delta Y_{\text{CP},R} + \Delta_{Y_{\text{HP},R}} \\ &= 1919.3 + 4.4 + 13.4 \\ &= 1937.1[\text{ft}] \end{aligned}$$

Determine the centerline elevation:

$$\begin{aligned} \text{elev}_{\text{CL}} &= \frac{\text{elev}_{\text{HP},L} + \text{elev}_{\text{HP},R}}{2} \\ &= \frac{1938.6 + 1937.1}{2} \\ &= \underline{\underline{1937.8[\text{ft}]}} \end{aligned}$$

(A) 1920.0[ft]

(B) 1921.2[ft]

(C) 1924.4[ft]

(D) 1937.8[ft]

Problem II.29

Field tape measurements, broken into three segments, are recorded in the table below. Readings were taken at a temperature of 92.5[F] using a nominally 100′ steel tape with calibrated length of $\ell = 100.34[\text{ft}]$. What is the corrected total length of the field measurements?

#	Measured Distance
1	54.782[ft]
2	98.462[ft]
3	14.325[ft]

Solution to Problem II.29

Total measured length:

$$\begin{aligned} L &= 54.782[\text{ft}] + 98.462[\text{ft}] + 14.325[\text{ft}] \\ &= 167.569[\text{ft}] \end{aligned}$$

Correction for temperature:

$$\begin{aligned} C_t &= \alpha_t (T - T_0) L \\ &= (6.45 \times 10^{-6})[^\circ\text{F}^{-1}] \cdot \\ &\quad (92.5 - 68)[^\circ\text{F}] \cdot 167.569[\text{ft}] \\ &= 0.02648[\text{ft}] \end{aligned}$$

Correction for nominal length:

$$\begin{aligned} C_\ell &= L \left(\frac{\ell}{\ell'} - 1 \right) \\ &= 167.569[\text{ft}] \left(\frac{100.34[\text{ft}]}{100[\text{ft}]} - 1 \right) \\ &= 0.5697[\text{ft}] \end{aligned}$$

Actual total length:

$$\begin{aligned} \overline{L} &= L + C_t + C_\ell \\ &= 167.569[\text{ft}] + 0.02648[\text{ft}] + 0.5697[\text{ft}] \\ &= \underline{\underline{168.165[\text{ft}]}} \end{aligned}$$

(A) 167.569[ft]

(B) 167.595[ft]

(C) 168.112[ft]

(D) 168.165[ft]

Problem II.30

The table below shows existing grades at certain stations of a proposed road extension. The proposed road extension starts with a 2.5% upward slope at point 0 at existing grade and ends at point 5 meeting the existing grade again. Determine the project station with zero fill. Assume the existing grade varies linearly between stations measured.

Point	Station	Elevation
0	(145+36.49)	949.54
1	(146+00.00)	926.25
2	(147+00.00)	930.41
3	(148+00.00)	932.40
4	(149+00.00)	967.03
5	(149+39.67)	959.62

Solution to Problem II.30

The problem statement asks for the project station, where existing grade intersects the proposed grade. The existing grade is interpolated between the given points, and the proposed grade is defined as a line with constant slope. In theory, one would need to check each segment between two points for a possible intersection. If we mentally visualize the existing grade, we see that up until point 3, the existing grade is always lower than the grade at project start. Because the proposed grade is going upwards, this means there cannot be any intersection. Considering that the existing and the proposed grade are supposed to meet at point 5 again, we can also rule out the last segment (between points 4 and 5). This is because the lines can not touch more than once per segment. Hence, only the segment between points 3 and 4 remains that possibly contains the grade intersection.

Note: Ideally, only one answer option would lie in this segment. But since all answer options are in this segment, the exact location of the intersection has to be computed.

To finally determine the location of intersection, define equations (in form of $y_(x) = \dots$) for two linear curves: One for the existing grade between points 3,4. And one for the proposed grade, starting at point 0. Then find the station x where both lines have the same elevation.

Equation for the proposed grade:

$$y_P(x) = y_0 + 2.5\% \cdot (x - x_0)$$

Equation for the existing grade between 3 and 4:

$$y_{34}(x) = y_3 + \underbrace{\left(\frac{y_4 - y_3}{x_4 - x_3}\right)}_{k_{34}} \cdot (x - x_3)$$

Equate the two lines:

$$\begin{aligned} y_P(x) &= y_{34}(x) \\ \leadsto x &= \frac{y_0 - 2.5x_0 - y_3 + k_{34}}{k_{34} - 2.5\%} \\ &= \frac{y_0 - 2.5 \cdot x_0 - y_3 + k_{34} \cdot x_3}{k_{34} - 2.5} \\ &= \frac{949.54 - 2.5 \cdot 145.36 - 932.4 + 34.63 \cdot 148}{34.63 - 2.5} \\ &= 148.7385[\text{sta}] \\ &= \underline{\underline{(148{+}73.85)}} \end{aligned}$$

Note: If you intend to solve this during a timed practice exam, use the numerical solver function on your calculator instead of rearranging for X.

(A) (148+26.15)

(B) (148+41.54)

(C) (148+62.64)

(D) <u>(148+73.85)</u>

Problem II.31

A shipping container is to be buried in sand. Two 12′ long ramps are to be dumped adjacent to long sides of the container. Determine how deep the container needs to be buried, such that the ramps can be built from the excavation material and no excess material remains.

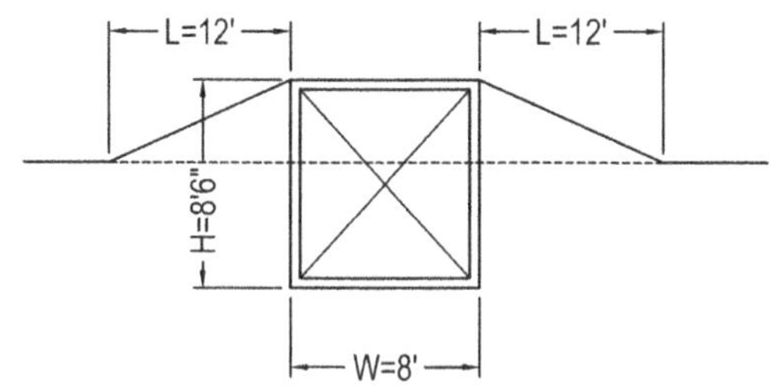

Solution to Problem II.31

This question is asking you to find the depth D at which the area of excavation ($= D \cdot W$) equals the area of the ramps ($= (H - D) \cdot L$):

$$D \cdot W = (H - D) \cdot L$$

This equation is then solved for D:

$$\begin{aligned} D &= \frac{H \cdot L}{W + L} \\ &= \frac{8.5[\text{ft}] \cdot 12[\text{ft}]}{8[\text{ft}] + 12[\text{ft}]} \\ &= \underline{\underline{5.1[\text{ft}]}} \end{aligned}$$

(A) 3.3[ft]

(B) 3.6[ft]

(C) 4.7[ft]

(D) 5.1[ft]

Problem II.32

From the field notes of a leveling exercise shown below, determine the linear misclosure of the vertical clearance of the bridge underpass.

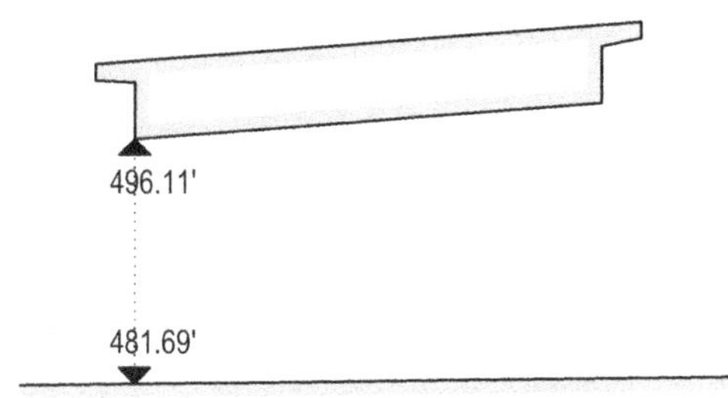

Point	BS	HI	FS	Elev	Notes
CL of Road	8.53			481.69	
Bot. Edge of Bridge			5.92	496.11	Rod held upside down.

Solution to Problem II.32

Compute the misclosure between the observed and the known clearance.

> **Note:** The question is asking for the linear misclosure of the *vertical clearance*, not the linear misclosure of the *bottom-of-bridge elevation*.

Expected vertical clearance:

$$\begin{aligned} \Delta H_{ref} &= \text{elev}_{bridge} - \text{elev}_{road} \\ &= 496.11' - 481.69' \\ &= 14.42' \end{aligned}$$

Measured vertical clearance:

$$\begin{aligned} \Delta H_{calc} &= \text{FS}_{bridge} - \text{BS}_{road} \\ &== 5.92' + 8.53' \\ &= 14.45' \end{aligned}$$

Linear Misclosure:

$$\begin{aligned} \varepsilon &= x_{observed} - x_{actual} \\ &= \Delta H_{calc} - \Delta H_{ref} \\ &= 14.45' - 14.42' \\ &= \underline{\underline{0.03'}} \end{aligned}$$

(A) $-0.01'$

(B) $-0.03'$

(C) $0.01'$

(D) $\underline{\underline{0.03'}}$

Problem II.33

A $R = 900[\text{ft}]$ curve is being staked out in the field. The table below contains layout data from the previous stake. Determine the required chord distance between points 3 and PT for backchecking the stakes.

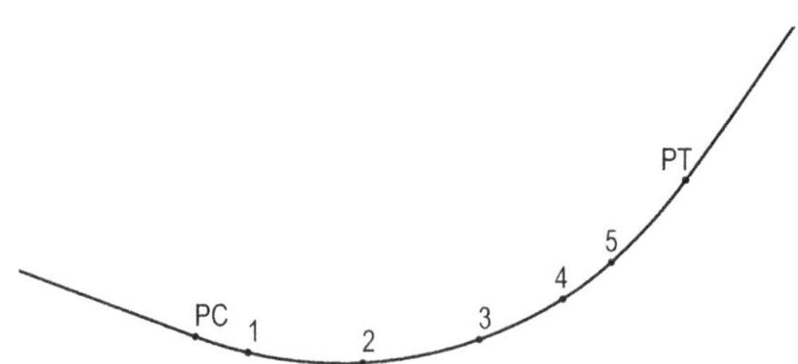

Point	Curve Length $x[\text{ft}]$	Deflection Angle $\delta[°]$	Chord Length $c[\text{ft}]$
PC	—	—	—
1	31.000	0.9868	30.998
2	100.000	3.1831	99.949
3	100.000	3.1831	99.949
4	70.000	2.2282	69.982
5	30.000	0.9549	29.999
PT	22.560	0.7181	22.559

Solution to Problem II.33

First, determine the interior angle between point 3 and PT:

$$\begin{aligned}\theta_{3,\text{PT}} &= 2 \cdot (\delta_4 + \delta_5 + \delta_{\text{PT}}) \\ &= 2 \cdot (2.2281° + 0.9549° + 0.7181°) \\ &= 7.8024°\end{aligned}$$

Then, compute the chord length between point 3 and PT:

$$\begin{aligned}c_{3,\text{PT}} &= 2 \cdot R \cdot \sin\left(\frac{\theta_{3,\text{PT}}}{2}\right) \\ &= 2 \cdot 900[\text{ft}] \cdot \sin\left(\frac{7.8024°}{2}\right) \\ &= \underline{\underline{122.465[\text{ft}]}}\end{aligned}$$

(A) 122.181[ft]

(B) $\underline{\underline{122.465[\text{ft}]}}$

(C) 220.298[ft]

(D) 221.993[ft]

Problem II.34

The temporary benchmark at point B got lost. Determine distance and azimuth to re-establish the benchmark from point A.

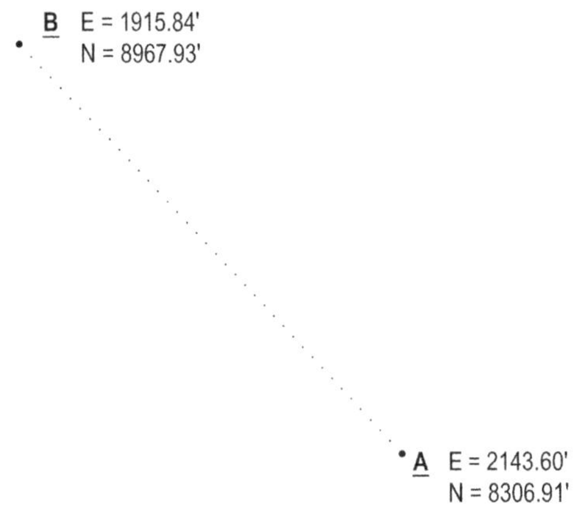

Solution to Problem II.34

Determine distance and azimuth from A to B using the coordinates provided.

Departure and latitude:

$$\begin{aligned}\Delta N &= N_B - N_A \\ &= 8967.93[\text{ft}] - 8306.91[\text{ft}] \\ &= 661.02[\text{ft}] \\ \Delta E &= E_B - E_A \\ &= 1915.84[\text{ft}] - 2143.6[\text{ft}] \\ &= -227.76[\text{ft}]\end{aligned}$$

Length to B''

$$\begin{aligned}L_{AB} &= \sqrt{(\Delta N)^2 + (\Delta E)^2} \\ &= \sqrt{(661.02[\text{ft}])^2 + (-227.76[\text{ft}])^2} \\ &= \underline{\underline{699.16[\text{ft}]}}\end{aligned}$$

Azimuth to B:

$$\begin{aligned}Az_{AB} &= \arctan\left(\frac{\Delta E}{\Delta N}\right) \\ &= \arctan\left(\frac{-227.76[\text{ft}]}{661.02[\text{ft}]}\right) \\ &= -19°0'43'' \\ &= \underline{\underline{341°0'43''}}\end{aligned}$$

(A) $L_{AB} = 699.16[\text{ft}]$, $Az_{AB} = 19°0'43''$

(B) $L_{AB} = 699.16[\text{ft}]$, $Az_{AB} = 71°0'43''$

(C) $L_{AB} = 699.16[\text{ft}]$, $Az_{AB} = 161°0'43''$

(D) $\underline{\underline{L_{AB} = 699.16[\text{ft}],\ Az_{AB} = 341°0'43''}}$

Problem II.35

The table below shows existing grades at all project stations of a proposed road. The proposed road starts with a 2.5[ft/sta] upward slope at point 0 at its existing elevation and ends at point 5 meeting the existing grade. Determine the project station with greatest cut. Assume the existing grade varies linearly between measured stations.

Point	Station	Elevation
0	(145+36.49)	949.54
1	(146+00.00)	926.25
2	(147+00.00)	930.41
3	(148+00.00)	932.40
4	(149+00.00)	967.03
5	(149+39.67)	959.62

Solution to Problem II.35

The problem statement asks for the project station, with the maximum difference between an existing and a proposed elevation. Because it is stated that the existing grade varies linearly between all stations, such an extreme may only occur at one of the given stations (and not in between). You can either check all four intermediate stations x_i by computing the amount of cut with:

$$\Delta_{Y,i} = \underbrace{y_{E,0} + (x_i - x_0) * (\text{grade})}_{\text{(proposed grade)}} \quad \underbrace{y_{E,i}}_{\text{(existing grade)}},$$

or you may take a look at the input table and realize that only at point 4, the existing elevation is greater than the elevation of project end and project start. Therefore, it must be the station with the maximum cut.

(A) (146+00.00) (Point 1)

(B) (147+00.00) (Point 2)

(C) (148+00.00) (Point 3)

(D) $\underline{\underline{\text{(149+00.00) (Point 4)}}}$

Problem II.36

The two construction stakes shown below were set for rough grading of a highway segment according to Caltrans' Surveys Manual. Determine the distance between left and right catch points.

(A) 88.9′

(B) 98.9′

(C) 108.9′

(D) 118.9′

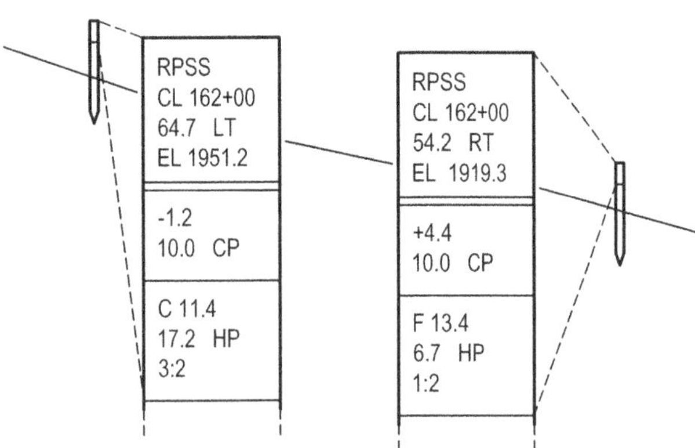

Solution to Problem II.36

Before solving this problem, sketch out the information shown on the stakes. Using this sketch, compute the sought quantity.

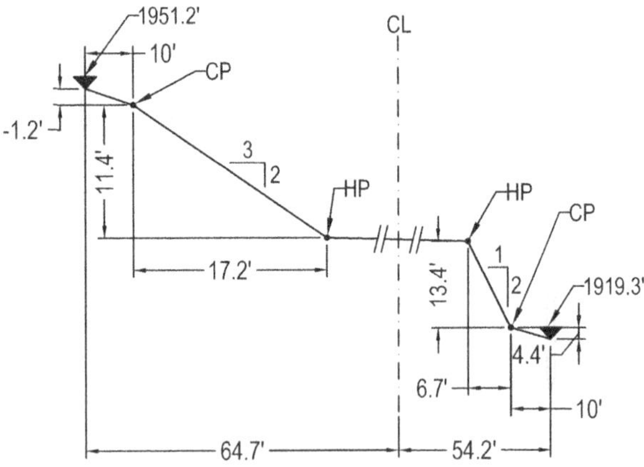

Distance between catch points:

$$\begin{aligned} d &= (64.7' - 10') + (54.2' - 10') \\ &= \underline{\underline{98.9'}} \end{aligned}$$

Problem II.37

For a construction project, two benchmarks—A and B—have been established. A third temporary benchmark C has been set out in the field; see the sketch below. Determine the easting and northing coordinates of this new temporary benchmark.

(A) $(E, N) = (5308.29[\text{ft}], 8965.23[\text{ft}])$

(B) $(E, N) = (5337.04[\text{ft}], 8650.38[\text{ft}])$

(C) $(E, N) = (5547.80[\text{ft}], 8650.38[\text{ft}])$

(D) $(E, N) = (5576.55[\text{ft}], 8965.23[\text{ft}])$

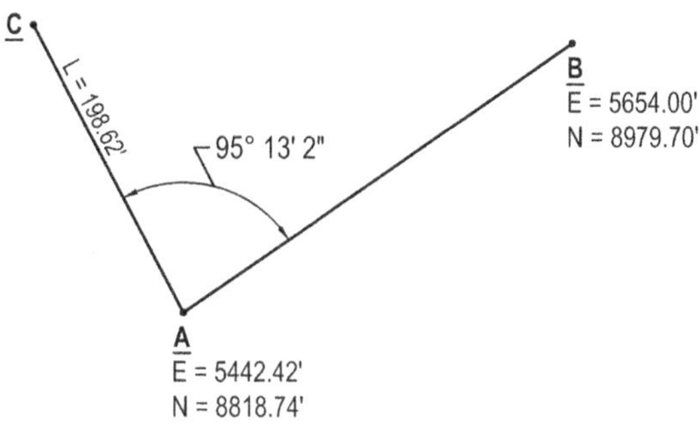

Solution to Problem II.37

Azimuth $A - B$:

$$\begin{aligned} \mathrm{Az}_{AB} &= \arctan\left(\frac{E_B - E_A}{N_B - N_A}\right) \\ &= 52°44'16'' \end{aligned}$$

Azimuth $A - C$:

$$\begin{aligned} \mathrm{Az}_{AC} &= \mathrm{Az}_{AB} - \Delta_{AC} \\ &= 52°44'16'' - 95°13'2'' \\ &= 317°31'14'' \end{aligned}$$

Coordinates of C:

$$\begin{aligned} E_C &= E_A + L_{AC} \cdot \sin \mathrm{Az}_{AC} \\ &= 5442.42 + 198.62 \cdot \sin(317°31'14'') \\ &= \underline{\underline{5308.29[\text{ft}]}} \\ N_C &= N_A + L_{AC} \cdot \cos \mathrm{Az}_{AC} \\ &= 8818.74 + 198.62 \cdot \cos(317°31'14'') \\ &= \underline{\underline{8965.23[\text{ft}]}} \end{aligned}$$

Problem II.38

The figure below shows a typical cross section of a proposed, 75[ft] wide highway. Using the tabulated dimensions and the prismoidal method, compute the excavation volume between the three cross sections.

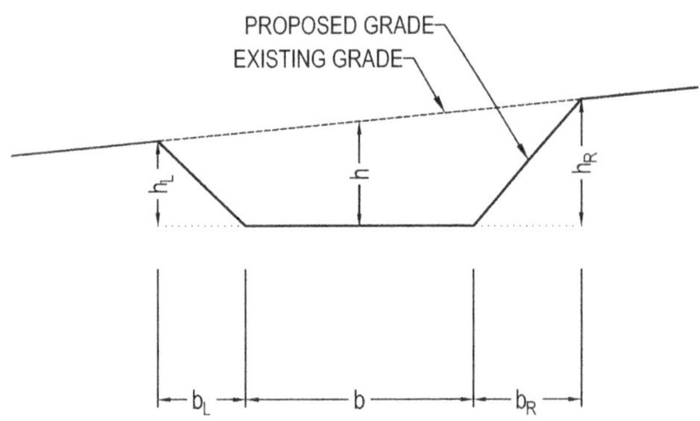

Station [sta]	b_L [ft]	b_R [ft]	h [ft]	h_L [ft]	h_R [ft]
161+00	19.62	39.35	18.85	13.08	26.23
162+00	25.15	50.54	23.81	16.77	33.69
163+00	40.62	52.96	29.00	27.08	35.31

Solution to Problem II.38

Compute the area of each cross section using the area of a trapezium formula. Then compute the volume using the prismoidal method.

Compute areas per cross section:

$$\begin{aligned} A_1 &= \frac{1}{2} \cdot (b_{L1} + b + b_{R1}) \cdot h_1 \\ &\quad + \frac{1}{4} \cdot b \cdot (h_{L1} + h_{R1}) \\ &= \frac{1}{2} \cdot (19.62 + 75 + 39.35) \cdot 18.85 + \\ &\quad \frac{1}{4} \cdot 75 \cdot (13.08 + 26.23) \\ &= 2000[\text{ft}^3] \end{aligned}$$

$$\begin{aligned} A_2 &= \frac{1}{2} \cdot (b_{L2} + b + b_{R2}) \cdot h_2 \\ &\quad + \frac{1}{4} \cdot b \cdot (h_{L2} + h_{R2}) \\ &= \frac{1}{2} \cdot (25.15 + 75 + 50.54) \cdot 23.81 + \\ &\quad \frac{1}{4} \cdot 75 \cdot (16.77 + 33.69) \\ &= 2740[\text{ft}^3] \end{aligned}$$

$$\begin{aligned} A_3 &= \frac{1}{2} \cdot (b_{L3} + b + b_{R3}) \cdot h_3 \\ &\quad + \frac{1}{4} \cdot b \cdot (h_{L3} + h_{R3}) \\ &= \frac{1}{2} \cdot (40.62 + 75 + 52.96) \cdot 29.0 + \\ &\quad \frac{1}{4} \cdot 75 \cdot (27.08 + 35.31) \\ &= 3614[\text{ft}^3] \end{aligned}$$

Volume by prismoidal method:

$$\begin{aligned} V &= \frac{L}{6} \cdot (A_1 + 4 \cdot A_2 + A_3) \\ &= \frac{200[\text{ft}]}{6} \cdot \left(2000[\text{ft}^3] + 4 \cdot 2740[\text{ft}^3] + 3614[\text{ft}^3]\right) \\ &= 552477[\text{ft}^3] \\ &= \underline{\underline{20462[\text{yd}^3]}} \end{aligned}$$

(A) 13696[yd³]

(B) 13838[yd³]

(C) 17458[yd³]

(D) $\underline{\underline{20462[\text{yd}^3]}}$

Problem II.39

For the all-rectangular building shown below, only the two corner points at the front have coordinates. Determine the coordinates for corner F.

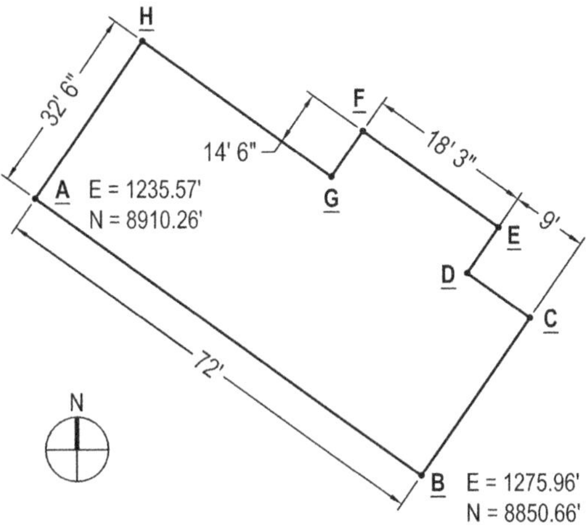

Solution to Problem II.39

The probably least error-prone approach to solve this problem is to compute the difference between a known point (A or B) to F in a coordinate system aligned with the building first. Then transform this difference into state plane coordinates.

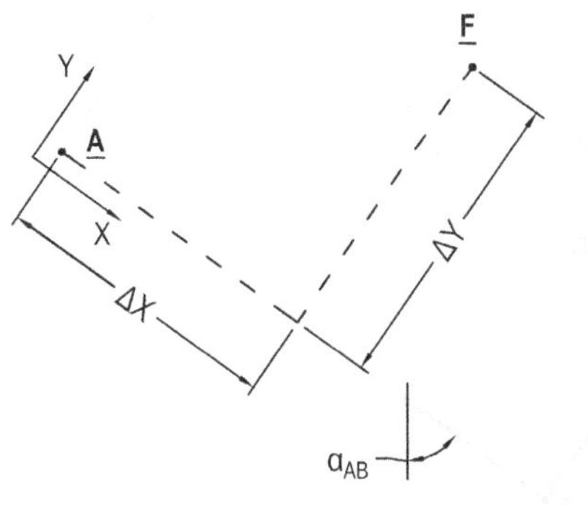

Difference in building coordinates:

$$\begin{aligned}\Delta_X &= L_{AB} - L_{CD} - L_{EF}\\ &= 72.0 - 9.0 - 18.25\\ &= 44.75[\text{ft}]\\ \Delta_Y &= L_{BC} + L_{DE}\\ &= 32.5 + 14.5\\ &= 47.00[\text{ft}]\end{aligned}$$

Angle between line $A - B$ and grid north:

$$\begin{aligned}\alpha_{AB} &= \arctan\left(\frac{E_B - E_A}{N_A - N_B}\right)\\ &= \arctan\left(\frac{1275.96 - 1235.57}{8910.26 - 8850.66}\right)\\ &= 34°7'30''\end{aligned}$$

Point F state-plane coordinates:

$$\begin{aligned}E_F &= E_A + \Delta_X \cdot \sin(\alpha_{AB}) + \Delta_Y \cdot \cos(\alpha_{AB})\\ &= 1235.57 + 44.75 \cdot \sin(34°7'30'')\\ &\quad + 47.00 \cdot \cos(34°7'30'')\\ &= \underline{\underline{1299.58[\text{ft}]}}\\ N_F &= N_A - \Delta_X \cdot \cos(\alpha_{AB}) + \Delta_Y \cdot \sin(\alpha_{AB})\\ &= 8910.26 - 44.75 \cdot \cos(34°7'30'')\\ &\quad + 47.00 \cdot \sin(34°7'30'')\\ &= \underline{\underline{8899.58[\text{ft}]}}\end{aligned}$$

(A) $(E,N)_F = (1228.90, 9003.89)[\text{ft}]$

(B) $\underline{\underline{(E,N)_F = (1299.58, 8899.58)[\text{ft}]}}$

(C) $(E,N)_F = (1309.68, 8884.68)[\text{ft}]$

(D) $(E,N)_F = (1320.06, 9003.89)[\text{ft}]$

Problem II.40

A 3½″ deep speed table, as shown below, will be added to a residential road. Compute the volume of this speed table using the average end area method.

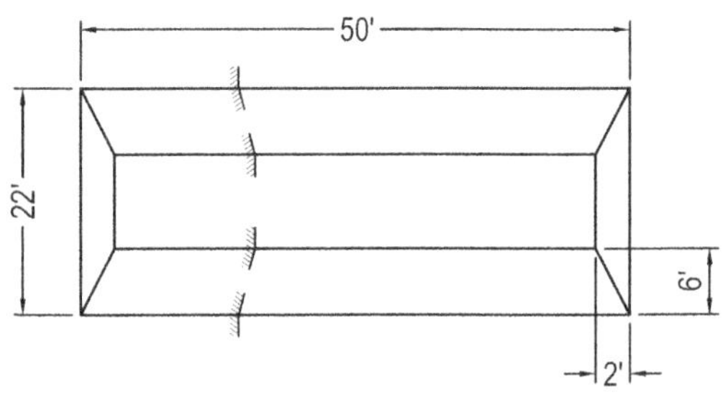

Solution to Problem II.40

The speed table volume can be estimated using the average end area method.

Area of base:

$$\begin{aligned} A_{base} &= W_{road} \cdot L_{table} \\ &= 50[\text{ft}] \cdot 22[\text{ft}] \\ &= 1100[\text{ft}^2] \end{aligned}$$

Area of top:

$$\begin{aligned} A_{top} &= \left(W_{road} - 2 \cdot w_{ramp}\right) \cdot \left(L_{table} - 2 \cdot L_{ramp}\right) \\ &= (50[\text{ft}] - 2 \cdot 2[\text{ft}]) \cdot (22[\text{ft}] - 2 \cdot 6[\text{ft}]) \\ &= 460[\text{ft}^2] \end{aligned}$$

Speeed table volume:

$$\begin{aligned} V &= \frac{t_{ramp}}{2} \cdot \left(A_{base} + A_{top}\right) \\ &= \frac{3.5''/(12[\text{in}/\text{ft}])}{2} \cdot \left(1100[\text{ft}^2] + 460[\text{ft}^2]\right) \\ &= \underline{\underline{228[\text{ft}^3]}} \end{aligned}$$

Note: In this case the average end area method does not give the exact result, but we have to use it because the problem statement has instructed us to do so. In case the question does not specify which method to use, before using an approximate formula make sure the possible answer choices are far enough apart. If they are not, consider computing the volume using an exact method.

(A) $\underline{\underline{228[\text{ft}^3]}}$

(B) $233[\text{ft}^3]$

(C) $308[\text{ft}^3]$

(D) $321[\text{ft}^3]$

Problem II.41

The creek on the topographic map shown below is most likely to flow in which direction?

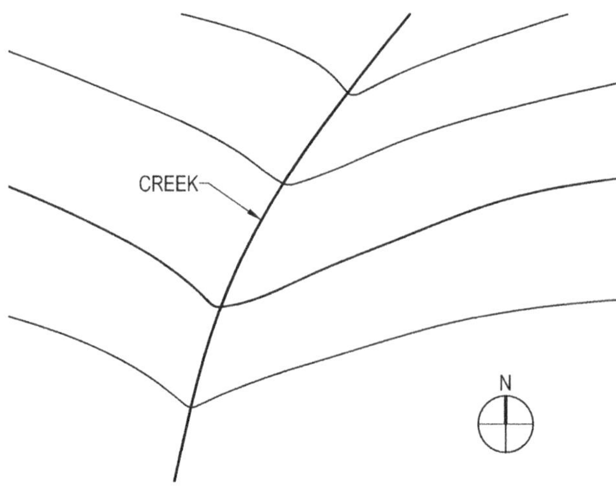

Solution to Problem II.41

Based on the map, the stream could either flow north or south. If it was flowing south, then it would have been flowing along a ridge, which is highly unlikely. Hence, north is the only plausible direction.

(A) <u>North</u>

(B) East

(C) South

(D) West

Problem II.42

For the turnaround shown below, determine its length L.

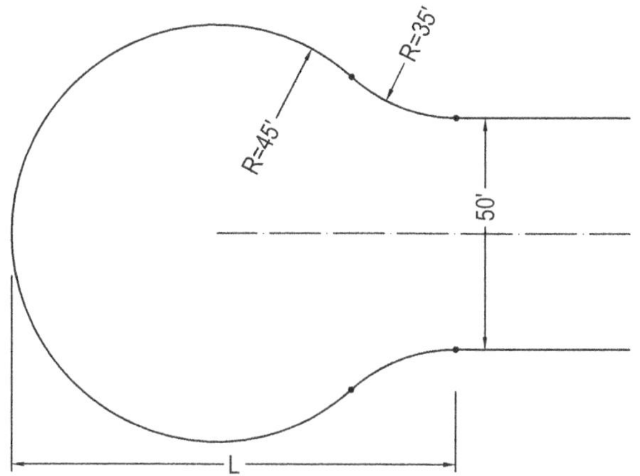

Solution to Problem II.42

This problem may seem daunting at first, but it can easily be solved with one or two equations. The key is to sketch out the geometric relationships and break down the geometries into their constituent parts.

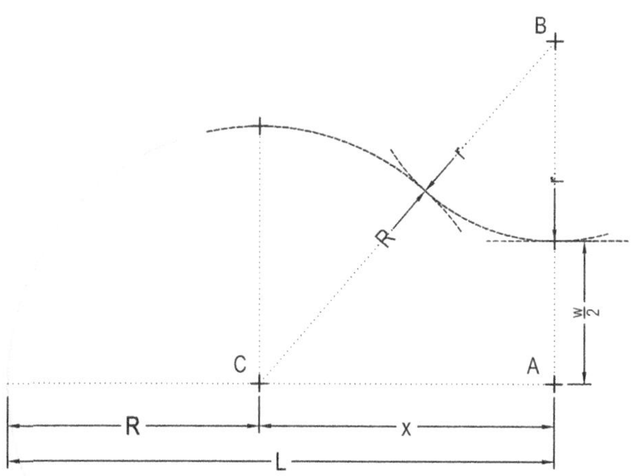

When this is done it becomes clear that the points A, B, C form a right triangle, from which the edge $\overline{A,C}$ can readily be computed by Pythagoras' theorem.

Length of edge $\overline{A,C}$:

$$
\begin{aligned}
x &= \sqrt{(R+r)^2 - \left(r + \frac{w}{2}\right)^2} \\
&= \sqrt{(45+35)^2 - \left(35 + \frac{50}{2}\right)^2} \\
&= 52.92[\text{ft}]
\end{aligned}
$$

Length of turnaround:

$$
\begin{aligned}
L &= R + x \\
&= 45[\text{ft}] + 52.92[\text{ft}] \\
&= \underline{\underline{97.92[\text{ft}]}}
\end{aligned}
$$

(A) 52.92[ft]

(B) $\underline{\underline{97.92[\text{ft}]}}$

(C) 106.80[ft]

(D) 145.00[ft]

Problem II.43

A brand-new metal tape was used to measure a distance at a temperature of 85.6[°F]. The distance after temperature correction is 68.72[ft]. After taking the measurement, the tape was sent in for calibration. The calibration gave a length of 99.94[ft] for this 100[ft]-tape. What would be the actual distance when incorporating the tape length correction?

Solution to Problem II.43

Because the temperature correction has already been applied, we only need to apply the tape length correction. Since this is the only correction that needs to be applied, we directly scale the length instead of computing a correction delta C_ℓ.

$$
\begin{aligned}
L_M &= L \cdot \frac{\ell}{\ell'} \\
&= 68.720[\text{ft}] \cdot \frac{99.94[\text{ft}]}{100[\text{ft}]} \\
&= \underline{\underline{68.679[\text{ft}]}}
\end{aligned}
$$

(A) $\underline{\underline{68.679[\text{ft}]}}$

(B) 68.687[ft]

(C) 68.720[ft]

(D) 68.761[ft]

Problem II.44

A 9 × 9[in] aerial photo was taken at 2400[ft] above ground level using a 152[mm] focal length lens. A feature was measured to be 4.35[in^2] on photo. Determine the actual area of the feature.

Solution to Problem II.44

Determine the scale factor for the aerial photo and scale the measured area accordingly. Note that because the scale factor is for line measures, it must to be squared for area measures.

Scale factor for line measures:

$$\begin{aligned} S &= \frac{f}{H} \\ &= \frac{152[\text{mm}] \cdot (1/25.4[\text{in/mm}] \cdot 1/12[\text{ft/in}])}{2400[\text{ft}]} \\ &= 2.0779 \times 10^{-4} \end{aligned}$$

Area on ground:

$$\begin{aligned} A_g &= \frac{A_{photo}}{S^2} \\ &= \frac{4.35[\text{in}^2]}{(2.0779 \times 10^{-4})^2} \\ &= 100752189[\text{in}^2] \end{aligned}$$

Conversion factor from[ac] to[in^2]:

$$\begin{aligned} \kappa &= (12[\text{in/ft}] \cdot 66[\text{ft/chain}])^2 \cdot 10[\text{chain}^2/\text{ac}] \\ &= 6272640[\text{in}^2/\text{ac}] \\ A_{g,ac} &= \frac{A_g}{\kappa} \\ &= \frac{100752189[\text{in}^2]}{6272640[\text{in}^2/\text{ac}]} \\ &= \underline{\underline{16.06[\text{ac}]}} \end{aligned}$$

(A) 145.38[ft^2]

(B) 2312[ft^2]

(C) <u>16.06[ac]</u>

(D) 824[ac]

Problem II.45

For the highway section shown below, if the minimum curve radius for each lane (measured at the lane centerline) is 2100[ft], what is the minimum possible curve radius at the median line M?

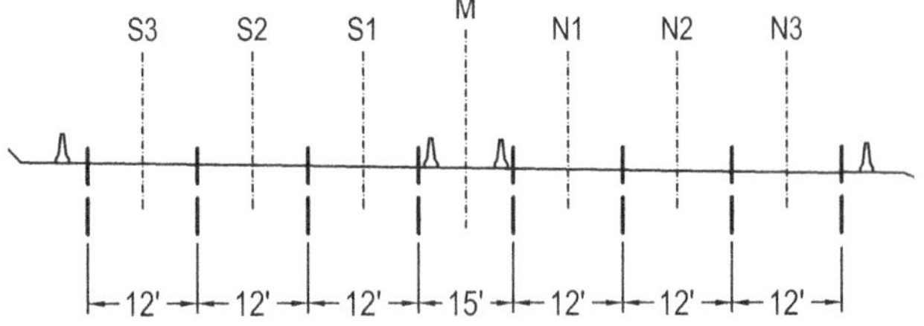

Solution to Problem II.45

By inspection, the lanes $N3$ and $S3$ control the median line radius, hence:

$$\begin{aligned} R_M &= R_3 + \frac{12[\text{ft}]}{2} + 2\,(12[\text{ft}]) + \frac{15[\text{ft}]}{2} \\ &= 2100[\text{ft}] + 37.5[\text{ft}] \\ &= 2137.5[\text{ft}] \\ &= \underline{\underline{2138[\text{ft}]}} \end{aligned}$$

(A) 2064[ft]

(B) 2136[ft]

(C) <u>2138[ft]</u>

(D) 2151[ft]

Problem II.46

The air strips of an airport are to be paved with asphalt. Each runway is 8000[ft] long and 300[ft] wide. Determine the total area to be asphalted.

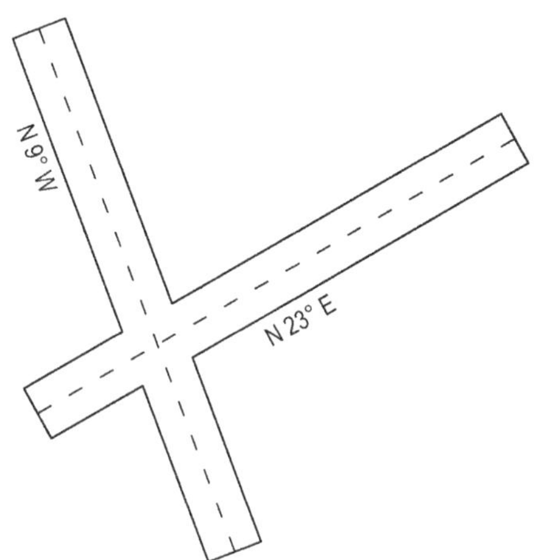

Solution to Problem II.46

The total area of both runways is the sum of each individual runway, minus the overlapping part. The area of the overlapping part can be computed as a parallelogram. The height is the runway width w and the length of the base is given in the figure below.

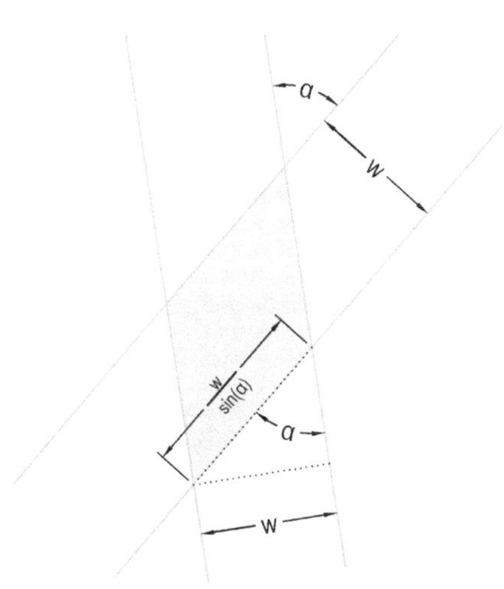

Area of a runway:

$$\begin{aligned} A_{rw} &= L \cdot W \\ &= 8000[\text{ft}] \cdot 300[\text{ft}] \\ &= 2400000[\text{ft}^2] \end{aligned}$$

Intersecting angle between the runways:

$$\begin{aligned} \alpha &= \text{brg}_1 + \text{brg}_2 \\ &= 9^\circ + 23^\circ \\ &= 32^\circ \end{aligned}$$

Overlapping runway area:

$$\begin{aligned} A_\diamond &= W \cdot \frac{W}{\sin(\alpha)} \\ &= 300[\text{ft}] \cdot \frac{300[\text{ft}]}{\sin(32^\circ)} \\ &= 169837[\text{ft}^2] \end{aligned}$$

Nonoverlapping area of both runways:

$$\begin{aligned} A &= 2 \cdot A_{rw} - A_\diamond \\ &= 2 \cdot 2400000[\text{ft}^2] - 169837[\text{ft}^2] \\ &= 4630163[\text{ft}^2] \\ &= \underline{\underline{106.29[\text{ac}]}} \end{aligned}$$

(A) $\underline{\underline{106.29[\text{ac}]}}$

(B) 107.76[ac]

(C) 108.13[ac]

(D) 114.09[ac]

Problem II.47

For the road segment depicted in the figure below, determine the station of the high point.

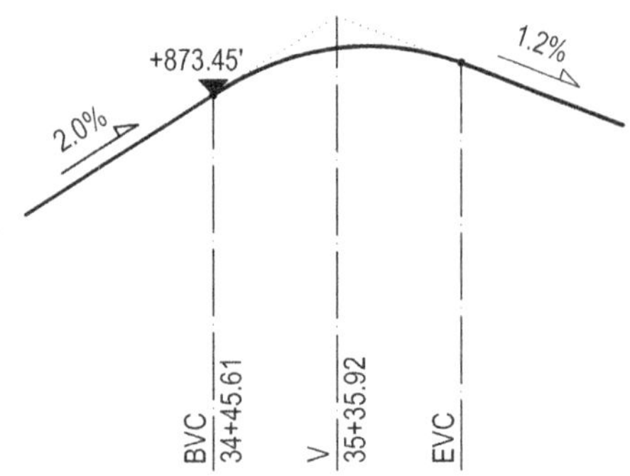

Solution to Problem II.47

Compute station of high point around the standard equation: $x_{TP} = {}^{-G_1}/_{R}$, which gives the offset from BVC to the turning point.

Length of vertical curve:

$$\begin{aligned} L &= 2 \cdot \left(\text{sta}_V - \text{sta}_{(\text{BVC})}\right) \\ &= 2 \cdot (35.3592[\text{sta}] - 34.4561[\text{sta}]) \\ &= 1.8062[\text{sta}] \end{aligned}$$

Rate of grade change:

$$\begin{aligned} R &= \frac{G_2 - G_1}{L} \\ &= \frac{-1.2\% - 2\%}{1.8062[\text{sta}]} \\ &= -1.7717[\%/\text{sta}] \end{aligned}$$

Distance from BVC to TP:

$$\begin{aligned} x_{(\text{TP})} &= \frac{-G_1}{R} \\ &= \frac{-2\%}{-1.7717[\%/\text{sta}]} \\ &= 1.1289[\text{sta}] \end{aligned}$$

Station of high point:

$$\begin{aligned} \text{sta}_{(\text{TP})} &= \text{sta}_{(\text{BVC})} + x_{(\text{TP})} \\ &= 34.4561[\text{sta}] + 1.1289[\text{sta}] \\ &= 35.5850[\text{sta}] \\ &= (35{+}58.50) \end{aligned}$$

(A) (35+58.50)

(B) (35+13.34)

(C) (36+02.05)

(D) (36+26.23)

Problem II.48

The open traverse shown below represents centerline points of a natural creek. The creek is to be streamlined from A to D in a straight line. If the average slope of the original path is 5.5%, what would be the slope of the streamlined path?

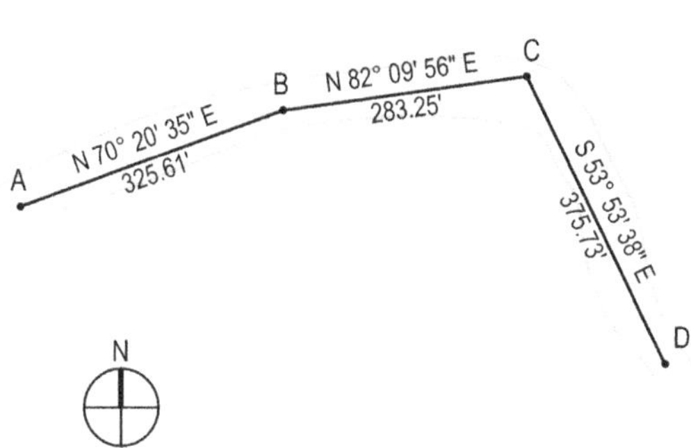

Solution to Problem II.48

To get the slope of the streamlined path, compute its length and divide by the elevation difference. The elevation difference is computed based on the original average slope and the original length.

Length of streamlined path:

$$\begin{aligned}\Delta E &= \ell_{AB}\sin(\alpha_{AB}) + \ell_{BC}\sin(\alpha_{BC}) \\ &\quad + \ell_{CD}\sin(\alpha_{CD}) \\ &= 325.61 \cdot \sin\left(70°0'35''\right) \\ &\quad + 283.25 \cdot \sin\left(82°9'56''\right) \\ &\quad + 375.73 \cdot \sin\left(180° - 53°53'38''\right) \\ &= 890.80[\text{ft}] \\ \Delta N &= \ell_{AB}\cos(\alpha_{AB}) + \ell_{BC}\cos(\alpha_{BC}) \\ &\quad + \ell_{CD}\cos(\alpha_{CD}) \\ &= 325.61 \cdot \cos\left(70°0'35''\right) \\ &\quad + 283.25 \cdot \cos\left(82°9'56''\right) \\ &\quad + 375.73 \cdot \cos\left(180° - 53°53'38''\right) \\ &= -73.27[\text{ft}] \\ \ell_{AD} &= \sqrt{(\Delta E)^2 + (\Delta N)^2} \\ &= \sqrt{(890.8)^2 + (-73.27)^2} \\ &= 893.81[\text{ft}]\end{aligned}$$

Elevation difference between A and D:

$$\begin{aligned}\Delta H &= (\ell_{AB} + \ell_{BC} + \ell_{CD}) \cdot (\text{existing slope}) \\ &= (325.61 + 283.25 + 375.73) \cdot 5.50\% \\ &= 54.15[\text{ft}]\end{aligned}$$

Slope of streamlined path:

$$\begin{aligned}(\text{streamlined slope}) &= \frac{\Delta H}{\ell_{AD}} \\ &= \frac{54.15[\text{ft}]}{893.81[\text{ft}]} \\ &= \underline{\underline{6.1\%}}\end{aligned}$$

> **Note:** Instead of computing ΔH, the streamlined slope can also be computed by scaling the existing slope by the old to new stream length ratio.

(A) <u>6.1%</u>

(B) 8.5%

(C) 11.6%

(D) 18.5%

Problem II.49

The two construction stakes shown below were set for rough grading of a highway segment according to Caltrans' Surveys Manual. Determine net cut or fill area of this cross section. Assume the horizontal distance between hinge points is 75[ft] and that there is no additional grade point in between hinge points. Also, the existing slope is constant between the catch points.

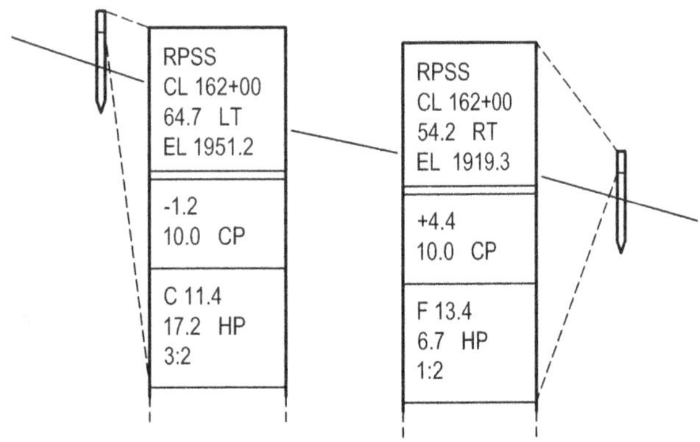

Solution to Problem II.49

Before solving this problem, it is recommended to sketch out the information shown on the stakes. Using this sketch, compute the sought quantity.

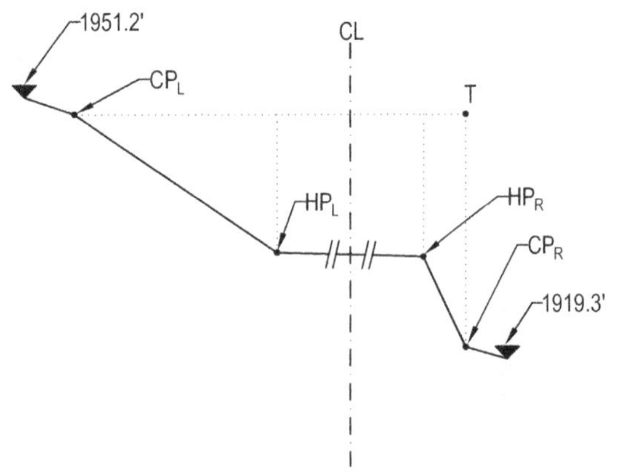

First compute the area between the line $CP_L - T$ and the polygon $CP_L - HP_L - HP_R - CP_R$. Then subtract the area of the triangle $CP_L - CP_R - T$.

Compute required distances:

$$
\begin{aligned}
Y_{HP,L} &= \Delta Y_{HP,L} = 11.4 \\
Y_{CP,R} &= \text{elev}_{RPSS,L} - \text{elev}_{RPSS,R} \\
&\quad - \Delta Y_{CP,L} - \Delta Y_{CP,R} \\
&= 1951.2 - 1919.3 - 1.2 - 4.4 \\
&= 26.3[\text{ft}] \\
Y_{HP,R} &= Y_{CP,R} - \Delta Y_{HP,R} \\
&= 26.3 - 13.4 \\
&= 12.9[\text{ft}] \\
X_1 &= \Delta X_{HP,L} = 17.2[\text{ft}] \\
X_3 &= \Delta X_{HP,R} = 6.7[\text{ft}] \\
X_2 &= 75[\text{ft}] \quad \text{(given)}
\end{aligned}
$$

Compute areas:

$$
\begin{aligned}
A_1 &= X_1 \cdot \frac{Y_{HP,L}}{2} \\
&= 17.2 \cdot \frac{11.4}{2} \\
&= 98.0[\text{ft}^2] \\
A_2 &= X_2 \cdot \frac{Y_{HP,L} + Y_{HP,R}}{2} \\
&= 75 \cdot \frac{11.4 + 12.9}{2} \\
&= 911.3[\text{ft}^2] \\
A_3 &= X_3 \cdot \frac{Y_{HP,R} + Y_{CP,R}}{2} \\
&= 6.7 \cdot \frac{12.9 + 26.3}{2} \\
&= 131.3[\text{ft}^2] \\
A_4 &= (X_1 + X_2 + X_3) \cdot \frac{Y_{CP,R}}{2} \\
&= (17.2 + 75 + 6.7) \cdot \frac{26.3}{2} \\
&= 1300.5[\text{ft}^2]
\end{aligned}
$$

Compute final area:

$$
\begin{aligned}
A &= A_1 + A_2 + A_3 - A_4 \\
&= 98.0 + 911.3 + 131.3 - 1300.5 \\
&= -160[\text{ft}^2] \\
&= \underline{\underline{160[\text{ft}^2]}} \quad \text{(net fill)}
\end{aligned}
$$

To determine if a negative A means net cut or net fill, think of it like this: A_1, A_2, A_3 (which were added with a positive sign) 'cut' away from existing soil; whereas A_4 (which can be imagined as additional fill to the exiting ground) was subtracted. Because of this, a $A > 0$ would mean a net cut. Consequently, a negative A means a net fill.

(A) $135[\text{ft}^2]$ (net cut)

(B) $135[\text{ft}^2]$ (net fill)

(C) $160[\text{ft}^2]$ (net cut)

(D) $\underline{\underline{160[\text{ft}^2] \quad \text{(net fill)}}}$

Problem II.50

A shipping container is to be buried in sand $6'$ deep and covered $1'6''$ on top with sand and ramps along the long edges. Determine the ramp length, such that the excavation material can be used to build the ramp and the top cover and no excess material remains.

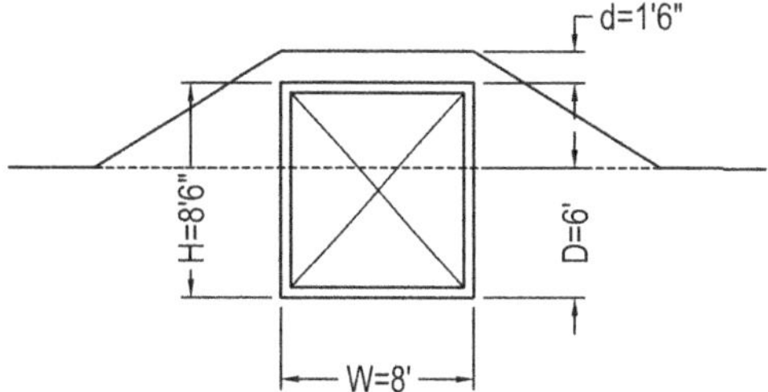

Solution to Problem II.50

This question is asking you to equate the excavation material volume with the material volume used for the top cover and the ramps. From this equation, the required ramp length L can be determined.

Excavation area:

$$\begin{aligned} A_x &= D \cdot W \\ &= 6[\text{ft}] \cdot 8[\text{ft}] \\ &= 48[\text{ft}^2] \end{aligned}$$

Top cover area:

$$\begin{aligned} A_c &= d \cdot W \\ &= 1.5[\text{ft}] \cdot 8[\text{ft}] \\ &= 12.0[\text{ft}^2] \end{aligned}$$

Area remaining for both ramps:

$$\begin{aligned} A_r &= A_x - A_c \\ &= 48[\text{ft}^2] - 12.0[\text{ft}^2] \\ &= 36.0[\text{ft}^2] \end{aligned}$$

Ramp length to maintain ramp area:

$$\begin{aligned} L &= \frac{A_r}{H - D + d} \\ &= \frac{36.0[\text{ft}^2]}{8.5[\text{ft}] - [\text{ft}]6 + 1.5[\text{ft}]} \\ &= \underline{\underline{9.0[\text{ft}]}} \end{aligned}$$

(A) 4.5[ft]

(B) 6.0[ft]

(C) 9.0[ft]

(D) 14.4[ft]

Problem II.51

Determine the area of the rectangular parcel shown below.

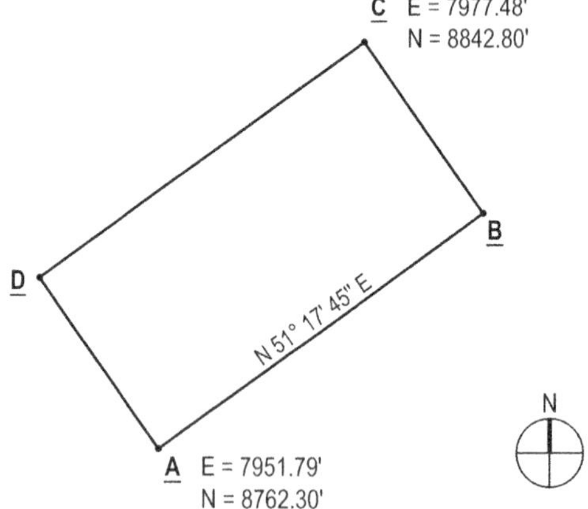

Solution to Problem II.51

Start with computing azimuth and length of the diagonal (line $\overline{AC}$). Then together with azimuth of line $\overline{AB}$ compute the lengths of $\overline{AB}$ and $\overline{BC}$ using trigonometry.

Azimuth of $\overline{AC}$:

$$\begin{aligned} Az_{AC} &= \arctan\left(\frac{E_C - E_A}{N_C - N_A}\right) \\ &= \arctan\left(\frac{7977.48 - 7951.79}{8842.8 - 8762.3}\right) \\ &= 17°41'58'' \end{aligned}$$

Interior angle between lines $\overline{AB}$, $\overline{AC}$:

$$\begin{aligned} \alpha_{CAB} &= Az_{AB} - Az_{AC} \\ &= 51°17'45'' - 17°41'58'' \\ &= 33°35'47'' \end{aligned}$$

Length of $\overline{AC}$:

$$\begin{aligned} L_{AC} &= \sqrt{(N_C - N_A)^2 + (E_C - E_A)^2} \\ &= \sqrt{(8842.8 - 8762.3)^2 + (7977.5 - 7951.8)^2} \\ &= 84.5[\text{ft}] \end{aligned}$$

Lengths of rectangular parcel:

$$\begin{aligned} L_{AB} &= L_{AC} \cdot \cos(\alpha_{CAB}) \\ &= 84.5 \cdot \cos(33°35'47'') \\ &= 70.38[\text{ft}] \end{aligned}$$

$$L_{BC} = L_{AC} \cdot \sin(\alpha_{CAB})$$
$$= 84.5 \cdot \sin(33°35'47'')$$
$$= 46.76[\text{ft}]$$

Area of the rectangular parcel:

$$A_{ABCD} = L_{AB} \cdot L_{BC}$$
$$= 70.38[\text{ft}] \cdot 46.76[\text{ft}]$$
$$= \underline{\underline{3291[\text{ft}^2]}}$$

(A) $2389[\text{ft}^2]$

(B) $\underline{\underline{3291[\text{ft}^2]}}$

(C) $4954[\text{ft}^2]$

(D) $7140[\text{ft}^2]$

Problem II.52

Using the leveling field notes and the sketch below, determine the slope of the flow line.

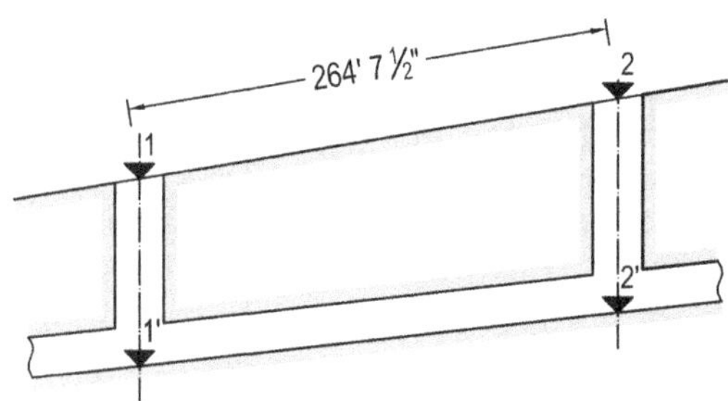

	BS	HI	FS	Elev
BM 12-06431	5.54			263.383
1			10.54	
1′			16.41	
2			5.37	
2′			12.46	

Solution to Problem II.52

From the rod readings, compute the elevation differences at the surface and at the invert. Use the surface elevation difference to reduce the sloped distance measurement into a horizontal one.

Height difference on ground:

$$\Delta H_{\text{ground}} = \text{FS}_1 - \text{FS}_2$$
$$= 10.54[\text{ft}] - 5.17[\text{ft}]$$
$$= 5.37[\text{ft}]$$

Horizontal distance between manholes:

$$L_h = \sqrt{L^2 - (\Delta H_{\text{ground}})^2}$$
$$= \sqrt{(264.625[\text{ft}])^2 + (5.37[\text{ft}])^2}$$
$$= 264.57[\text{ft}]$$

Height difference on flow line:

$$\Delta H_{\text{flowline}} = \text{FS}_{1'} - \text{FS}_{2'}$$
$$= 16.41[\text{ft}] - 12.46[\text{ft}]$$
$$= 3.95[\text{ft}]$$

Slope of flow line:

$$G = \frac{\Delta H_{\text{flowline}}}{\Delta H_{\text{ground}}} \cdot 100\% = \frac{3.95[\text{ft}]}{264.57[\text{ft}]} \cdot 100\% = \underline{\underline{1.49\%}}$$

Note: Computing the pipe slope using the sloped distance measurement might also lead to answer A, even if the result strictly speaking is incorrect.

(A) <u>1.49%</u>

(B) 1.55%

(C) 1.64%

(D) 1.79%

Problem II.53

Referring to the figure below, points A and B have been established in a previous survey. Later, a third point, C, was added to the survey. Since only a tape measure was at hand, no direction angles are available. Determine the grid coordinates of point C.

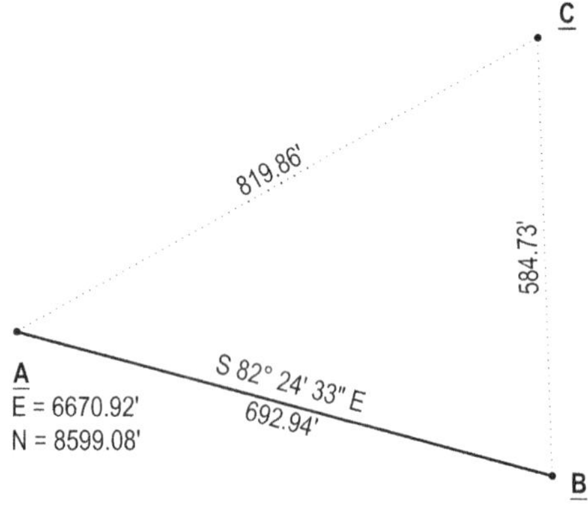

Solution to Problem II.53

Solve this problem by using one of the equations of the law of the cosines. For example: $\cos\alpha = {-a^2+b^2+c^2}/{2bc}$, which gives the enclosing angle of the triangle at point A. With α, compute the azimuth from A to C and finally the grid coordinates.

Enclosing angle at point A, α:

$$\begin{aligned}\alpha &= \arccos\frac{-(L_{BC})^2 + (L_{AB})^2 + (L_{AC})^2}{2 \cdot L_{AB} \cdot L_{AC}} \\ &= \arccos\frac{-(584.73)^2 + (692.94)^2 + (819.86)^2}{2 \cdot 692.94 \cdot 819.86} \\ &= 44^\circ 29' 57''\end{aligned}$$

Azimuth from A to C:

$$\begin{aligned}\text{Az}_{AC} &= 180^\circ - \text{brg}_{AB} - \alpha \\ &= 180^\circ - 82^\circ 24' 33'' - 44^\circ 29' 57'' \\ &= 53^\circ 5' 30''\end{aligned}$$

Grid coordinates:

$$\begin{aligned}E_C &= E_A + L_{AC} \cdot \sin(\text{Az}_{AC}) \\ &= 6670.92[\text{ft}] + 819.86[\text{ft}] \cdot \sin(53^\circ 5' 30'') \\ &= \underline{\underline{7326.48[\text{ft}]}}\end{aligned}$$

$$N_C = N_A + L_{AC} \cdot \cos(\text{Az}_{AC})$$

$$= 8599.08[\text{ft}] + 819.86[\text{ft}] \cdot \cos\left(53°5'30''\right)$$
$$= \underline{\underline{9091.44[\text{ft}]}}$$

Note: Storing the lengths a, b, c as variables in the calculator greatly improves your speed and reduces the probability of mistyping values.

(A) $(E, N)_C = (7163.28, 9254.64)[\text{ft}]$

(B) $(E, N)_C = (7245.56, 9183.85)[\text{ft}]$

(C) $(E, N)_C = (7255.69, 9173.72)[\text{ft}]$

(D) $\underline{\underline{(E, N)_C = (7326.48, 9091.44)[\text{ft}]}}$

Problem II.54

A 415[ft] long $R = 330[\text{ft}]$ curve is being staked out in the field. Starting at the beginning of curve, stakes are to be set at every station along the curve. For back-checking, what must be the chord distance between the last stake and the PT?

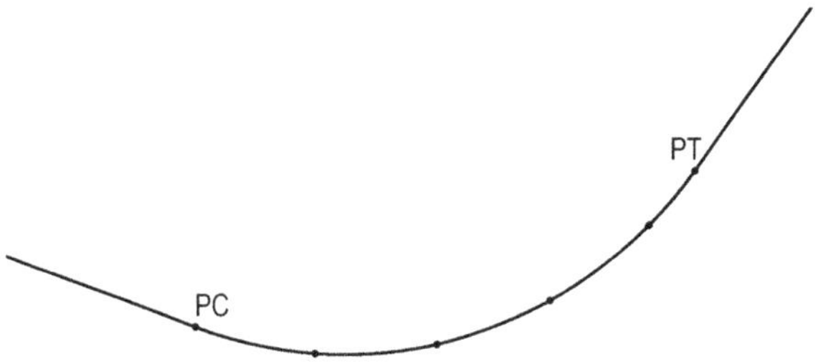

Solution to Problem II.54

When staking out 100[ft] stations, the remainder is $415[\text{ft}] - (4)(100[\text{ft}]) = 15[\text{ft}]$. Therefore, compute chord length of this 15[ft] segment.

$$\theta_x = \frac{x}{R}$$
$$= \frac{15[\text{ft}]}{330[\text{ft}]}$$
$$= 2.6043°$$

Finally, compute the chord length:

$$c_x = 2R\sin\left(\frac{\theta_x}{2}\right)$$
$$= (2)(330[\text{ft}])\sin\left(\frac{2.6043°}{2}\right)$$
$$= \underline{\underline{14.9987[\text{ft}]}}$$

(A) 14.7998[ft]

(B) 14.8799[ft]

(C) 14.9879[ft]

(D) $\underline{\underline{\text{14.9987[ft]}}}$

Problem II.55

Using the information provided in the figure below, determine the minimum vertical clearance between the riverbed and the top of the sewer pipe.

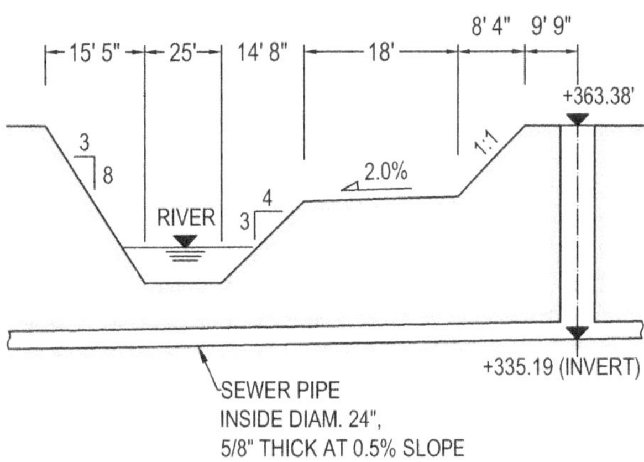

Solution to Problem II.55

Based on the information in the figure, the vertical clearance is minimal at the toe of the right river embankment. Compute the elevations of riverbed and pipe at this location and subtract them.

Elevation at the toe of right embankment:

$$\begin{aligned} \text{elev}_{\text{toe}} &= (\text{manhole cover elev.}) \\ &\quad - \sum(\text{horiz. slope dist.}) \cdot (\text{slope grades}) \\ &= 363.38' - (8'4'' \cdot 1 + 18 \cdot 2\% + 14'8'' \cdot 3/4) \\ &= 343.69' \end{aligned}$$

Distance from center of manhole to toe:

$$\begin{aligned} x_{\text{toe}} &= \sum(\text{horiz. slope dist.}) \\ &= 9'9'' + 8'4'' + 18' + 14'8'' \\ &= 50.75' \end{aligned}$$

Top of pipe elevation at toe:

$$\begin{aligned} \text{elev}_{\text{top}} &= (\text{manhole invert elevation}) \\ &\quad + (\text{inside diam.}) + (\text{pipe thickness}) \\ &\quad - x_{\text{toe}} \cdot (\text{slope of pipe}) \\ &= 335.19' + 24'' + 5/8'' - 50.75' \cdot 0.5\% \\ &= 336.99' \end{aligned}$$

Vertical Clearance:

$$\begin{aligned} \Delta Y &= \text{elev}_{\text{toe}} - \text{elev}_{\text{top}} \\ &= 343.69' - 336.99' \\ &= \underline{\underline{6.70'}} \end{aligned}$$

(A) 1.86′

(B) 6.65′

(C) <u>6.70′</u>

(D) 6.80′

Jakob Stanford is also the author of

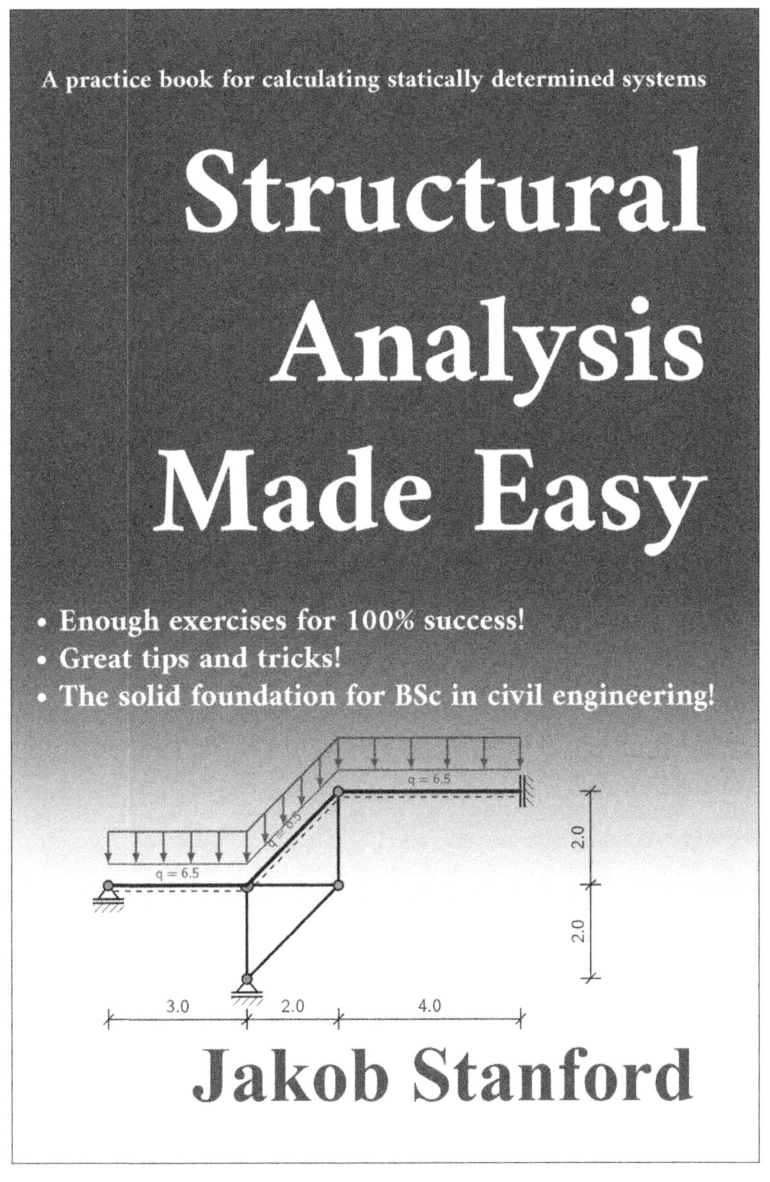

Made in the USA
Las Vegas, NV
10 October 2023